Mometrix TEST PREPARATION

Virginia SOL Grade 6 Secrets Study Guide

DEAR FUTURE EXAM SUCCESS STORY

First of all, **THANK YOU** for purchasing Mometrix study materials!

Second, congratulations! You are one of the few determined test-takers who are committed to doing whatever it takes to excel on your exam. **You have come to the right place.** We developed these study materials with one goal in mind: to deliver you the information you need in a format that's concise and easy to use.

In addition to optimizing your guide for the content of the test, we've outlined our recommended steps for breaking down the preparation process into small, attainable goals so you can make sure you stay on track.

We've also analyzed the entire test-taking process, identifying the most common pitfalls and showing how you can overcome them and be ready for any curveball the test throws you.

Standardized testing is one of the biggest obstacles on your road to success, which only increases the importance of doing well in the high-pressure, high-stakes environment of test day. Your results on this test could have a significant impact on your future, and this guide provides the information and practical advice to help you achieve your full potential on test day.

Your success is our success

We would love to hear from you! If you would like to share the story of your exam success or if you have any questions or comments in regard to our products, please contact us at **800-673-8175** or **support@mometrix.com**.

Thanks again for your business and we wish you continued success!

Sincerely,
The Mometrix Test Preparation Team

Written and edited by the Mometrix Exam Secrets Test Prep Team
Printed in the United States of America

TABLE OF CONTENTS

Introduction

Thank you for purchasing this resource! You have made the choice to prepare yourself for a test that could have a huge impact on your future, and this guide is designed to help you be fully ready for test day. Obviously, it's important to have a solid understanding of the test material, but you also need to be prepared for the unique environment and stressors of the test, so that you can perform to the best of your abilities.

For this purpose, the first section that appears in this guide is the **Secret Keys**. We've devoted countless hours to meticulously researching what works and what doesn't, and we've boiled down our findings to the five most impactful steps you can take to improve your performance on the test. We start at the beginning with study planning and move through the preparation process, all the way to the testing strategies that will help you get the most out of what you know when you're finally sitting in front of the test.

We recommend that you start preparing for your test as far in advance as possible. However, if you've bought this guide as a last-minute study resource and only have a few days before your test, we recommend that you skip over the first two Secret Keys since they address a long-term study plan.

If you struggle with **test anxiety**, we strongly encourage you to check out our recommendations for how you can overcome it. Test anxiety is a formidable foe, but it can be beaten, and we want to make sure you have the tools you need to defeat it.

Secret Key #1 – Plan Big, Study Small

There's a lot riding on your performance. If you want to ace this test, you're going to need to keep your skills sharp and the material fresh in your mind. You need a plan that lets you review everything you need to know while still fitting in your schedule. We'll break this strategy down into three categories.

Information Organization

Start with the information you already have: the official test outline. From this, you can make a complete list of all the concepts you need to cover before the test. Organize these concepts into groups that can be studied together, and create a list of any related vocabulary you need to learn so you can brush up on any difficult terms. You'll want to keep this vocabulary list handy once you actually start studying since you may need to add to it along the way.

Time Management

Once you have your set of study concepts, decide how to spread them out over the time you have left before the test. Break your study plan into small, clear goals so you have a manageable task for each day and know exactly what you're doing. Then just focus on one small step at a time. When you manage your time this way, you don't need to spend hours at a time studying. Studying a small block of content for a short period each day helps you retain information better and avoid stressing over how much you have left to do. You can relax knowing that you have a plan to cover everything in time. In order for this strategy to be effective though, you have to start studying early and stick to your schedule. Avoid the exhaustion and futility that comes from last-minute cramming!

Study Environment

The environment you study in has a big impact on your learning. Studying in a coffee shop, while probably more enjoyable, is not likely to be as fruitful as studying in a quiet room. It's important to keep distractions to a minimum. You're only planning to study for a short block of time, so make the most of it. Don't pause to check your phone or get up to find a snack. It's also important to **avoid multitasking**. Research has consistently shown that multitasking will make your studying dramatically less effective. Your study area should also be comfortable and well-lit so you don't have the distraction of straining your eyes or sitting on an uncomfortable chair.

The time of day you study is also important. You want to be rested and alert. Don't wait until just before bedtime. Study when you'll be most likely to comprehend and remember. Even better, if you know what time of day your test will be, set that time aside for study. That way your brain will be used to working on that subject at that specific time and you'll have a better chance of recalling information.

Finally, it can be helpful to team up with others who are studying for the same test. Your actual studying should be done in as isolated an environment as possible, but the work of organizing the information and setting up the study plan can be divided up. In between study sessions, you can discuss with your teammates the concepts that you're all studying and quiz each other on the details. Just be sure that your teammates are as serious about the test as you are. If you find that your study time is being replaced with social time, you might need to find a new team.

Secret Key #2 – Make Your Studying Count

You're devoting a lot of time and effort to preparing for this test, so you want to be absolutely certain it will pay off. This means doing more than just reading the content and hoping you can remember it on test day. It's important to make every minute of study count. There are two main areas you can focus on to make your studying count.

Retention

It doesn't matter how much time you study if you can't remember the material. You need to make sure you are retaining the concepts. To check your retention of the information you're learning, try recalling it at later times with minimal prompting. Try carrying around flashcards and glance at one or two from time to time or ask a friend who's also studying for the test to quiz you.

To enhance your retention, look for ways to put the information into practice so that you can apply it rather than simply recalling it. If you're using the information in practical ways, it will be much easier to remember. Similarly, it helps to solidify a concept in your mind if you're not only reading it to yourself but also explaining it to someone else. Ask a friend to let you teach them about a concept you're a little shaky on (or speak aloud to an imaginary audience if necessary). As you try to summarize, define, give examples, and answer your friend's questions, you'll understand the concepts better and they will stay with you longer. Finally, step back for a big picture view and ask yourself how each piece of information fits with the whole subject. When you link the different concepts together and see them working together as a whole, it's easier to remember the individual components.

Finally, practice showing your work on any multi-step problems, even if you're just studying. Writing out each step you take to solve a problem will help solidify the process in your mind, and you'll be more likely to remember it during the test.

Modality

Modality simply refers to the means or method by which you study. Choosing a study modality that fits your own individual learning style is crucial. No two people learn best in exactly the same way, so it's important to know your strengths and use them to your advantage.

For example, if you learn best by visualization, focus on visualizing a concept in your mind and draw an image or a diagram. Try color-coding your notes, illustrating them, or creating symbols that will trigger your mind to recall a learned concept. If you learn best by hearing or discussing information, find a study partner who learns the same way or read aloud to yourself. Think about how to put the information in your own words. Imagine that you are giving a lecture on the topic and record yourself so you can listen to it later.

For any learning style, flashcards can be helpful. Organize the information so you can take advantage of spare moments to review. Underline key words or phrases. Use different colors for different categories. Mnemonic devices (such as creating a short list in which every item starts with the same letter) can also help with retention. Find what works best for you and use it to store the information in your mind most effectively and easily.

Secret Key #3 – Practice the Right Way

Your success on test day depends not only on how many hours you put into preparing, but also on whether you prepared the right way. It's good to check along the way to see if your studying is paying off. One of the most effective ways to do this is by taking practice tests to evaluate your progress. Practice tests are useful because they show exactly where you need to improve. Every time you take a practice test, pay special attention to these three groups of questions:

- The questions you got wrong
- The questions you had to guess on, even if you guessed right
- The questions you found difficult or slow to work through

This will show you exactly what your weak areas are, and where you need to devote more study time. Ask yourself why each of these questions gave you trouble. Was it because you didn't understand the material? Was it because you didn't remember the vocabulary? Do you need more repetitions on this type of question to build speed and confidence? Dig into those questions and figure out how you can strengthen your weak areas as you go back to review the material.

Additionally, many practice tests have a section explaining the answer choices. It can be tempting to read the explanation and think that you now have a good understanding of the concept. However, an explanation likely only covers part of the question's broader context. Even if the explanation makes perfect sense, **go back and investigate** every concept related to the question until you're positive you have a thorough understanding.

As you go along, keep in mind that the practice test is just that: practice. Memorizing these questions and answers will not be very helpful on the actual test because it is unlikely to have any of the same exact questions. If you only know the right answers to the sample questions, you won't be prepared for the real thing. **Study the concepts** until you understand them fully, and then you'll be able to answer any question that shows up on the test.

It's important to wait on the practice tests until you're ready. If you take a test on your first day of study, you may be overwhelmed by the amount of material covered and how much you need to learn. Work up to it gradually.

On test day, you'll need to be prepared for answering questions, managing your time, and using the test-taking strategies you've learned. It's a lot to balance, like a mental marathon that will have a big impact on your future. Like training for a marathon, you'll need to start slowly and work your way up. When test day arrives, you'll be ready.

Start with the strategies you've read in the first two Secret Keys—plan your course and study in the way that works best for you. If you have time, consider using multiple study resources to get different approaches to the same concepts. It can be helpful to see difficult concepts from more than one angle. Then find a good source for practice tests. Many times, the test website will suggest potential study resources or provide sample tests.

Practice Test Strategy

If you're able to find at least three practice tests, we recommend this strategy:

Untimed and Open-Book Practice

Take the first test with no time constraints and with your notes and study guide handy. Take your time and focus on applying the strategies you've learned.

Timed and Open-Book Practice

Take the second practice test open-book as well, but set a timer and practice pacing yourself to finish in time.

Timed and Closed-Book Practice

Take any other practice tests as if it were test day. Set a timer and put away your study materials. Sit at a table or desk in a quiet room, imagine yourself at the testing center, and answer questions as quickly and accurately as possible.

Keep repeating timed and closed-book tests on a regular basis until you run out of practice tests or it's time for the actual test. Your mind will be ready for the schedule and stress of test day, and you'll be able to focus on recalling the material you've learned.

Secret Key #4 – Pace Yourself

Once you're fully prepared for the material on the test, your biggest challenge on test day will be managing your time. Just knowing that the clock is ticking can make you panic even if you have plenty of time left. Work on pacing yourself so you can build confidence against the time constraints of the exam. Pacing is a difficult skill to master, especially in a high-pressure environment, so **practice is vital**.

Set time expectations for your pace based on how much time is available. For example, if a section has 60 questions and the time limit is 30 minutes, you know you have to average 30 seconds or less per question in order to answer them all. Although 30 seconds is the hard limit, set 25 seconds per question as your goal, so you reserve extra time to spend on harder questions. When you budget extra time for the harder questions, you no longer have any reason to stress when those questions take longer to answer.

Don't let this time expectation distract you from working through the test at a calm, steady pace, but keep it in mind so you don't spend too much time on any one question. Recognize that taking extra time on one question you don't understand may keep you from answering two that you do understand later in the test. If your time limit for a question is up and you're still not sure of the answer, mark it and move on, and come back to it later if the time and the test format allow. If the testing format doesn't allow you to return to earlier questions, just make an educated guess; then put it out of your mind and move on.

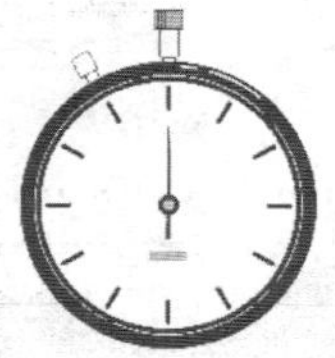

On the easier questions, be careful not to rush. It may seem wise to hurry through them so you have more time for the challenging ones, but it's not worth missing one if you know the concept and just didn't take the time to read the question fully. Work efficiently but make sure you understand the question and have looked at all of the answer choices, since more than one may seem right at first.

Even if you're paying attention to the time, you may find yourself a little behind at some point. You should speed up to get back on track, but do so wisely. Don't panic; just take a few seconds less on each question until you're caught up. Don't guess without thinking, but do look through the answer choices and eliminate any you know are wrong. If you can get down to two choices, it is often worthwhile to guess from those. Once you've chosen an answer, move on and don't dwell on any that you skipped or had to hurry through. If a question was taking too long, chances are it was one of the harder ones, so you weren't as likely to get it right anyway.

On the other hand, if you find yourself getting ahead of schedule, it may be beneficial to slow down a little. The more quickly you work, the more likely you are to make a careless mistake that will affect your score. You've budgeted time for each question, so don't be afraid to spend that time. Practice an efficient but careful pace to get the most out of the time you have.

Secret Key #5 – Have a Plan for Guessing

When you're taking the test, you may find yourself stuck on a question. Some of the answer choices seem better than others, but you don't see the one answer choice that is obviously correct. What do you do?

The scenario described above is very common, yet most test takers have not effectively prepared for it. Developing and practicing a plan for guessing may be one of the single most effective uses of your time as you get ready for the exam.

In developing your plan for guessing, there are three questions to address:

- When should you start the guessing process?
- How should you narrow down the choices?
- Which answer should you choose?

When to Start the Guessing Process

Unless your plan for guessing is to select C every time (which, despite its merits, is not what we recommend), you need to leave yourself enough time to apply your answer elimination strategies. Since you have a limited amount of time for each question, that means that if you're going to give yourself the best shot at guessing correctly, you have to decide quickly whether or not you will guess.

Of course, the best-case scenario is that you don't have to guess at all, so first, see if you can answer the question based on your knowledge of the subject and basic reasoning skills. Focus on the key words in the question and try to jog your memory of related topics. Give yourself a chance to bring the knowledge to mind, but once you realize that you don't have (or you can't access) the knowledge you need to answer the question, it's time to start the guessing process.

It's almost always better to start the guessing process too early than too late. It only takes a few seconds to remember something and answer the question from knowledge. Carefully eliminating wrong answer choices takes longer. Plus, going through the process of eliminating answer choices can actually help jog your memory.

Summary: Start the guessing process as soon as you decide that you can't answer the question based on your knowledge.

How to Narrow Down the Choices

The next chapter in this book (**Test-Taking Strategies**) includes a wide range of strategies for how to approach questions and how to look for answer choices to eliminate. You will definitely want to read those carefully, practice them, and figure out which ones work best for you. Here though, we're going to address a mindset rather than a particular strategy.

Your odds of guessing an answer correctly depend on how many options you are choosing from.

Number of options left	5	4	3	2	1
Odds of guessing correctly	20%	25%	33%	50%	100%

You can see from this chart just how valuable it is to be able to eliminate incorrect answers and make an educated guess, but there are two things that many test takers do that cause them to miss out on the benefits of guessing:

- Accidentally eliminating the correct answer
- Selecting an answer based on an impression

We'll look at the first one here, and the second one in the next section.

To avoid accidentally eliminating the correct answer, we recommend a thought exercise called **the $5 challenge**. In this challenge, you only eliminate an answer choice from contention if you are willing to bet $5 on it being wrong. Why $5? Five dollars is a small but not insignificant amount of money. It's an amount you could afford to lose but wouldn't want to throw away. And while losing $5 once might not hurt too much, doing it twenty times will set you back $100. In the same way, each small decision you make—eliminating a choice here, guessing on a question there—won't by itself impact your score very much, but when you put them all together, they can make a big difference. By holding each answer choice elimination decision to a higher standard, you can reduce the risk of accidentally eliminating the correct answer.

The $5 challenge can also be applied in a positive sense: If you are willing to bet $5 that an answer choice *is* correct, go ahead and mark it as correct.

Summary: Only eliminate an answer choice if you are willing to bet $5 that it is wrong.

Which Answer to Choose

You're taking the test. You've run into a hard question and decided you'll have to guess. You've eliminated all the answer choices you're willing to bet $5 on. Now you have to pick an answer. Why do we even need to talk about this? Why can't you just pick whichever one you feel like when the time comes?

The answer to these questions is that if you don't come into the test with a plan, you'll rely on your impression to select an answer choice, and if you do that, you risk falling into a trap. The test writers know that everyone who takes their test will be guessing on some of the questions, so they intentionally write wrong answer choices to seem plausible. You still have to pick an answer though, and if the wrong answer choices are designed to look right, how can you ever be sure that you're not falling for their trap? The best solution we've found to this dilemma is to take the decision out of your hands entirely. Here is the process we recommend:

Once you've eliminated any choices that you are confident (willing to bet $5) are wrong, select the first remaining choice as your answer.

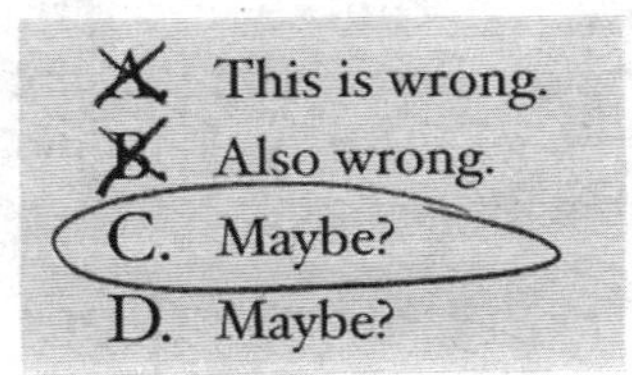

Whether you choose to select the first remaining choice, the second, or the last, the important thing is that you use some preselected standard. Using this approach guarantees that you will not be enticed into selecting an answer choice that looks right, because you are not basing your decision on how the answer choices look.

This is not meant to make you question your knowledge. Instead, it is to help you recognize the difference between your knowledge and your impressions. There's a huge difference between thinking an answer is right because of what you know, and thinking an answer is right because it looks or sounds like it should be right.

Summary: To ensure that your selection is appropriately random, make a predetermined selection from among all answer choices you have not eliminated.

Test-Taking Strategies

This section contains a list of test-taking strategies that you may find helpful as you work through the test. By taking what you know and applying logical thought, you can maximize your chances of answering any question correctly!

It is very important to realize that every question is different and every person is different: no single strategy will work on every question, and no single strategy will work for every person. That's why we've included all of them here, so you can try them out and determine which ones work best for different types of questions and which ones work best for you.

Question Strategies

⊘ Read Carefully

Read the question and the answer choices carefully. Don't miss the question because you misread the terms. You have plenty of time to read each question thoroughly and make sure you understand what is being asked. Yet a happy medium must be attained, so don't waste too much time. You must read carefully and efficiently.

⊘ Contextual Clues

Look for contextual clues. If the question includes a word you are not familiar with, look at the immediate context for some indication of what the word might mean. Contextual clues can often give you all the information you need to decipher the meaning of an unfamiliar word. Even if you can't determine the meaning, you may be able to narrow down the possibilities enough to make a solid guess at the answer to the question.

⊘ Prefixes

If you're having trouble with a word in the question or answer choices, try dissecting it. Take advantage of every clue that the word might include. Prefixes can be a huge help. Usually, they allow you to determine a basic meaning. *Pre-* means before, *post-* means after, *pro-* is positive, *de-* is negative. From prefixes, you can get an idea of the general meaning of the word and try to put it into context.

⊘ Hedge Words

Watch out for critical hedge words, such as *likely, may, can, often, almost, mostly, usually, generally, rarely,* and *sometimes.* Question writers insert these hedge phrases to cover every possibility. Often an answer choice will be wrong simply because it leaves no room for exception. Be on guard for answer choices that have definitive words such as *exactly* and *always.*

⊘ Switchback Words

Stay alert for *switchbacks*. These are the words and phrases frequently used to alert you to shifts in thought. The most common switchback words are *but, although*, and *however*. Others include *nevertheless, on the other hand, even though, while, in spite of, despite*, and *regardless of.* Switchback words are important to catch because they can change the direction of the question or an answer choice.

⊘ Face Value

When in doubt, use common sense. Accept the situation in the problem at face value. Don't read too much into it. These problems will not require you to make wild assumptions. If you have to go beyond creativity and warp time or space in order to have an answer choice fit the question, then you should move on and consider the other answer choices. These are normal problems rooted in reality. The applicable relationship or explanation may not be readily apparent, but it is there for you to figure out. Use your common sense to interpret anything that isn't clear.

Answer Choice Strategies

⊘ Answer Selection

The most thorough way to pick an answer choice is to identify and eliminate wrong answers until only one is left, then confirm it is the correct answer. Sometimes an answer choice may immediately seem right, but be careful. The test writers will usually put more than one reasonable answer choice on each question, so take a second to read all of them and make sure that the other choices are not equally obvious. As long as you have time left, it is better to read every answer choice than to pick the first one that looks right without checking the others.

⊘ Answer Choice Families

An answer choice family consists of two (in rare cases, three) answer choices that are very similar in construction and cannot all be true at the same time. If you see two answer choices that are direct opposites or parallels, one of them is usually the correct answer. For instance, if one answer choice says that quantity x increases and another either says that quantity x decreases (opposite) or says that quantity y increases (parallel), then those answer choices would fall into the same family. An answer choice that doesn't match the construction of the answer choice family is more likely to be incorrect. Most questions will not have answer choice families, but when they do appear, you should be prepared to recognize them.

⊘ Eliminate Answers

Eliminate answer choices as soon as you realize they are wrong, but make sure you consider all possibilities. If you are eliminating answer choices and realize that the last one you are left with is also wrong, don't panic. Start over and consider each choice again. There may be something you missed the first time that you will realize on the second pass.

⊘ Avoid Fact Traps

Don't be distracted by an answer choice that is factually true but doesn't answer the question. You are looking for the choice that answers the question. Stay focused on what the question is asking for so you don't accidentally pick an answer that is true but incorrect. Always go back to the question and make sure the answer choice you've selected actually answers the question and is not merely a true statement.

⊘ Extreme Statements

In general, you should avoid answers that put forth extreme actions as standard practice or proclaim controversial ideas as established fact. An answer choice that states the "process should be used in certain situations, if…" is much more likely to be correct than one that states the "process should be discontinued completely." The first is a calm rational statement and doesn't even make a definitive, uncompromising stance, using a hedge word *if* to provide wiggle room, whereas the second choice is far more extreme.

⊘ Benchmark

As you read through the answer choices and you come across one that seems to answer the question well, mentally select that answer choice. This is not your final answer, but it's the one that will help you evaluate the other answer choices. The one that you selected is your benchmark or standard for judging each of the other answer choices. Every other answer choice must be compared to your benchmark. That choice is correct until proven otherwise by another answer choice beating it. If you find a better answer, then that one becomes your new benchmark. Once you've decided that no other choice answers the question as well as your benchmark, you have your final answer.

⊘ Predict the Answer

Before you even start looking at the answer choices, it is often best to try to predict the answer. When you come up with the answer on your own, it is easier to avoid distractions and traps because you will know exactly what to look for. The right answer choice is unlikely to be word-for-word what you came up with, but it should be a close match. Even if you are confident that you have the right answer, you should still take the time to read each option before moving on.

General Strategies

⊘ Tough Questions

If you are stumped on a problem or it appears too hard or too difficult, don't waste time. Move on! Remember though, if you can quickly check for obviously incorrect answer choices, your chances of guessing correctly are greatly improved. Before you completely give up, at least try to knock out a couple of possible answers. Eliminate what you can and then guess at the remaining answer choices before moving on.

⊘ Check Your Work

Since you will probably not know every term listed and the answer to every question, it is important that you get credit for the ones that you do know. Don't miss any questions through careless mistakes. If at all possible, try to take a second to look back over your answer selection and make sure you've selected the correct answer choice and haven't made a costly careless mistake (such as marking an answer choice that you didn't mean to mark). This quick double check should more than pay for itself in caught mistakes for the time it costs.

⊘ Pace Yourself

It's easy to be overwhelmed when you're looking at a page full of questions; your mind is confused and full of random thoughts, and the clock is ticking down faster than you would like. Calm down and maintain the pace that you have set for yourself. Especially as you get down to the last few minutes of the test, don't let the small numbers on the clock make you panic. As long as you are on track by monitoring your pace, you are guaranteed to have time for each question.

⊘ Don't Rush

It is very easy to make errors when you are in a hurry. Maintaining a fast pace in answering questions is pointless if it makes you miss questions that you would have gotten right otherwise. Test writers like to include distracting information and wrong answers that seem right. Taking a little extra time to avoid careless mistakes can make all the difference in your test score. Find a pace that allows you to be confident in the answers that you select.

⊘ Keep Moving

Panicking will not help you pass the test, so do your best to stay calm and keep moving. Taking deep breaths and going through the answer elimination steps you practiced can help to break through a stress barrier and keep your pace.

Final Notes

The combination of a solid foundation of content knowledge and the confidence that comes from practicing your plan for applying that knowledge is the key to maximizing your performance on test day. As your foundation of content knowledge is built up and strengthened, you'll find that the strategies included in this chapter become more and more effective in helping you quickly sift through the distractions and traps of the test to isolate the correct answer.

Now that you're preparing to move forward into the test content chapters of this book, be sure to keep your goal in mind. As you read, think about how you will be able to apply this information on the test. If you've already seen sample questions for the test and you have an idea of the question format and style, try to come up with questions of your own that you can answer based on what you're reading. This will give you valuable practice applying your knowledge in the same ways you can expect to on test day.

Good luck and good studying!

Mathematics

Number and Number Sense

Classifying Numbers

Whole numbers, **integers**, and **rational numbers** are three categories used to classify numbers. Let's explore these categories from broad to specific. The broadest category is rational numbers.

Rational Numbers

Rational numbers are all numbers that can be written as a fraction. **Rational numbers** can be positive or negative and include fractions, improper fractions, terminating decimals, and some repeating decimals. If it can be written as a fraction, it is rational. Some examples include 6, which can be written as $\frac{6}{1}$; −23, which can be written as $\frac{-23}{1}$; $\frac{1}{4}$, which is already written as a fraction, as is $\frac{-7}{2}$; 0.46, which can be written as $\frac{46}{100}$ or $\frac{23}{50}$; $0.3\overline{3}$, which can be written as $\frac{1}{3}$; and $\sqrt{64}$, which can be written as 8, or $\frac{8}{1}$. The number π, or 3.14159265... is not a rational number because it is a decimal that continues infinitely without repeating and cannot be written as a fraction. It is an **irrational number**.

Review Video: Rational and Irrational Numbers
Visit mometrix.com/academy and enter code: 280645

Integers

Integers are numbers that can be written without a fraction or a decimal. They can be positive, negative, or zero. Some examples include 7; −56; $\frac{8}{4}$, which can be written as 2; and $-\sqrt{81}$, which can be written as −9. If it can be written as a number without a fraction or decimal component, it is an integer. All integers are rational numbers, because they can be written as a fraction, but not all rational numbers are integers, because not all of them can be written *without* a fraction.

Whole Numbers

Whole numbers include the positive integers and zero. 0, 1, 2, 3... and so on, are all whole numbers. Some whole numbers can be written as fractions, like $\frac{7}{1}$, or $\frac{9}{3}$, but because they can be written without the fraction component and they are not negative, they are whole numbers. So, rational numbers are the largest category including fractions, integers, and whole numbers. Integers are the next largest category including negative numbers and whole numbers. Whole numbers are the smallest category, including only zero and positive numbers that are not fractions.

Review Video: Classification of Numbers
Visit mometrix.com/academy and enter code: 461071

Opposites and Absolute Value

A number's **opposite** is the number that is opposite to it on a number line or has an opposite sign. The opposite of –53 is 53. The opposite of 187 is –187. The opposite of a number can be found by multiplying the number by –1. They both have the same distance from zero on a number line, just in different directions. Opposite numbers have the same **absolute value**.

The **absolute value** of a number is its distance from zero. Absolute value is notated by placing a vertical line on each side of a number. For instance, $|-46|$ means the absolute value of –46. We know the names of numbers based on their distance from zero. Numbers and their opposite have the same distance from zero. –2 and 2 have a distance of 2 from zero. So, the absolute value of –2 is 2, or $|-2| = 2$. Also, the absolute value of 2 is 2, or $|2| = 2$. This may be noted by words, or with symbols. You may see something like "$|-89| = 89$," or "the absolute value of $|543|$ is 543," or "find the absolute value of $-\frac{1}{3}$ on a number line." In the last case, you would select $\frac{1}{3}$ on a number line.

Zero is its own opposite. The absolute value of zero is zero.

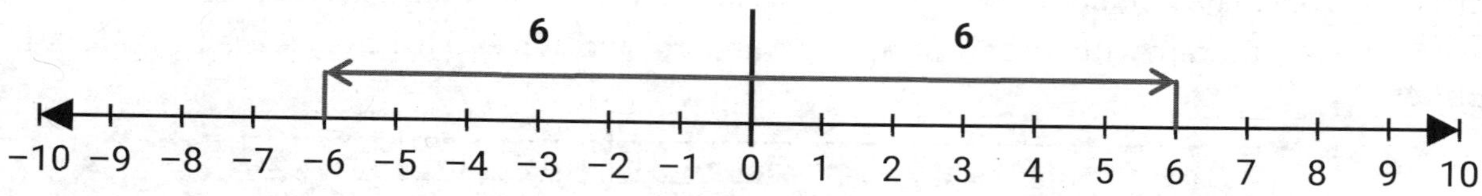

Review Video: Absolute Value
Visit mometrix.com/academy and enter code: 314669

Rational Numbers

Locating Rational Numbers on a Number Line

When locating the placement of integers and rational numbers on a number line, we use whole numbers and negative numbers as a guide. We can easily locate, compare, and order whole numbers like 0, 1, 2, 5, 9, and 258 on a number line. They lie in ascending order to the right of zero. Negative numbers lie on the number line to the left of zero in ascending order. An integer that is in the form of an improper fraction or square root, such as $\frac{12}{3}$ or $-\sqrt{49}$, should be converted into its whole number or negative number counterpart, so $\frac{12}{3}$ simplifies to 4, and $-\sqrt{49}$ simplifies to –7, and can now be placed appropriately on a number line.

Rational numbers can be slightly more complicated. When you are given a rational number, a number that can be written as a fraction, it is best to convert it to a number that is easy for you to use. Are you more familiar with the values of fractions or decimals? That is a decision only you can make. Regardless of which you choose, convert the rational number to a number that is easier to work with, and find its place on the number line.

EXAMPLE

Place $-\frac{8}{3}$ on the number line.

There are three strategies to approach this task:

Strategy 1: Convert to a decimal using division.

$$\begin{array}{r} 2.6\overline{6} \\ 3\overline{)\,8.00} \\ \underline{6} \\ 2\,0 \\ \underline{1\,8} \\ 20 \\ \underline{18} \\ 2 \end{array}$$

$$-\frac{8}{3} = -2.\overline{6}$$

Given this value, we can determine that this number belongs to the left of the number line because it is less than zero. It is between −3 and −2. And we can divide the section between −3 and −2 into tenths, and estimate that this value is slightly to the right of −2.7.

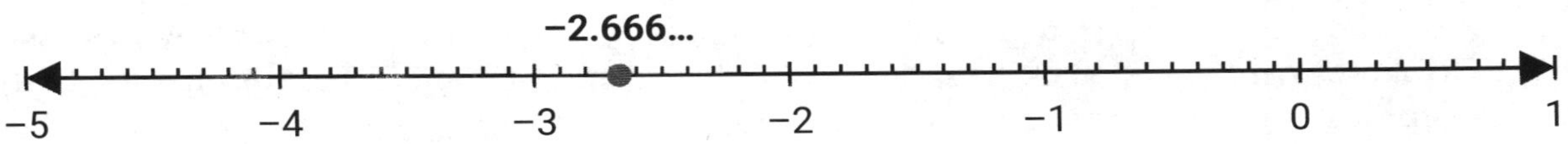

Strategy 2: Convert to a mixed number.

Ask yourself, how many times will 3 go into 8 evenly, or how many $\frac{3}{3}$ are in $\frac{8}{3}$?

3 goes into 8 two times and has a remainder of 2.

In other words, there are two $\frac{3}{3}$ in $\frac{8}{3}$ with $\frac{2}{3}$ left over.

$$-\frac{8}{3} = -2\frac{2}{3}$$

Given this value, we can determine that this number is between −3 and −2. We can divide this section further into thirds, and count two to the left to place this value at $-2\frac{2}{3}$.

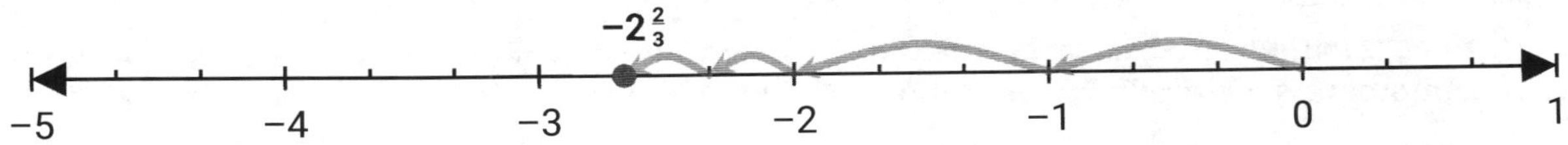

Strategy 3:

Place $-\frac{8}{3}$ on the number line using thirds.

Given this value, we can determine that this value is less than one and will be to the left of 0. We can also determine that each section between whole numbers should be divided into 3 sections to represent thirds.

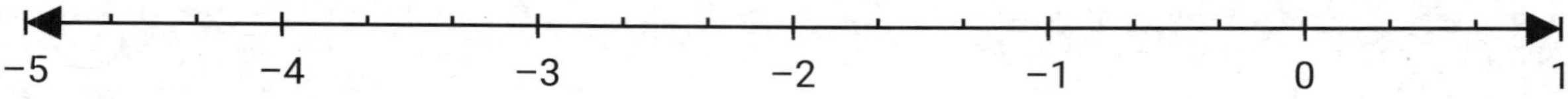

We can now count 8 thirds to the left because we are dealing with a negative fraction.

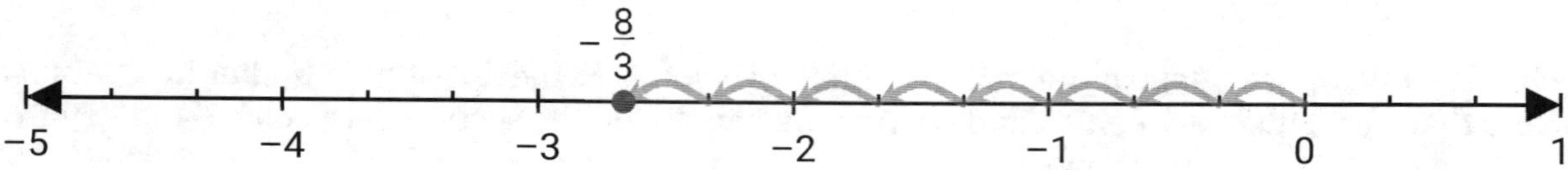

Each strategy will give you the same approximate placement on the number line. The strategy that is chosen is dependent on which type of value is the simplest for you. Each person has number preferences. Choose the best strategy for you based on your preferences. Which strategy was easier for you to follow? Which version of the same value (decimal, mixed number, or improper fraction) was simpler for you to estimate? You may choose more than one strategy!

Comparing and Ordering Rational Numbers

Comparing numbers involves making decisions about whether one number is greater than, less than, or equal to another. Ordering numbers involves making comparisons between more than two numbers to order them from least to greatest, or greatest to least. When you compare and order a set of rational numbers, it is important to first identify where you can make simple judgments. Can you identify the negative and positive numbers? That can help narrow down which numbers are greater and less than others. Can you identify a number that is much larger or much smaller than the rest of the set of numbers? Great! Use your knowledge of numbers to make some judgments and narrow down the set from there. Each set of numbers is different, and you will have to make observations and judgments based on the values given.

Once you have made preliminary judgments, next it is time to rewrite the remaining values as a representation that is easy to work with and convert them appropriately. The goal is to have forms that are easy to visualize so you may make comparisons between numbers. When you are given a list of fractions, it is often helpful to find a common denominator. When working with a mix of decimals and fractions, it is often helpful to convert the values to a common format: all fractions or all decimals. When you are given a rational number using an exponent or a square root, express these numbers in their integer form. Remember, place value is very important when comparing and ordering numbers, specifically integers and decimals.

Do not make the mistake of comparing numbers correctly but not ordering them the way the question is asked. Pay attention and double check if the question is asking for numbers to be ordered from greatest to least, or least to greatest.

Review Video: Ordering Rational Numbers
Visit mometrix.com/academy and enter code: 419578

EXAMPLE

Order the values from greatest to least.

$$-3.48, -\frac{3}{5}, 4, \frac{17}{4}, -3\frac{1}{2}$$

Step 1: Start by making some judgments about the numbers in this list. We can see that there are some negative values and some positive values. Using this judgment, we can determine that 4 and $\frac{17}{4}$ are greater than the other values just by their signs alone. These two values will be first in our list because they are the greatest. Let's compare these values first to create the beginning of our list.

4 is a value that is easy to work with, but $\frac{17}{4}$ is a little tougher. This should be converted to a number that is easier to work with. You may choose to perform the division problem, $17 \div 4$, to find this value as a decimal. Or, you may choose to find the mixed number form of this improper fraction. Let's find both.

Converting to decimal:

```
    4.25
4) 17.00
   16
    1 0
      8
      20
      20
       0
```

So, $\frac{17}{4} = 4.25$.

Converting to mixed number:

To find the whole number, we can ask ourselves, how many times does 4 go into 17 evenly, or how many times does $\frac{4}{4}$ go into $\frac{17}{4}$? 4 times, so 4 is our whole number.

Now, to find the fractional part of this number, we can ask, what is left over. Since $\frac{4}{4} \times 4 = \frac{16}{4}$, we can subtract and find that $\frac{17}{4} - \frac{16}{4} = \frac{1}{4}$. So, 4 is our whole number, and $\frac{1}{4}$ is our fraction.

This means that $\frac{17}{4} = 4\frac{1}{4}$.

Step 2: Now that we have a decimal or mixed number, we can compare this value to 4. We make the judgment that $4 < \frac{17}{4}$.

Now we have our first two values. We are ordering numbers from greatest to least, so the greatest value is $\frac{17}{4}$ and the next greatest value is 4.

Step 3: Continue to make judgments about the remaining values. We can see that there are two values that include −3 as a whole number and then a negative proper fraction. Without doing any conversions, we can determine that the numbers that have −3 as a whole number are smaller than the negative proper fraction. This tells us that $-\frac{3}{5} > -3.47$ and $-\frac{3}{5} > 3\frac{1}{2}$.

We can now include this value to our list from greatest to least. So far, we know:

$$\frac{17}{4} > 4 > -\frac{3}{5}$$

Step 4: Compare the remaining values. We only have two values left, −3.48 and $-3\frac{1}{2}$. We can now make judgments on these values. To compare these numbers, we can convert them both to decimals, convert them both to fractions, or use our number sense. You may be able to look at these values and make an automatic judgment. Let's convert our values to decimals to make sure. I know that $\frac{1}{2}$ is equivalent to 0.5, so I can say that $-3\frac{1}{2} = -3.5$.

Now that our values are in similar forms, we can compare.

When dealing with negative numbers, remember the "larger" the number, the smaller the value. Given −3.48 and −3.5, we will start with the largest place value and compare. We can say that they each have a 3 in the ones place, so we will move to the tenths. The tenths are different. −3.48 has a 4 in the tenths place and −3.5 has a 5 in the tenths place. Because these are negative numbers, we can determine that $-3.48 > -3.5$, or $-3.5 < -3.48$.

Step 5: Review the order and rewrite the values.

We are asked to order this list from greatest to least and we have all the information needed to do this. We have found that $\frac{17}{4} > 4 > -\frac{3}{5} > -3.48 > -3.5$. We can now order these values from greatest to least.

$$\frac{17}{4}, 4, -\frac{3}{5}, -3.48, -3\frac{1}{2}$$

USING MULTIPLICATION AND DIVISION TO IDENTIFY EQUIVALENT VALUES

Division is commonly represented using language, symbols, and fractions, but division can also be represented by using the multiplication operation. Sometimes it makes sense to use different methods of division, and reciprocal multiplication is one of those ways. Division can be considered backwards multiplication. We find this when we are looking at fact families, such as the set of equations involving the numbers 3, 2, and 6. We know that $2 \times 3 = 6$, $3 \times 2 = 6$, $6 \div 2 = 3$, and $6 \div 3 = 2$. If multiplication is the inverse operation of division, we can use that fact to deal with reciprocals in multiplication and division.

A **reciprocal number** is a number's multiplicative inverse. This is directly related to the inverse property of multiplication. When reciprocal numbers are multiplied, their product is always 1. Reciprocal numbers have their numerators and denominators flipped. They are like mirror images of each other.

2 and $\frac{1}{2}$ are reciprocal numbers. Their numerators and denominators are in switched positions, and when they are multiplied, the product is 1.

$$2 = \frac{2}{1}$$
$$\frac{2}{1} \times \frac{1}{2} = \frac{2}{2} = 1$$

When a number is divided by another number, we can get an equivalent value when that same number is multiplied by its reciprocal. Let's look at the known fact $6 \div 2 = 3$, and test the theory that dividing by a number and multiplying by its reciprocal are equivalent. That would mean that $6 \div 2$ and $6 \cdot \frac{1}{2}$ are equivalent.

$$6 \div 2 = \frac{6}{2} = 6 \times \left(\frac{1}{2}\right) = \left(\frac{1}{2}\right) \times 6$$

If we complete the computation, we can see that these are equivalent.

$$6 \times \frac{1}{2} = \frac{6}{1} \times \frac{1}{2} = \frac{6 \times 1}{1 \times 2} = \frac{6}{2} = 6 \div 2 = 3$$

This works for all rational numbers: whole numbers and fractions.

Modeling Fractions, Decimals, and Percentages

There are a group of fractions, decimals, and percentages that are commonly expressed in the real world and that are very important to understand as reference points when working with other values. One category of common part-whole representations is **base 10 values**. These are $\frac{1}{10}, \frac{2}{10}, \frac{3}{10}$... $\frac{10}{10}, \frac{11}{10}$ and so on. As decimals they appear as 0.1, 0.2, 0.3...1.0, 1.1 and so on. And as percentages, 10%, 20%, 30%... 100%, 110% and so on.

Another common category is **quarter values**. As fractions they look like $\frac{1}{4}, \frac{1}{2}, \frac{3}{4}$, 1, $1\frac{1}{4}$, and so on. As decimals, they look like 0.25, 0.5, 0.75, 1, 1.25, and so on. As percentages, they look like 25%, 50%, 75%, 100%, 125%, and so on.

The last category is **thirds**. As fractions these look like $\frac{1}{3}, \frac{2}{3}$, 1, $1\frac{1}{3}$ and so on. As decimals these look like $0.3\overline{3}$, $0.6\overline{6}$, 1, $1.3\overline{3}$, and so on. And as percentages, 33%, 66%, 100%, 133%, and so on.

Benchmark Values

These **benchmark values**, or common values, can be represented through 10 × 10 grids, strip diagrams, and number lines. It is important to be able to identify common fractions, decimals, and percentages using these visual representations.

$$\frac{10}{100} = \frac{1}{10} = 0.1$$

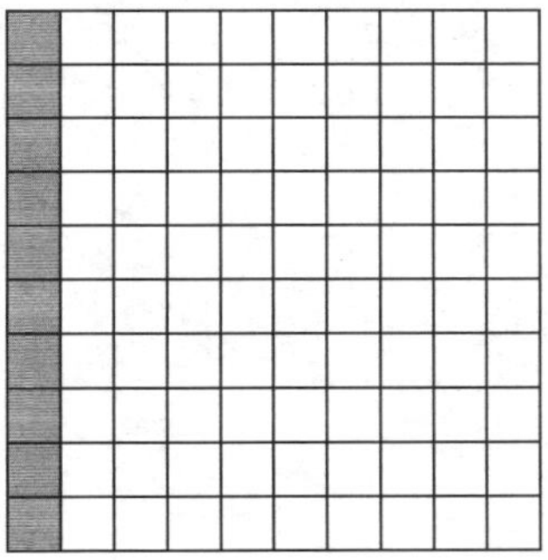

10%

$$\frac{20}{100} = \frac{2}{10} = 0.2$$

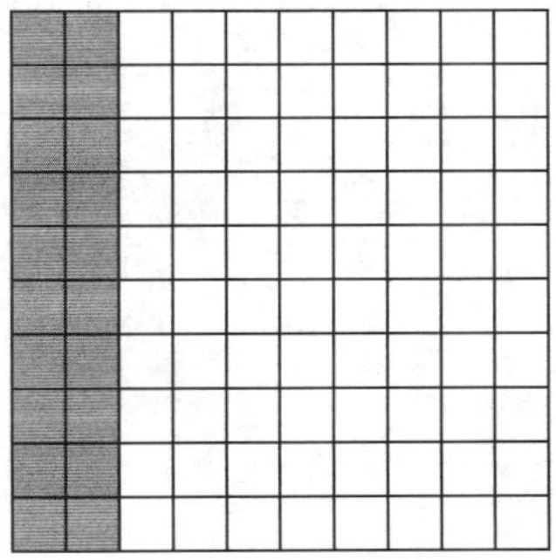

20%

$$\frac{25}{100} = \frac{2.5}{10} = 0.25$$

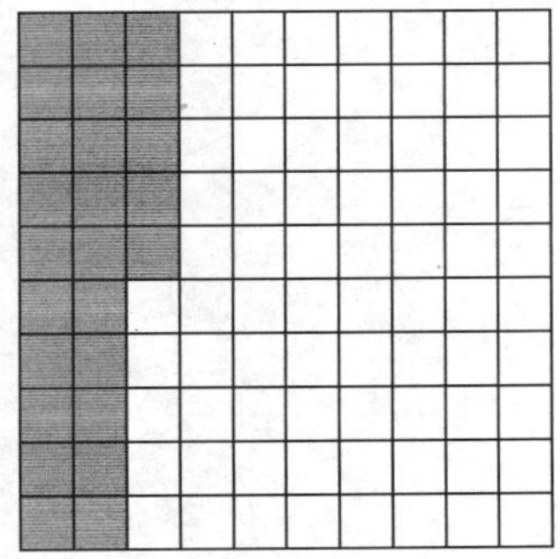

25%

$$\frac{30}{100} = \frac{3}{10} = 0.3$$

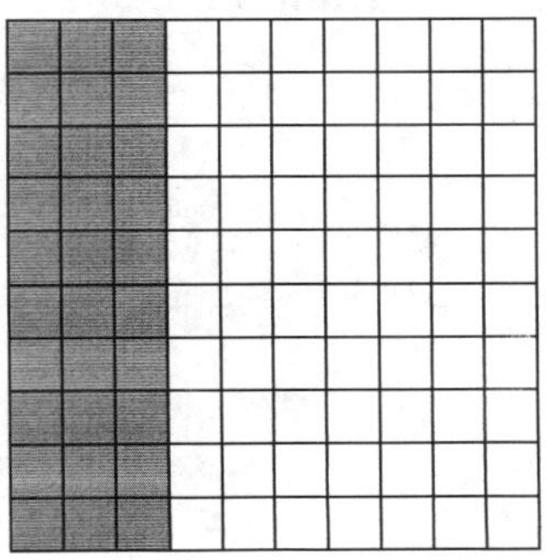

30%

$$\frac{50}{100} = \frac{5}{10} = 0.5$$

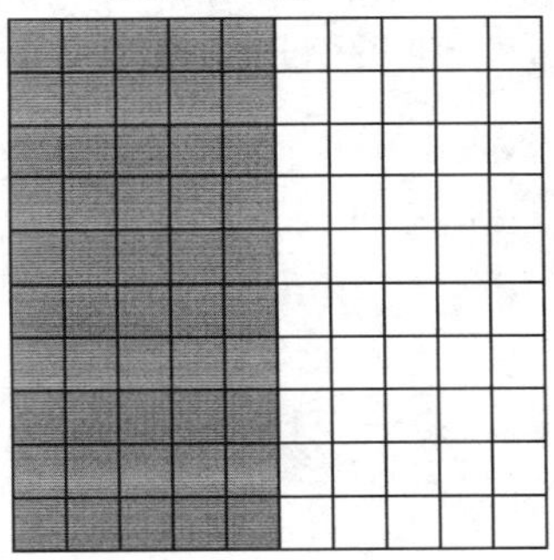

50%

$$\frac{75}{100} = \frac{7.5}{10} = 0.75$$

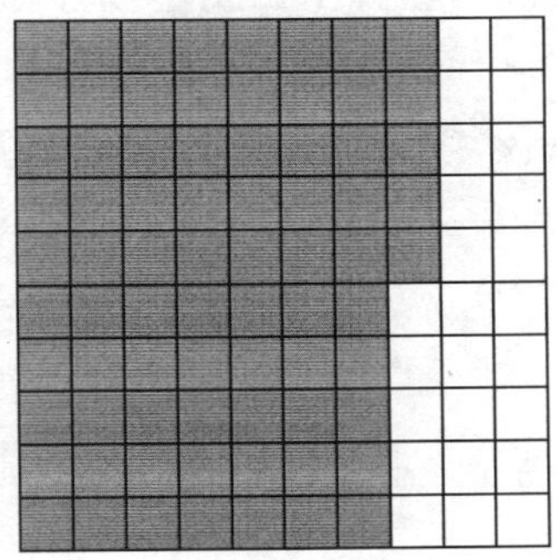

75%

$$\frac{100}{100} = \frac{10}{10} = 1.0$$

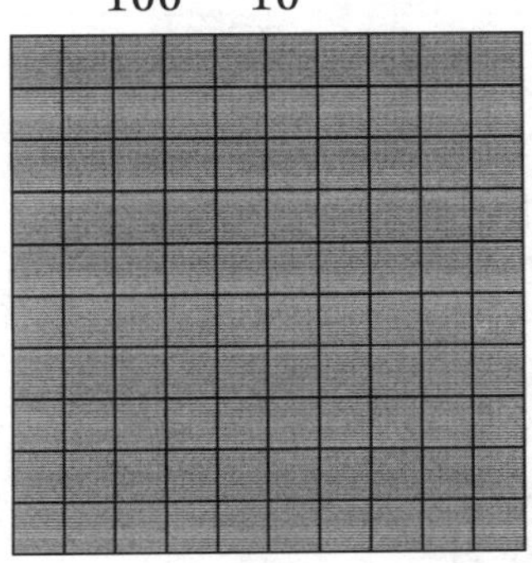

100%

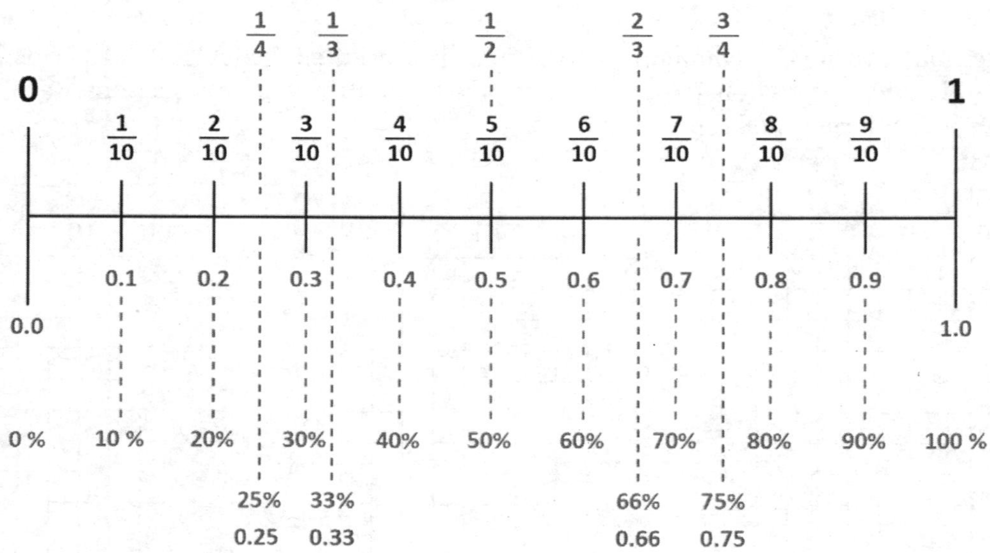

Converting Fractions, Decimals, and Percentages

Fractions, decimals, and percentages compare parts to a whole and are another way to represent division. Sometimes you are required to find equivalent values for given fractions, decimals, and percentages. You can generate equivalent values through models like strip diagrams and number lines, but you can also calculate conversions using multiplication or division.

Converting Fractions to Decimals

To convert a fraction to a decimal, you will divide the numerator by the denominator. For example, $\frac{2}{5}$ can be converted to a decimal by performing the division problem 2 divided by 5 to get the value 0.4, so 0.4 is equivalent to $\frac{2}{5}$.

$$\begin{array}{r} 0.4 \\ 5\overline{)\,2.0} \\ \underline{2\,0} \\ 0 \end{array}$$

$$\frac{2}{5} = 0.4$$

<u>Example</u>

Convert $\frac{7}{20}$ to a decimal.

In this problem, we need to convert a fraction to a decimal. First, rewrite the fraction as a division problem.

$$\frac{7}{20} = 7 \div 20$$

Now, we can solve the new division problem by extending the decimal and using long division.

$$\begin{array}{r} 0.35 \\ 20\overline{)7.00} \\ \underline{6\,0} \\ 1\,00 \\ \underline{1\,00} \\ 0 \end{array}$$

Once we have completed the long division, we can express the conversion as an equation.

$$\frac{7}{20} = 0.35$$

Converting Decimals to Percentages

To convert a decimal to a percent, multiply the decimal by 100 and rewrite using the percent sign. For example, 0.4 can be converted to a percent by performing the calculation 0.4 times 100 to give the value 40, or 40%.

$$0.4 \times 100 = 40$$
$$0.4 = 40\%$$

Example

Convert 0.735 to a percent.

In this problem, we need to convert a decimal to a percentage. Multiply the decimal by 100.

$$0.735 \times 100 = 73.5$$

Now, we can express the conversion as an equation using the percentage sign.

$$0.735 = 73.5\%$$

Example

Convert $\frac{3}{5}$ to a percent.

In this problem we need to convert a fraction to a percentage. First, convert the fraction to a decimal, and then convert the decimal to a percentage.

Rewrite the fraction as a division problem.

$$\frac{3}{5} = 5\overline{)3}$$

Next, we will solve the new division problem by extending the decimal and using long division.

$$\begin{array}{r} 0.6 \\ 5\overline{)3.0} \\ \underline{3\,0} \\ 0 \end{array}$$

Now that we have a decimal form, we can multiply the decimal quotient by 100.

$$0.6 \times 100 = 60$$

Last, we can express the conversion as an equation using the percent sign.

$$\frac{3}{5} = 60\%$$

Another way to approach this problem is to convert the fraction to a value out of 100, and then convert the fraction out of 100 to a percentage.

First, we will use equivalent fractions to convert $\frac{3}{5}$ to a fraction out of 100. We know that $5 \times 20 = 100$, so we can multiply $\frac{3}{5}$ by $\frac{20}{20}$ to get a fraction out of 100.

$$\frac{3}{5} \times \frac{20}{20} = \frac{60}{100}$$

Now, a percentage is a value out of 100, so we can rewrite this value as a percentage with the percentage sign.

$$\frac{60}{100} = 60\%$$

Last, we can rewrite the conversion as an equation.

$$\frac{3}{5} = 60\%$$

Converting Decimals to Fractions

To convert decimals to fractions, keep in mind place value and how a decimal is read. If you can remember the proper way to *read* a decimal, this will really help in generating a fraction that can then be simplified. If reading the decimal is difficult for you, you will need to identify each place value. For example, when you see a decimal like 0.20, you know that you can read this number as 20 hundredths, but also you can see that the smallest value is the zero in the hundredths place, so the fraction will be a part of 100. This can be represented as the fraction $\frac{20}{100}$, also read as 20 hundredths. Since 0.20 is equivalent to 0.2, you may also see this this decimal as 2 tenths and represent the fraction $\frac{2}{10}$, also read as 2 tenths. Once you have this value, you can simplify by finding a common factor between the numerator and denominator to find $\frac{1}{5}$, so $0.20 = \frac{1}{5}$.

$$0.20 = \frac{20}{100} = \frac{2}{10} = \frac{1}{5}$$

Example

Convert 1.225 to a fraction.

In this problem, we need to convert a decimal to a fraction. To approach this problem, we need to identify the place values in this decimal. Notice that there is a 1 in the ones place, a 2 in the tenths place, a 2 in the hundredths place, and a 5 in the thousandths place. We can also read this fraction as one and two hundred twenty-five thousandths.

Next, we will rewrite the decimal as a part compared to the smallest place value. The smallest place value, or the value farthest to the right, is the thousandths place. Because of this, our fraction will be part of 1,000.

$$\frac{1{,}225}{1{,}000}$$

Notice that we are writing this as an improper fraction. As we simplify, we can convert to a mixed number if that is needed. Sometimes improper fractions are easier to work with. It depends on the situation.

Next, we will reduce the fraction to simplest terms. Find the greatest common factor to reduce it in one step or find a common factor and reduce it in multiple steps. Both terms are divisible by 5, so we can start there. We will divide both the numerator and denominator by 5.

$$1{,}225 \div 5 = 245$$
$$1{,}000 \div 5 = 200$$

These terms can be reduced further. The new numerator and denominator are both divisible by 5, so we will divide both values by 5, again.

$$245 \div 5 = 49$$
$$200 \div 5 = 40$$

These terms cannot be simplified further.

The last step is to rewrite the conversion as an equation.

$$1.225 = \frac{49}{40}$$

Converting Percentages to Fractions

To convert percentages to fractions, keep in mind that a percentage is a rate per 100. Any percent can be written as a part of 100. For example, 54% can be converted to a fraction by writing it as $\frac{54}{100}$. Now, this fraction can be simplified using common factors to find that $54\% = \frac{27}{50}$.

Example

Convert 63% to a fraction.

In this problem, we need to convert a percentage to a fraction. We know that a percent is a rate per 100 or a part per 100. This means we can rewrite 60% as a fraction out of 100.

$$60\% = \frac{60}{100}$$

Now that we have written the percentage as a fraction out of 100, we can reduce the fraction to simplest terms. 60 and 100 are divisible by 20, so we will divide both the numerator and denominator by 20.

$$60 \div 20 = 3$$
$$100 \div 20 = 5$$

These terms cannot be simplified further, so the last step is to rewrite the conversion as an equation.

$$60\% = \frac{3}{5}$$

Review Video: Converting Fractions to Percentages and Decimals
Visit mometrix.com/academy and enter code: 306233

Review Video: Converting Decimals to Fractions and Percentages
Visit mometrix.com/academy and enter code: 986765

Solve Problems Involving Decimal, Percentage, and Fraction Conversions

You Bought a Milkshake with $4 out of the $20 in Your Wallet. What Percentage Represents the Amount of Your Money That Was Spent?

a. 2%
b. 20%
c. 16%
d. 5%

In this problem, you are given a story. You used $4 out of the $20 in your wallet and need to find what percent represents the amount you spent.

To approach this problem, we need to understand what information is given, and what you need to find. If you spent $4 out of $20, that means that you spent 4 out of 20, which can be written as the fraction $\frac{4}{20}$.

We want to find what percentage this represents. We can use conversions to find the equivalent percentage to $\frac{4}{20}$.

To convert a fraction to a percentage, we can use equivalent fractions, or we can use division.

Let's start with division. Remember, fractions are another way to write a division problem, so $\frac{4}{20}$ is the same thing as 4 divided by 20. We can set this up using long division.

$$\begin{array}{r} 0.2 \\ 20\overline{)\,4.0} \\ \underline{0} \\ 4\,0 \end{array}$$

So, if you spent $4 out of a total of $20, you spent 0.2 of your money. We want this as a percent, so we can multiply this decimal number by 100, to find the percent.

$$0.2 \times 100 = 20$$

So, you spent 20% of your money.

We can also find this value using equivalent fractions. To use equivalent fractions to find a percentage, we want to find an equivalent fraction where the denominator is 100. We can see that

20 times 5 is 100, so if we multiply the numerator and denominator by 5, we will get an equivalent fraction out of 100.

$$\frac{4}{20} \times \frac{5}{5} = \frac{20}{100} = 20\%$$

$\frac{20}{100}$ is equivalent to 20%, so this also shows that we spent 20% of our money.

The correct answer is B.

Showing Equal Parts

Fractions, decimals, and percentages share a common function: they each compare a part to a whole. One example of this is a quarter. A quarter is 25 cents, or $0.25. We can express the relationship between quarters and dollars multiple ways. We could express this as a fraction. A quarter is $\frac{25}{100}$ of a dollar because it is 25 cents out of 100 cents. This could be simplified to $\frac{1}{4}$ of a dollar. We could express this as a decimal. A quarter is 0.25 of a dollar. And we could express this as a percent. A quarter is 25% of a dollar. Each of these representations show the same *value* of part compared to the whole. You may use strip diagrams or similar models to show equivalent values with fractions, decimals, and percentages.

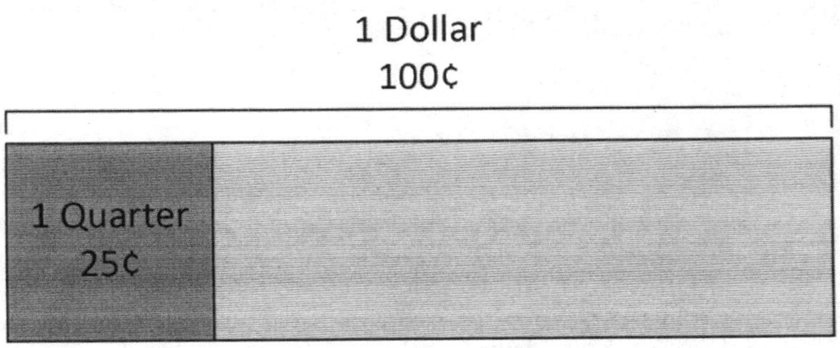

Percentage Problems

Percentage problems come in three possible categories: missing part, missing whole, and missing percent. Within every percentage problem, there is a whole value, a percent of the whole, and a value of the part. First, let's dissect the relationship between whole, percent, and part. Consider a value of 20, which will represent our whole value.

Now, any percent is going to be part of this whole value of 20.

50% would be half of the value of 20, which is 10.

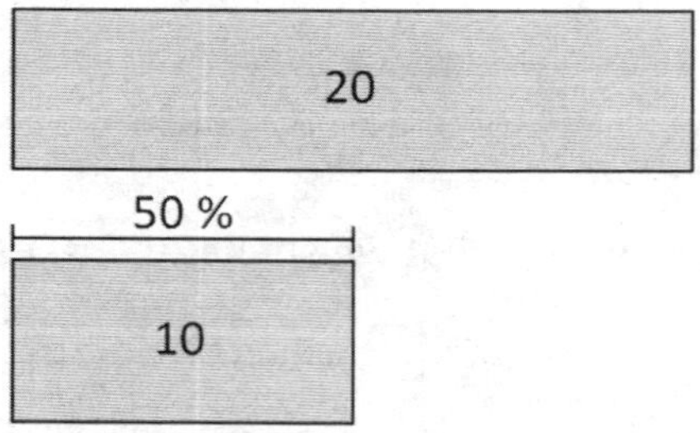

What is the relationship between these parts? How do we use equations to solve this?

Missing Part

Let's start with a missing part problem. This would look like, "What is 50% of 20?"

In this problem, we need to find 50% of a whole value 20. We know that 50% of 20 is 10, but let's figure out how we can solve this mathematically, so we have a strategy to solve more difficult problems.

To find the value of the missing part, we multiply the whole by the percent in decimal form. The decimal form of 50% is 0.5, so we multiply 20 by 0.5 to find the value of the part.

$$20 \times 0.5 = 10$$

So, in a missing part problem, our equation is:

$$\text{whole} \times \text{percent as a decimal} = \text{part}$$

Missing Whole

Now, let's look at missing whole problems. This will look like, "10 is 50% of what value?"

In this type of problem, we know the part, we know the percentage, but we need to find the value of the whole.

To find the value of the whole, we need to divide the value of the part by the decimal form of the percent. In this example, we need to divide 10 by the decimal form of 50%, which is 0.5.

$$10 \div 0.5 = 20$$

So, in a missing whole problem, our equation is:

$$\text{part} \div \text{percent as a decimal} = \text{whole}$$

Missing Percent

Lastly, we will look at a missing percent problem. A missing percent problem will look like, "10 is what percentage of 20?"

In this problem, we have a whole value and a part value, but we need to find the percent.

To find the percent, we need to divide the part by the whole. Our answer will be in decimal form, so we will need to convert it to percent form by multiplying by 100%. In this example, we need to take

10 (the part) and divide it by 20 (the whole) and multiply the answer by 100% to get the percent value.

$$10 \div 20 = 0.5 \times 100\% = 50\%$$

So, in a missing percent problem, our equation is:

$$\text{part} \div \text{whole} = \text{decimal} \times 100 = \text{percent}$$

RATIOS

A **ratio** expresses the relationship between two values. For example, comparisons of the amount of green paint to the amount of white paint, the number of dogs to number of cats, or the volume of flour to volume of sugar could be described using ratios. These items can all be expressed using a value, and the relationship between these values is called a ratio. Ratios are expressed in a few ways: using the ratio symbol, using words, using division, and using equivalent ratios. Let's say a veterinarian sees 35 dogs and 25 cats per week. What is the relationship between the number of animals of each type that are seen? You could use words to explain the ratio of dogs to cats as 35 to 25, or there are 35 dogs seen for every 25 cats seen. You could use the ratio symbol to show the ratio of dogs to cats is $35 : 25$. You can show the ratio of dogs to cats as a fraction, $\frac{35}{25}$. You can simplify a ratio by finding the greatest common factor and dividing each term. In this example the greatest common factor of 35 and 25 is 5. We use the same process used to simplify fractions. So, the ratio of dogs to cats is $7 : 5$, or there are 7 dogs seen for every 5 cats, or the ratio is 7 to 5. We can also express the ratio of cats to dogs. When expressing the ratio of cats to dogs, the same values apply, only reversed. The ratio of cats to dogs is 25 to 35, 5 to 7, $25 : 35$, $5 : 7$, $\frac{25}{35}$, $\frac{5}{7}$, or there are 5 cats seen for every 7 dogs. Ratios can be expressed in a variety of ways, but each way expresses the same relationship between two values.

Review Video: Ratios
Visit mometrix.com/academy and enter code: 996914

RATES

A **rate** is a comparison of two values with different units. A **constant rate** means that the relationship between units remains the same. Some common examples are the comparison of dollars to hour, miles to hours, and beats to seconds. Rates can be expressed in a variety of ways, including using language, as quotients, using equivalent rates, algebraically, using tables, or graphically.

Rates can be expressed through language. Let's say you get your first job working at a store making $12 for every hour of work. This is a rate, a comparison between two unlike units, dollars and hours. This rate can be expressed through words. We use the word *per* when expressing rates. You could say that you make 12 dollars per hour.

Rates can be expressed as a fraction, or division. If you make 12 dollars per hour, you could express that as $12/hour, or $\frac{12 \text{ dollars}}{1 \text{ hour}}$. You could even say that the rate of dollars per hour is $\frac{12}{1}$.

Rates can be expressed using equivalent rates. \$12/hour can be expressed as \$24/2 hours. Or, if you work 20 hours per week, you could say you make \$240/week. Regardless of the number of hours worked, the number of dollars made per hour remains constant, or the same.

Review Video: Rates and Unit Rates
Visit mometrix.com/academy and enter code: 185363

Modeling Ratios

Ratios can be expressed through models. You will often encounter ratio models as strip diagrams and picture models. Suppose we are tiling a bathroom floor with a cool design and for every 4 hexagon tiles, there are 6 square tiles. We can express this ratio using a picture model or a strip diagram.

Model 1

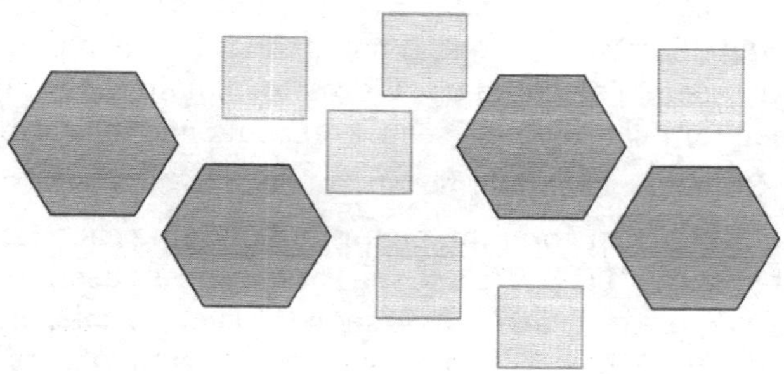

Model 2

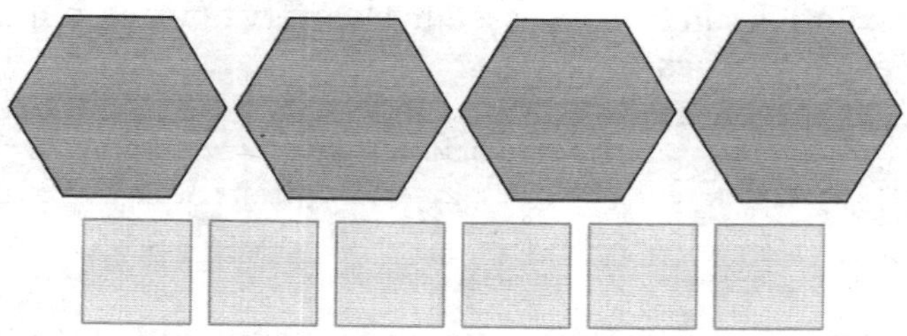

Model 3

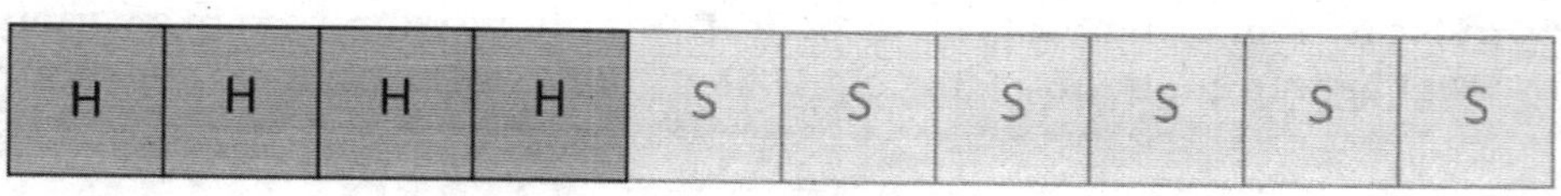

Model 4

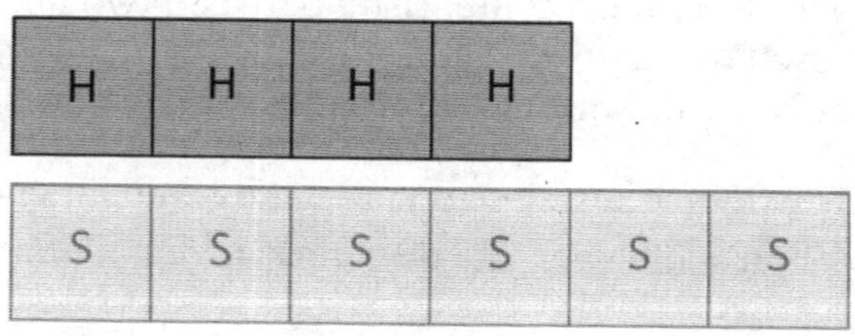

Strip diagrams and picture models can also help you simplify a ratio. You may group like terms to identify a simplified ratio.

MODEL 5

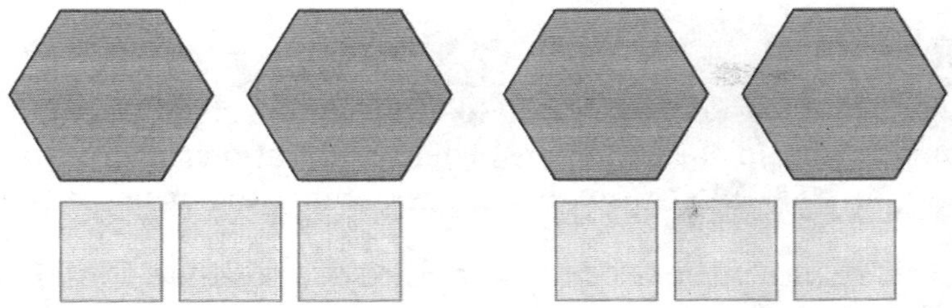

MODEL 6

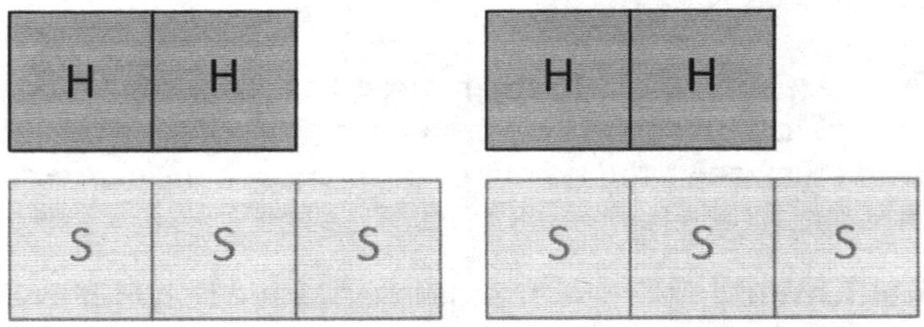

So, from these models, we can conclude that the ratio of hexagon tiles to square tiles is 4 : 6, and we can also express it as 2 : 3 because we can divide our diagrams into two equal groups and in each group, there are 2 hexagons and 3 squares.

EXPONENTS

An **exponent** is a superscript number placed next to another number at the top right. It indicates how many times the base number is to be multiplied by itself. Exponents provide a shorthand way to write what would be a longer mathematical expression, Example: $2^4 = 2 \times 2 \times 2 \times 2$. A number with an exponent of 2 is said to be "squared," while a number with an exponent of 3 is said to be "cubed." The value of a number raised to an exponent is called its power. So 8^4 is read as "8 to the 4th power," or "8 raised to the power of 4."

Review Video: Exponents
Visit mometrix.com/academy and enter code: 600998

A **root**, such as a square root, is another way of writing a fractional exponent. Instead of using a superscript, roots use the radical symbol ($\sqrt{\ }$) to indicate the operation. Nearly all of the roots you encounter will be square roots. A square root is the same as a number raised to the one-half power. When we say that a is the square root of b ($a = \sqrt{b}$), we mean that a multiplied by itself equals b: ($a \times a = b$). A **perfect square** is a number that has an integer for its square root. There are 10 perfect squares from 1 to 100: 1, 4, 9, 16, 25, 36, 49, 64, 81, 100 (the squares of integers 1 through 10).

Review Video: Perfect Squares and Square Roots
Visit mometrix.com/academy and enter code: 648063

Computation and Estimation

ORDER OF OPERATIONS

The **order of operations** is a mathematical term to describe the correct sequence of steps to simplify an expression or solve an equation. The order of operations is very specific and important to remember. The acronym **PEMDAS** is used to help remember the order of operations.

The first two operations are **parentheses** and **exponents**. This is the PE in PEMDAS. When given an expression or equation that includes parentheses or exponents, these items should be dealt with first. If you have an expression or equation with both items, or more than one, you will first simplify or solve the items in parentheses, then the items with exponents.

If there are parentheses or exponents within other parentheses or exponents, you should simplify from the inside out. For instance, given the expression $3 \times (5 - 2)^2$, you first solve the part inside the parentheses, $5 - 2$, and then solve the exponent, 3^2. But given the expression $3 \times (5 - 2^2)$, you first solve the exponent, 2^2, and then the parentheses, $5 - 4$.

The next group is **multiplication** and **division**. This is the M and D in PEMDAS. When given an expression or equation that includes multiplication or division, these operations are dealt with *after* parentheses and exponents if they are present. If multiplication and division are present, simplify from left to right. For example, given the expression $24 \div 4 + 3 \times 5$, we would simplify the expression $24 \div 4$ and then the expression 3×5.

The last category is **addition** and **subtraction**, the A and S in PEMDAS. This is the last category that is dealt with when simplifying an expression. Addition and subtraction are dealt with after parentheses, exponents, multiplication, and division, and when there is more than one addition or subtraction operation, they are solved or simplified from left to right. For example, given the expression $2 + 4 - 3 + 7$, we would simplify from left to right. First, $2 + 4$, then $6 - 3$ (note that we are using the result of the previous expression because it is simplified first), and last, $3 + 7$.

Review Video: Order of Operations
Visit mometrix.com/academy and enter code: 259675

FRACTION OPERATIONS

PROPER FRACTIONS AND MIXED NUMBERS

A fraction whose denominator is greater than its numerator is known as a **proper fraction**, while a fraction whose numerator is greater than its denominator is known as an **improper fraction**. Proper fractions have values *less than one* and improper fractions have values *greater than one.*

A **mixed number** is a number that contains both an integer and a fraction. Any improper fraction can be rewritten as a mixed number. Example: $\frac{8}{3} = \frac{6}{3} + \frac{2}{3} = 2 + \frac{2}{3} = 2\frac{2}{3}$. Similarly, any mixed number can be rewritten as an improper fraction. Example: $1\frac{3}{5} = 1 + \frac{3}{5} = \frac{5}{5} + \frac{3}{5} = \frac{8}{5}$.

Review Video: Proper and Improper Fractions and Mixed Numbers
Visit mometrix.com/academy and enter code: 211077

ADDING AND SUBTRACTING FRACTIONS

If two fractions have a common denominator, they can be added or subtracted simply by adding or subtracting the two numerators and retaining the same denominator. If the two fractions do not already have the same denominator, one or both of them must be manipulated to achieve a common denominator before they can be added or subtracted. Example: $\frac{1}{2}+\frac{1}{4}=\frac{2}{4}+\frac{1}{4}=\frac{3}{4}$.

Review Video: Adding and Subtracting Fractions
Visit mometrix.com/academy and enter code: 378080

Multiplying Fractions

Two fractions can be multiplied by multiplying the two numerators to find the new numerator and the two denominators to find the new denominator. Example: $\frac{1}{3}\times\frac{2}{3}=\frac{1\times2}{3\times3}=\frac{2}{9}$.

Dividing Fractions

Two fractions can be divided by flipping the numerator and denominator of the second fraction and then proceeding as though it were a multiplication problem. Example: $\frac{2}{3}\div\frac{3}{4}=\frac{2}{3}\times\frac{4}{3}=\frac{8}{9}$.

Review Video: Multiplying and Dividing Fractions
Visit mometrix.com/academy and enter code: 473632

Multiplying a Mixed Number by a Whole Number or a Decimal

When multiplying a mixed number by something, it is usually best to convert it to an improper fraction first. Additionally, if the multiplicand is a decimal, it is most often simplest to convert it to a fraction. For instance, to multiply $4\frac{3}{8}$ by 3.5, begin by rewriting each quantity as a whole number plus a proper fraction. Remember, a mixed number is a fraction added to a whole number and a decimal is a representation of the sum of fractions, specifically tenths, hundredths, thousandths, and so on:

$$4\frac{3}{8}\times 3.5=\left(4+\frac{3}{8}\right)\times\left(3+\frac{1}{2}\right)$$

Next, the quantities being added need to be expressed with the same denominator. This is achieved by multiplying and dividing the whole number by the denominator of the fraction. Recall that a whole number is equivalent to that number divided by 1:

$$=\left(\frac{4}{1}\times\frac{8}{8}+\frac{3}{8}\right)\times\left(\frac{3}{1}\times\frac{2}{2}+\frac{1}{2}\right)$$

When multiplying fractions, remember to multiply the numerators and denominators separately:

$$=\left(\frac{4\times 8}{1\times 8}+\frac{3}{8}\right)\times\left(\frac{3\times 2}{1\times 2}+\frac{1}{2}\right)$$
$$=\left(\frac{32}{8}+\frac{3}{8}\right)\times\left(\frac{6}{2}+\frac{1}{2}\right)$$

Now that the fractions have the same denominators, they can be added:

$$=\frac{35}{8}\times\frac{7}{2}$$

Finally, perform the last multiplication and then simplify:

$$= \frac{35 \times 7}{8 \times 2} = \frac{245}{16} = \frac{240}{16} + \frac{5}{16} = 15\frac{5}{16}$$

Decimal Operations

Adding and Subtracting Decimals

When adding and subtracting decimals, the decimal points must always be aligned. Adding decimals is just like adding regular whole numbers. Example: $4.5 + 2.0 = 6.5$.

If the problem-solver does not properly align the decimal points, an incorrect answer of 4.7 may result. An easy way to add decimals is to align all of the decimal points in a vertical column visually. This will allow you to see exactly where the decimal should be placed in the final answer. Begin adding from right to left. Add each column in turn, making sure to carry the number to the left if a column adds up to more than 9. The same rules apply to the subtraction of decimals.

Review Video: Adding and Subtracting Decimals
Visit mometrix.com/academy and enter code: 381101

Multiplying Decimals

A simple multiplication problem has two components: a **multiplicand** and a **multiplier**. When multiplying decimals, work as though the numbers were whole rather than decimals. Once the final product is calculated, count the number of places to the right of the decimal in both the multiplicand and the multiplier. Then, count that number of places from the right of the product and place the decimal in that position.

For example, 12.3×2.56 has a total of three places to the right of the respective decimals. Multiply 123×256 to get 31,488. Now, beginning on the right, count three places to the left and insert the decimal. The final product will be 31.488.

Review Video: How to Multiply Decimals
Visit mometrix.com/academy and enter code: 731574

Dividing Decimals

Every division problem has a **divisor** and a **dividend**. The dividend is the number that is being divided. In the problem $14 \div 7$, 14 is the dividend and 7 is the divisor. In a division problem with decimals, the divisor must be converted into a whole number. Begin by moving the decimal in the divisor to the right until a whole number is created. Next, move the decimal in the dividend the same number of spaces to the right. For example, 4.9 into 24.5 would become 49 into 245. The decimal was moved one space to the right to create a whole number in the divisor, and then the same was done for the dividend. Once the whole numbers are created, the problem is carried out normally: $245 \div 49 = 5$.

Review Video: Dividing Decimals
Visit mometrix.com/academy and enter code: 560690

Review Video: Dividing Decimals by Whole Numbers
Visit mometrix.com/academy and enter code: 535669

Integer Operations

It is very important to be able to **add**, **subtract**, **multiply**, and **divide** integers quickly and easily. This includes operations with positive and negative numbers. Addition, subtraction, multiplication, and division with positive numbers should be automatic. Now you will use what you know about whole number operations to help you with integer operations involving negative numbers. When you are solving operations with integers, the most common way to get a question wrong is by mixing up your signs. There are a few rules that you can use to remember and practice frequently so the process is solid and automatic.

Addition

When you add two positive numbers, your answer will be positive.

$$7 + 32 = 39$$

When you add two negative numbers, your answer will be negative.

$$-7 + (-32) = -39$$

When you add a negative number to a positive number, the total value will be less than the positive number. Adding a negative number is the same as subtracting the positive version of that negative number.

$$\begin{aligned} &= 25 + (-5) \\ &= 25 - 5 \\ &= 20 \end{aligned}$$

When you add a positive number to a negative number, the total value will be greater than the negative number. When adding a positive number to a negative number, use subtraction.

$$\begin{aligned} &= -6 + 36 \\ &= 36 + -6 \\ &= 36 - 6 \\ &= 30 \end{aligned}$$

Subtraction

When you subtract two positive numbers, and the first number is larger, your answer will be positive.

$$24 - 3 = 21$$

When you subtract two positive numbers, and the first number is smaller, your answer will be negative.

$$3 - 24 = -21$$

When you subtract two negative numbers, your answer will be greater than the starting value. Subtracting a negative number is equivalent to adding the number.

$$-16 - (-4) = -16 + 4 = -12$$
$$-4 - (-16) = -4 + 16 = 12$$

MULTIPLICATION AND DIVISION

When multiplying and dividing positive and negative rational numbers, it is important to remember the rules for integer multiplication and division. Whether the answer is positive or negative depends on the number of negative numbers in your problem. If the total number of negative signs is even, your answer will be positive. If you have an odd number of negative numbers, your answer will be negative.

When multiplying or dividing two positive numbers, the answer will be positive.

$$5 \cdot 6 = 30$$
$$72 \div 9 = 8$$

When multiplying or dividing two negative numbers, the answer will be positive.

$$-7 \cdot (-3) = 21$$
$$-16 \div (-4) = 4$$

When multiplying or dividing a negative number and a positive number, the answer will be negative.

$$-2 \cdot 8 = -16$$
$$24 \div -6 = -4$$

REPRESENTING DIVISION

Division can be represented in many ways. A scenario for division is typically expressed as a group of items being divided among multiple groups with a certain number of items per group. Perhaps a group of flowers are divided among multiple vases, or a collection of pictures is being put in a photo album with multiple pages. Whatever the scenario, there are many ways to express it numerically. Let's say Terrance has 24 photos and can put 4 photos on each page. What are some ways to express this division problem?

- We could write it out: 24 divided by 4
- We could use the division symbol: $24 \div 4$
- We could write it using the long division symbol:
- We could write it as a fraction: $\frac{24}{4}$

Every division problem can be represented in these four ways.

Review Video: Mathematical Operations
Visit mometrix.com/academy and enter code: 208095

EXAMPLE

Simplify the expression using order of operations: $4(-3) + (-25 \times -4)$.

When approaching this expression, we will simplify in multiple steps using the order of operations, PEMDAS, as a guide. The first step is to simplify the items in parentheses.

$$4(-3) + (-25 \times -4)$$
$$4(-3) + (100)$$

-25×-4 is 100 because 25×4 is 100, and both signs are negative. There are an even number of negative signs, so the answer is positive.

Now we can continue simplifying by solving the multiplication problem.

$$4(-3) + 100$$
$$-12 + 100$$

$4(-3)$ is -12 because 4×3 is 12 and there is 1 negative number. There is an odd number of negative signs, so the answer is negative.

Now we can use addition to simplify further.

$$-12 + 100 = 100 - 12 = 88$$

The simplified expression is 88.

Representing Integer Operations on a Number Line

Integer operations include adding, subtracting, multiplying, and dividing using positive numbers, negative numbers, and zero. These operations can be represented on a number line.

We can represent operations of integers on a number line. Think about the problem $4 + (-7)$. This can be represented on a number line by starting at 4 and counting to the left 7 times because we are adding a -1 to 4 each time we move to the left. You can tell we are moving to the left because of the arrows in the figure.

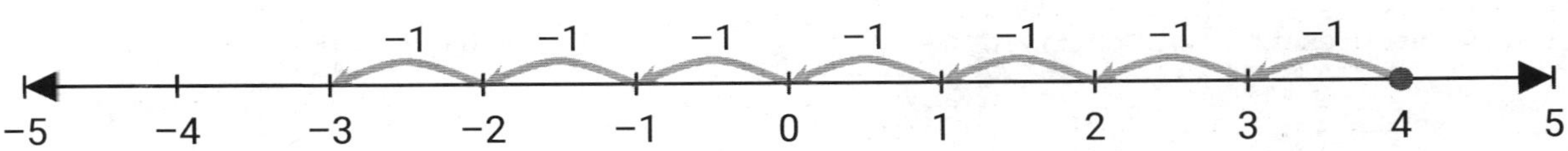

This number line also represents the problem $4 - 7$. We could also say that the number line shows $4 + (7 \times (-1))$ because we started at 4 and moved 7 "jumps" of -1.

Consider this number line that does not have any arrows. What expressions can you generate from this number line?

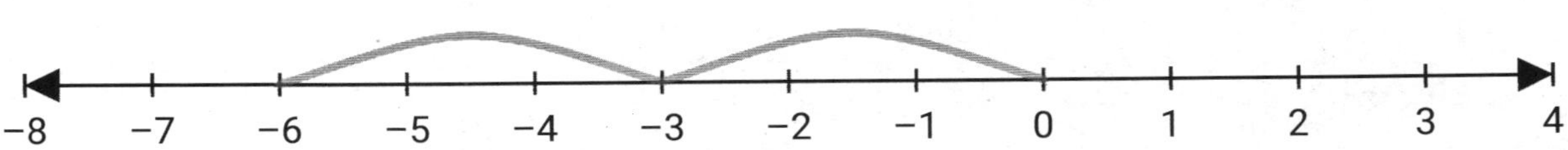

Since there are no arrows, it is open to interpretation. Let's look at our options.

An addition expression can be found. We could say $-6 + 3 + 3$ because it could be viewed that we started at -6 and added 3 twice.

A subtraction expression can be found in this number line. We could say $0 - 3 - 3$ because it could be viewed that we started at 0 and subtracted 3, twice.

A multiplication expression can also be found. We could say that we started at 0 and added -3 times 2. We could say this because there are two "jumps" of -3.

There are other possibilities that can be generated through equivalent expressions. When looking at a number line to find the expression, it is important to break each part down by considering the following questions. Where does the expression start? Which direction are the arrows moving? How many jumps are there and what is the value of each jump? All these will help you determine the correct expression.

Review Video: Negative and Positive Number Line
Visit mometrix.com/academy and enter code: 816439

Multiplying and Dividing Large Numbers, Decimals, and Fractions

Multiplying Large Numbers

Multiplying large numbers takes practice. When you set up a multiplication problem with large numbers, it is very important to line up place values and understand the concept of **partial products**. Partial products are the pieces of a larger multiplication problem that, when added together, give the whole product. When multiplying these numbers, you can approach the problem using the distributive property. This allows the values in the problem to be broken into small pieces based on place value.

Consider the following scenario: The soccer league is holding a bake sale. Each team made $1,542, and there are 12 teams in the league. How much money did the league raise?

This problem gives two values, 1,542 and 12, and this is a multiplication problem. We can set up this problem using expanded form and the distributive property.

One way to represent $1{,}542 \times 12$ is to break 12 into $10 + 2$ and distribute.

$$(1{,}542 \times 10) + (1{,}542 \times 2)$$

$$15{,}420 + 3{,}084$$

$$18{,}504$$

We can also use this strategy the other way, where 1,542 is written in expanded form and the 12 is distributed.

$$(12 \times 1{,}000) + (12 \times 500) + (12 \times 40) + (12 \times 2)$$

$$12{,}000 + 6{,}000 + 480 + 24$$

$$18{,}504$$

We can also set up a problem using the standard algorithm.

$$\begin{array}{r} ^{1}\quad\ \ \\ 1{,}542 \\ \times\quad 12 \\ \hline 3\,084 \end{array}$$

$$\begin{array}{r} 1{,}542 \\ \times\quad 1\not{2} \\ \hline 3{,}084 \\ 15{,}420 \end{array}$$

$$\begin{array}{r} ^{1}\quad\ \ \\ 3{,}084 \\ +15{,}420 \\ \hline 18{,}504 \end{array}$$

EXAMPLE

You are making an art project that includes beading 35 strands of beads. Each strand holds 1,254 beads. How many beads will you need to complete the project?

We can set up our problem in a few ways.

Using the distributive property and expanded notation:

$$(1{,}254 \times 30) + (1{,}254 \times 5)$$

or

$$(1{,}000 \times 35) + (200 \times 35) + (50 \times 35) + (4 \times 35)$$

We can expand each of these expressions further to find easier numbers to work with.

$$(1{,}000 \times 30) + (1{,}000 \times 5) + (200 \times 30) + (200 \times 5) + (50 \times 30) + (50 \times 5) + (4 \times 30) + (4 \times 5)$$
$$30{,}000 + 5{,}000 + 6{,}000 + 1{,}000 + 1{,}500 + 250 + 120 + 20$$

Once at this step, add all your partial products. You can add them in any order. In this example, we added two at a time until the answer was simplified completely.

$$35{,}000 + 7{,}000 + 1{,}750 + 140$$
$$42{,}000 + 1{,}890$$
$$43{,}890$$

We can also set this problem up traditionally and get the same product.

To solve traditionally, line up your factors based on place value where the ones, tens, hundreds, etc. line up. Then, you will begin with the ones place and multiply each digit. This is the same process as the expanded notation, just a shorthand version.

$$\begin{array}{r} ^{1\ 2\ 2}\quad \\ 1{,}254 \\ \times\quad 35 \\ \hline 6{,}270 \end{array}$$

Multiplying the ones gives us the first partial product. This is the product of 1,254 times 5.

Now, we need to multiply the tens. When we multiply the tens, we write our product starting in the tens place. You can put a zero in the ones place or use a placeholder. θ will be our placeholder.

```
  1 1
  1,254
×    35
  6,270
 37,62θ
```

Now we have our second partial product. This is the product of 1,254 times 30.

Now we can add our partial products.

```
   6,270
+37,620
  43,890
```

The answer is 43,890, which means that we need 43,890 beads.

MULTIPLYING DECIMALS

When multiplying decimals, you use the same strategy as multiplying whole numbers. The difference is that you have digits to the right of the decimal. Using the traditional strategy of multiplication is the most common way to solve problems with decimals, because the distributive property and expanded form would be extremely tedious. When using the traditional method, you will solve the multiplication with no decimals, and add a decimal to your solution at the end of the problem.

When you are setting up a multiplication problem, the number with more digits will be on the top, and the number with fewer digits will be on the bottom.

For example, find the value of 23.142 times 0.045.

We will set up this problem traditionally, with no decimal places. The number 23,142 has more digits than 45, so 23,142 will be at the top of our problem, and 45 will be at the bottom.

```
 23,142
×    45
```

When using this strategy, you add the decimal at the end. To figure out how many decimal places the answer will have, you count the number of digits behind the decimal point in each factor to find the decimal in the product. In this example, there are 3 decimal places in the first number (23.142) and 3 in the second number (0.045), so the answer will have 6 decimal places. Once the product is found, you would count back 6 digits and place the decimal in the appropriate place.

```
   1   1
   1   2 1
   23,142
×      45
---------
  115,710
+ 925,680
---------
1,041,390
```

1041390.

So, 23.142 times 0.045 is 1.04139, which can be rounded to the nearest thousandth to get 1.041.

Review Video: How to Multiply Decimals
Visit mometrix.com/academy and enter code: 731574

EXAMPLE

You are making a blanket for a friend, and you cut 244 squares. Each square is 2.125 inches across. If you laid the squares out in a line, how long would the line be?

In this problem, we are multiplying 244 and 2.125.

2.125 has more digits than 244, so place 2,125 on top when multiplying.

```
  2,125
×   244
-------
```

We can multiply each place value to find the partial products.

```
      1
    1 2
    1 2
  2,125
×   244
-------
  8,500
 85,000
425,000
```

Then we will add the partial products.

```
 1 1
    8,500
   85,000
+ 425,000
---------
  518,500
```

And finally, add our decimal point. The original problem was $244 \cdot 2.125$. Here, the first factor has zero decimal places and the second factor has 3, so this answer has 3 decimal places.

$$518500.$$

So, if we lined all 244 squares in a line, it would be 518.5 inches long.

Multiplying Fractions

When you multiply fractions, you must convert each factor to a fraction, and multiply across the denominators and numerators.

If you are multiplying 3 by $\frac{2}{3}$, you convert each factor to a fraction, and multiply across.

$$3 = \frac{3}{1}$$

$$\frac{3}{1} \times \frac{2}{3} = \frac{3 \times 2}{1 \times 3} = \frac{6}{3}$$

We should convert $\frac{6}{3}$ to a simplified fraction or whole number.

$$\frac{6}{3} = \frac{6 \div 3}{3 \div 3} = \frac{2}{1} = 2$$

Follow the same process to find the value of 3 times $\frac{5}{5}$.

$$3 = \frac{3}{1}$$

$$\frac{3}{1} \times \frac{5}{5} = \frac{3 \times 5}{1 \times 5} = \frac{15}{5} = \frac{3}{1} = 3$$

And for $3 \times \frac{5}{2}$.

$$3 = \frac{3}{1}$$

$$\frac{3}{1} \times \frac{5}{2} = \frac{3 \times 5}{1 \times 2} = \frac{15}{2}$$

$\frac{15}{2}$ is in simplest form.

Review Video: Multiplying and Dividing Fractions
Visit mometrix.com/academy and enter code: 473632

EXAMPLE

Solve $7 \cdot \frac{4}{5}$.

In this problem, we are multiplying 7 and $\frac{4}{5}$, a fraction that is less than 1. This tells us that our answer will be less than 7.

We will start by writing 7 as a fraction.

$$7 = \frac{7}{1}$$

Now, we can set up our multiplication problem.

$$\frac{7}{1} \times \frac{4}{5}$$

Now, we can multiply each numerator and each denominator to find our answer.

$$\frac{7 \times 4}{1 \times 5} = \frac{28}{5}$$

ESTIMATING THE VALUE OF A NUMBER MULTIPLIED BY A FRACTION

FRACTIONS LESS THAN 1

A fraction is less than 1 when the numerator is smaller than the denominator. The fractions $\frac{1}{8}, \frac{1}{2}, \frac{2}{3}, \frac{7}{8}$, and $\frac{23}{50}$ are all examples of fractions less than one. When we multiply a number by a fraction less than one, we get a smaller value than what we started with. Think about what happens when we multiply by a number that is greater than one. When we multiply 5 by a number greater than 1, we get a number larger than 5, like $5 \cdot 10 = 50$. When we multiply 5 by 1, we get 5. But when we multiply 5 by a number less than 1, we get a number that is smaller than 5. This is true for all multiplication by a fraction whose value is less than 1. You may be asked to estimate the value of a number multiplied by a fraction less than 1, or asked what may be true about a value when multiplied by a fraction less than 1. Remember, if you are multiplying by a value that is less than 1, you are going to get a smaller value.

FRACTIONS GREATER THAN 1

When you review a problem where a number is being multiplied by a fraction that is greater than 1, it is important to be able to estimate its value. Fractions are greater than 1 when the numerator is greater than the denominator. Some examples are $\frac{2}{1}, \frac{4}{3}, \frac{9}{7}$, and $\frac{100}{25}$. When a number is being multiplied by a given factor, it follows a general rule: if the factor is less than one, the value will be smaller, if the factor is equal to 1, the value will be the same, and if the factor is greater than 1, the value will be greater. If we are multiplying 5 by a number, we know a few things about it. If 5 is being multiplied by a number greater than 1, the product will be greater than 5, like $5 \times \frac{3}{2} = \frac{15}{2}$ or 7.5. If 5 is multiplied by 1, the product is 5. If 5 is being multiplied by a number less than 1, the product will be less than 5, like $5 \times \frac{1}{10} = \frac{1}{2}$. Knowing this, if a number is being multiplied by a fraction that is greater than 1, we can determine that the product will be greater than the original number.

Dividing Large Numbers

Dividing large numbers takes practice. The most common strategy for large-digit division is using long division. Long division is a shorthand way to divide large numbers by place value. There are a couple of ways to complete long division problems. Let's look at the problem 6,585 divided by 25.

When using long division, we set up our problems like this:

```
25)6,585
```

The first step in this problem is to ask how many times 25 goes into 6. 25 is larger than 6, so the answer would be zero. We will put a zero in the thousands place.

```
    0
25)6,585
```

Now we move to the hundreds place. How many times will 25 go into 65? Twice. We would say twice because $2 \cdot 25 = 50$ and $3 \cdot 25 = 75$; 75 is greater than 65, so we will choose $25 \cdot 2$.

```
    0 2
25)6,585
```

Now we multiply $25 \cdot 2$, place this under 65, subtract, and bring down the next digit.

```
    0 2
25)6,585
    5 0
    1 58
```

Now we ask, "how many times will 25 go into 158?" 6, because $6 \cdot 5 = 150$.

So, we place a 6 in the tens place, multiply, subtract, and bring down the last digit.

```
    0 26
25)6,585
    5 0
    1 58
    1 50
       85
```

Now, we follow the same process. How many times does 25 go into 85? 3 times. Place a 3 in the ones place, multiply, and subtract.

```
    0 263
25)6,585
    5 0
    158
    150
       85
       75
       10 ←remainder
```

There is nothing else to bring down, but we have 10 left over. This is our remainder, so we can say that $6{,}585 \div 25 = 263$ with a remainder of 10, or $263\frac{10}{25}$.

The fraction $\frac{10}{25}$ can be simplified, so in simplest terms, this is $263\frac{2}{5}$.

Using Expanded Form

We can also complete division problems using expanded form. In the problem 6,585 divided by 25, we can set up our problem by dividing each place value by 25 and adding them together.

$$(6{,}000 \div 25) + (500 \div 25) + (80 \div 25) + (5 \div 25)$$

$$240 + 20 + \frac{80}{25} + \frac{5}{25}$$

$$260 + \frac{85}{25}$$

$$260 + 3\frac{10}{25}$$

$$263\frac{10}{25}$$

$$263\frac{2}{5}$$

Dividing Decimals

Dividing decimal numbers involves the same process as dividing by whole numbers. The most common, and most efficient, way to solve these problems is to use long division. When using long division to solve decimal problems, you will set up your division problem and multiply the dividend and divisor by base 10 values until you get a value without decimals. The concept is that $2 \div 10$ is equivalent to $20 \div 100$ which is also equivalent to $2{,}000 \div 10{,}000$. If you multiply both values by the same number, you will get the same quotient.

Let's look at the problem 725.6 divided by 0.125. We would need to multiply each number by 1,000 to remove the decimal places.

$$0.125 \times 1{,}000 = 125$$
$$725.6 \times 1{,}000 = 725{,}600$$

Now, we can set this problem up using long division and divide using the long division process. Divide, multiply, subtract, and bring down.

```
      0 05,8 04
125) 7 25,6 00
     6 25
     1,00 6
     1,00 0
          6 0
            0
          6 00
          5 00
          1 00
```

When we are dividing by decimals, we want our answer in decimal form. You may be asked to round your answer to the nearest tenths, hundredths, or thousandths. Typically, you will not have more than 3 decimal places.

So, we can keep dividing by adding a decimal and a zero to the dividend. This is because 725,600 is equivalent to 725,600.0.

```
     005804.8
125) 725600.0
     625
     1006
     1000
        60
         0
        600
        500
        100 0
        100 0
            0
```

$725.6 \div 0.125 = 5{,}804.8$

Review Video: Dividing Decimals
Visit mometrix.com/academy and enter code: 560690

Dividing Fractions

We use the inverse property to help us solve fraction division problems. The inverse property tells us that dividing by a number is the same as multiplying by its reciprocal. The reciprocal of a number is its "flipped" version, where the numerator is flipped with the denominator. We can multiply the reciprocal of a fraction to get the same value as dividing by the original fraction. To multiply fractions, make sure each term is in fraction form and multiply the numerators and multiply the denominators.

Let's look at the problem $4 \div \frac{1}{2}$.

When we divide by a fraction, we get the same value by multiplying by its reciprocal.

This means that $4 \div \frac{1}{2}$ is equivalent to $4 \times \frac{2}{1}$. Write 4 as a fraction and multiply to find $\frac{4}{1} \times \frac{2}{1} = 8$.

Example

Solve $\frac{3}{4} \div \frac{1}{6}$.

When you see a problem like this, rewrite the problem by inverting the second fraction, then multiply the fractions instead of dividing. We are dividing $\frac{3}{4}$ by $\frac{1}{6}$, so we can also say we are multiplying $\frac{3}{4}$ by $\frac{6}{1}$.

$$\frac{3}{4} \div \frac{1}{6} = \frac{3}{4} \times \frac{6}{1}$$

Now multiply the numerators and denominators.

$$\frac{3}{4} \times \frac{6}{1} = \frac{3 \times 6}{4 \times 1} = \frac{18}{4}$$

The last step is to simplify.

$$\frac{18}{4} = \frac{9}{2}$$

So,

$$\frac{3}{4} \div \frac{1}{6} = \frac{9}{2}$$

Measurement and Geometry

Area of a Rectangle

The **area** of a polygon describes the total measure of the amount of space inside the polygon. We describe area using **square units** because area can be described as the number of squares that cover the inside of a polygon. A rectangle is a polygon with four sides, two sets of parallel sides, and four right angles.

If we have a rectangle that is 5 inches by 3 inches, we can count the number of square inches inside the rectangle to find the area.

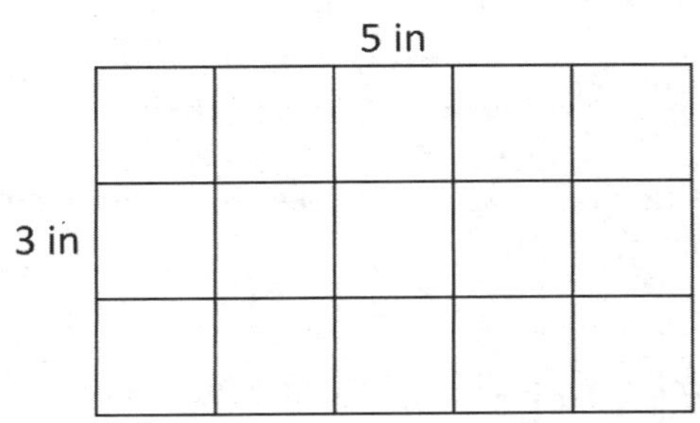

By counting the square inches in this rectangle, we can see that the area is 15 square units.

AREA FORMULA FOR RECTANGLES

We can also use formulas to find the area of a rectangle. Instead of counting the square units, we can find the area of a rectangle by multiplying the base and the height, or multiplying perpendicular sides. **Perpendicular sides** create right angles. Sides can be described as a base and a height, or length and width.

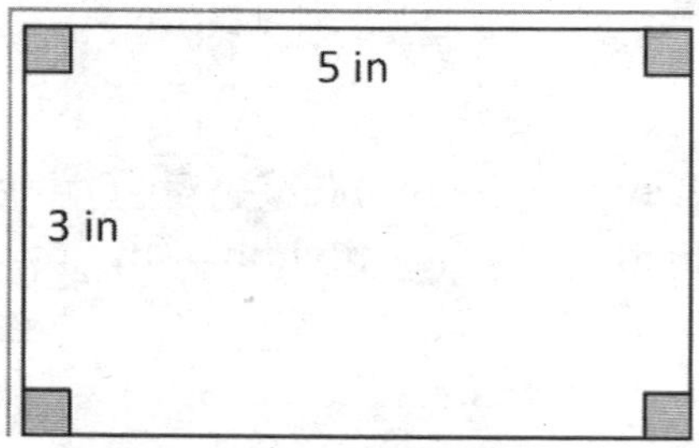

$$5 \text{ in} \times 3 \text{ in} = 15 \text{ sq in}$$

The side length that is 3 inches is perpendicular to the side length that is 5 inches, so the area is 15 square inches.

The area of a shape does not change if it is positioned differently. Consider the rectangle below.

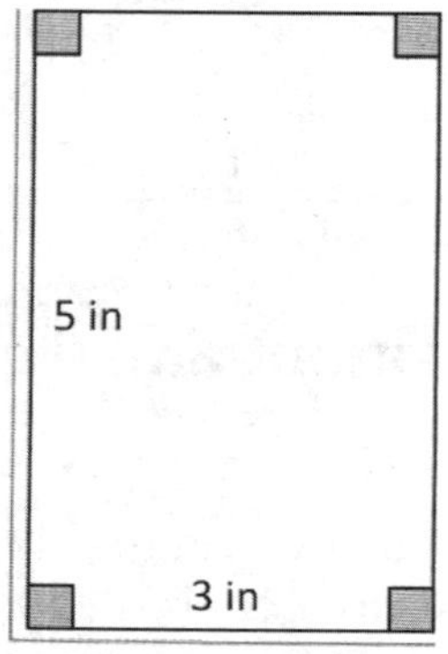

In this example, the base is 3 inches and the height is 5 inches. These sides are still perpendicular to each other, so we can still multiply the base and height to find the area.

$$\begin{aligned} \text{Area} &= \text{base} \times \text{height} \\ A &= b \times h \\ A &= 3 \text{ in} \times 5 \text{ in} \\ A &= 15 \text{ square inches} \end{aligned}$$

The formula for finding the area of a rectangle is area equals the base times the height, or $A = b \cdot h$, where the base and height are perpendicular.

EXAMPLE

If we have a rectangle with a given area and a given side length, we can use the area formula to find a missing side length.

A rectangle has an area of 20 square units, and a base of 5 units, we can use the area formula to find the height.

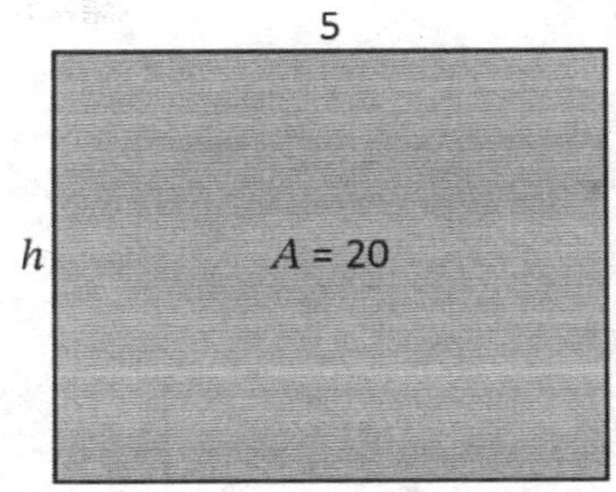

$$A = b \times h$$
$$\frac{20}{5} = \frac{5 \times h}{5}$$
$$\frac{20}{5} = h$$
$$h = 4$$

If we have a rectangle with an area of 20 square units, and a base of 5 units, the height is 4 units because 20 divided by 5 is 4.

We can use equivalent equations to find alternative area formulas. For example, to find a missing height, we can use the equation $h = \frac{A}{b}$, or to find a missing base, we can use the equation $b = \frac{A}{h}$. We can divide the total area by the side length to find the missing perpendicular side length.

$\frac{A}{b} = \frac{b \times h}{b}$ $\frac{A}{b} = h$ $h = \frac{A}{b}$	$\frac{A}{h} = \frac{b \times h}{h}$ $\frac{A}{h} = b$ $b = \frac{A}{h}$

Example

A garden has an area of A square feet. The length of the garden is 15 feet and the width of the garden is x feet. Which equation represents the width of the garden?

a. $x = A \times 15$
b. $x = A - (2 \times 15)$
c. $x = \frac{A}{15}$
d. $x = \frac{15}{A}$

In this problem, we are given some elements of a rectangle and need to select the equation that can be used to find a missing side length.

The best way to start a problem like this is to draw a picture. Pictures are useful in geometry because they can help you get an idea of what is really being asked in the question. Draw a rectangle and label the given information.

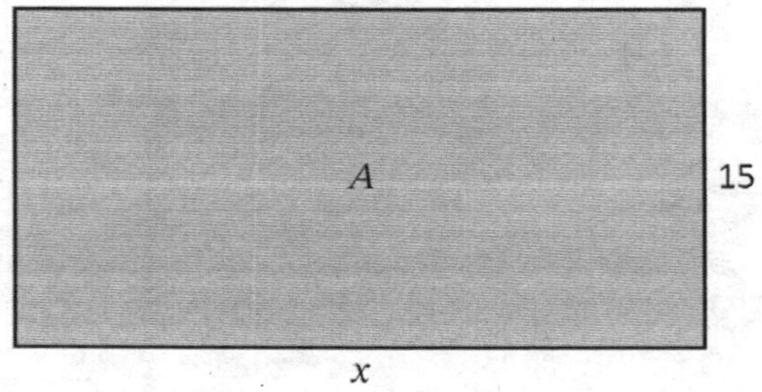

The area formula for a rectangle is $A = b \cdot h$. So, we can use the equation $A = b \cdot h$ and use equivalent equations to describe the width, x.

First, we need to input our given values. The area is A; the length, or height, is 15; and the width, or base, is x.

$$\text{A} = 15 \times x$$

Now, divide both sides by 15.

$$\frac{A}{15} = \frac{15 \times x}{15}$$
$$\frac{A}{15} = x$$

Now, we can reverse the sides so x is on the left side of the equal sign.

$$x = \frac{A}{15}$$

The correct answer is C.

EXAMPLE

Josie is designing a mural. The wall that the mural will be painted on is a rectangle where the height is 8 feet and the width is 11.5 feet. What is the total area of the space in square feet?

In this problem, we are given the perpendicular sides of a rectangle and need to calculate the area. We will use the area formula to help us.

Let's draw a picture and label the given values to help us visualize the problem.

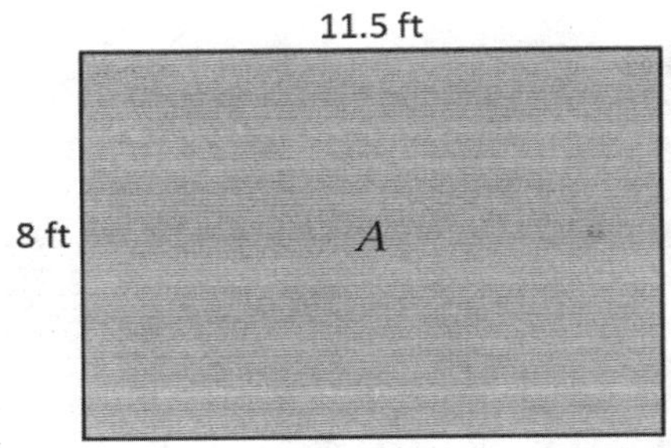

We know that the area of a rectangle is calculated by multiplying the base and the height, or the length and the width. We can use the formula $A = b \cdot h$ and input the given values in the formula.

$$A = b \times h$$
$$A = 11.5 \times 8$$

Multiply to find the area.

$$A = 11.5 \times 8$$
$$A = 92.0$$
$$A = 92 \text{ ft}^2$$

The area of the space is 92 square feet.

EXAMPLE

The area of a rectangle is $4\frac{1}{2}$ square centimeters. The height of the rectangle measures $\frac{1}{2}$ centimeters. What is the base of the rectangle in centimeters?

In this problem, we are given the area and one side length of a rectangle, and we need to find a missing side length.

Let's start by drawing a picture and labeling the given values to visualize the problem.

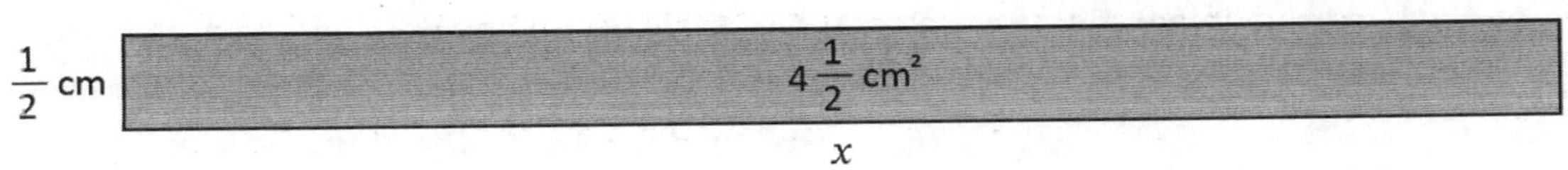

We know that the area of a rectangle is found by multiplying the base times the height, but when we have missing side lengths, we can find a missing side length by dividing the area by the given side length, in this case area divided by the height.

$$A = b \times h$$
$$h = \frac{A}{b}$$

Now, we can input the given values and solve. Remember that dividing by a fraction is equivalent to multiplying by the reciprocal.

$$h = \frac{a}{b}$$
$$h = 4\frac{1}{2} \div \frac{1}{2}$$
$$h = 4\frac{1}{2} \times \frac{2}{1}$$
$$h = 4\frac{1}{2} \times 2$$
$$h = 9$$

The base of the rectangle is 9 centimeters.

Area of a Triangle

We can dissect and rearrange simple shapes to find the areas of difficult shapes. The formula for the area of a rectangle is $A = b \cdot h$, and we can use this formula to help us model the area of a triangle.

A triangle has half of the area of a rectangle with the same base and height measurements as the triangle. We can represent this visually.

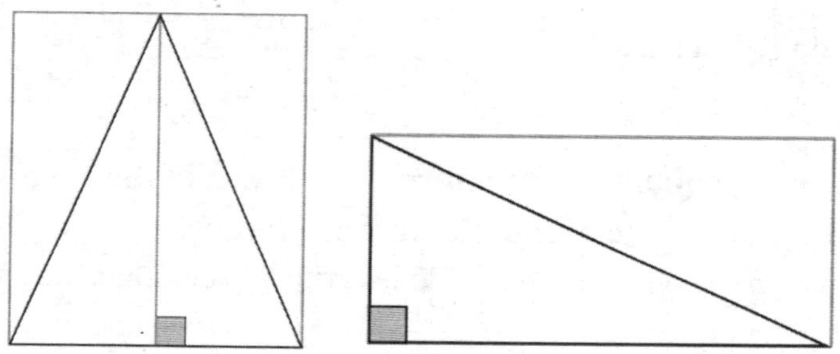

When looking at an obtuse triangle in this way, the triangle will extend outside the rectangle formed by the base and height. But the area of the triangle is still equal to half the area of the rectangle made from the base and height.

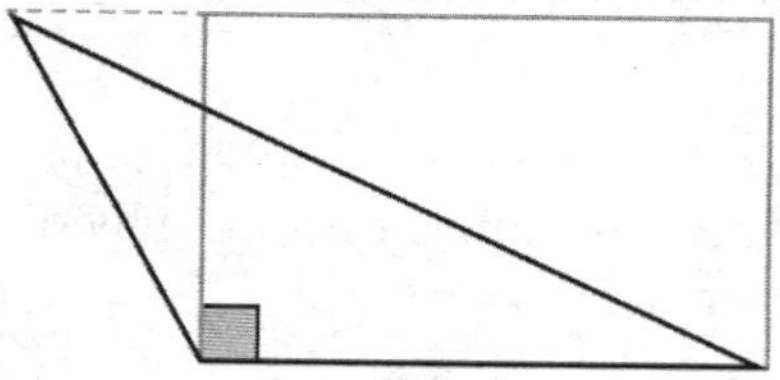

Remember, the base and height of a polygon will always be perpendicular and will create a right angle.

AREA FORMULA FOR TRIANGLES

Knowing that a triangle is half of a rectangle with the same base and height, we can determine that the area of a triangle can be found by multiplying the base and height of the triangle and dividing this product by 2.

When we multiply the base and height of a triangle, we are finding the area of the surrounding rectangle which is twice the area of the triangle. We need to divide this area by 2 to find the area of the triangle. The formula $A = \frac{1}{2}bh$ is used to find the area of a triangle.

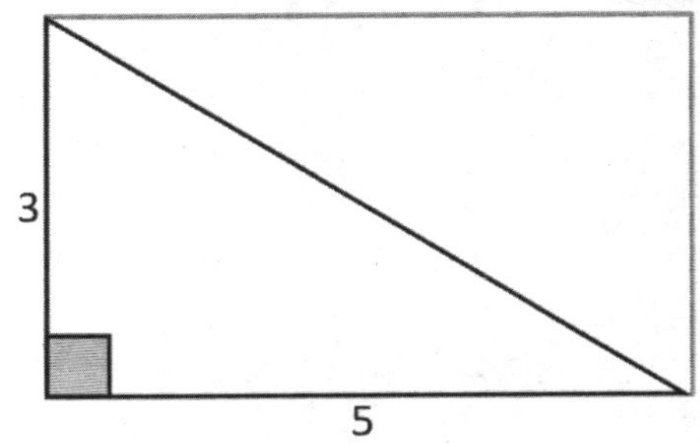

$$A = \frac{1}{2}(3 \times 5)$$
$$A = 7.5$$

The area of a rectangle with a base and height of 5 and 3 is 15 square units. A triangle with the same base and height will be half of that, so 7.5 square units.

Review Video: Area and Perimeter of a Triangle
Visit mometrix.com/academy and enter code: 853779

EXAMPLE

A small triangular tile has a base of $\frac{1}{2}$ inch and a height of $3\frac{1}{2}$ inches. What formula can be used to find the area, *A*, in inches?

a. $A = \frac{1}{2} \times 3\frac{1}{2}$
b. $A = \frac{1}{2}\left(\frac{1}{2} \times 3\frac{1}{2}\right)$
c. $A = 2\left(\frac{1}{2} \times 3\frac{1}{2}\right)$
d. $A = \frac{1}{2} + 3\frac{1}{2}$

In this problem, we are given the height and base measurement of a triangle and need to select the equation that represents the area, *A*, of the triangle.

Let's start by drawing a picture and labeling the given values to visualize this problem.

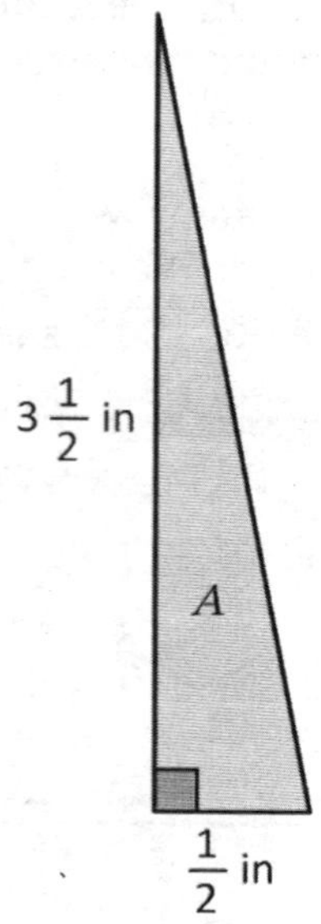

Now that we can see what is being asked, let's think about the area of a triangle. We know that the area of a triangle is half of the area of the surrounding rectangle, and the formula for the area of a triangle is $A = \frac{1}{2}b \times h$. We can use this formula and substitute the given values.

$$A = \frac{1}{2}b \times h$$
$$A = \frac{1}{2}\left(\frac{1}{2} \times 3\frac{1}{2}\right)$$

The correct answer is B.

Example

A triangle is pictured below. What is the area of the triangle in square meters?

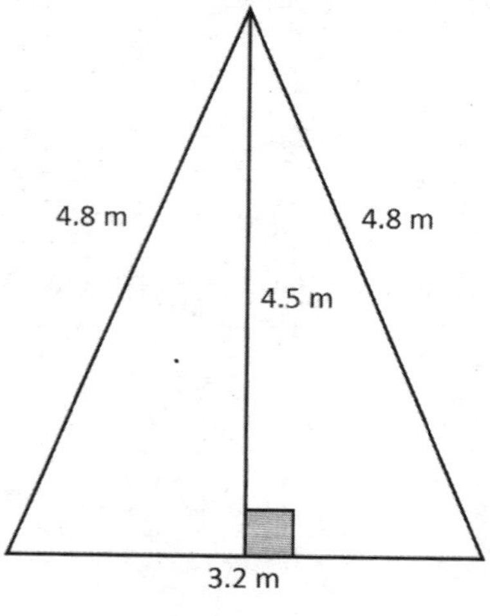

In this problem, we are given a picture of a triangle with the base, height, and all side lengths labeled. We need to first identify the base and the height out of all these measurements.

Remember, the base and height will always be perpendicular and will form a right angle, and only two measurements form a right angle, which is depicted by a square in the corner.

The base of the triangle is 3.2 meters and the height of the triangle is 4.5 meters.

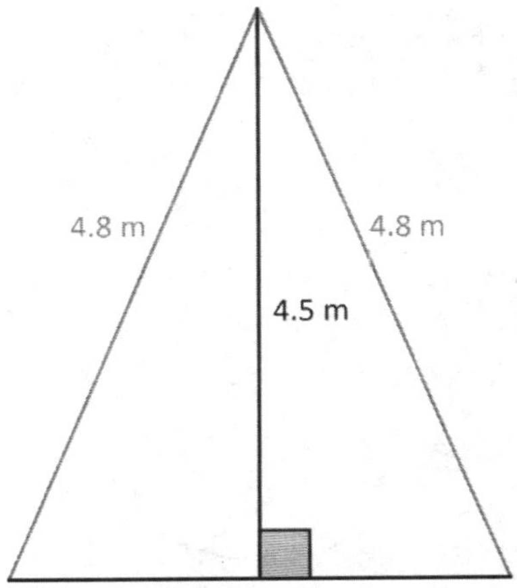

Now that we have identified the base and height of the triangle, we can use the triangle formula to find the area in square meters.

The triangle area formula is half of the base times the height, or half of the area of the surrounding rectangle. We can use the triangle area formula, input the given values, and solve.

$$A = \frac{1}{2} b \times h$$
$$A = \frac{1}{2}(3.2 \times 4.5)$$
$$A = \frac{1}{2}(14.4)$$
$$A = 7.2 \text{ m}^2$$

The area of the triangle is 7.2 square meters.

Solving for Measurements of Circles

The relationships between the measurements of a circle are unique. A circle does not have any sides or angles. The perimeter of a circle is called the **circumference**, and the width of a circle is called the **diameter**. The **radius** of a circle is the length from the center to any point along the circumference. The radius is half of the diameter.

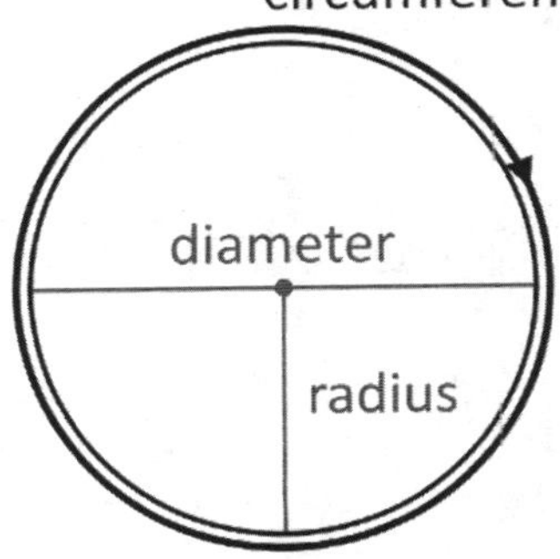

Pi, represented by the symbol π, is the constant for the proportional relationship between a circle's circumference and diameter. Pi is often rounded to 3.14. Formulas are used to find the circumference and area of circles and they all involve π.

CIRCUMFERENCE

The circumference of a circle can be found by multiplying the diameter by π. The formula to solve for the circumference of a circle is $C = \pi d$ where C represents the circumference and d represents the diameter.

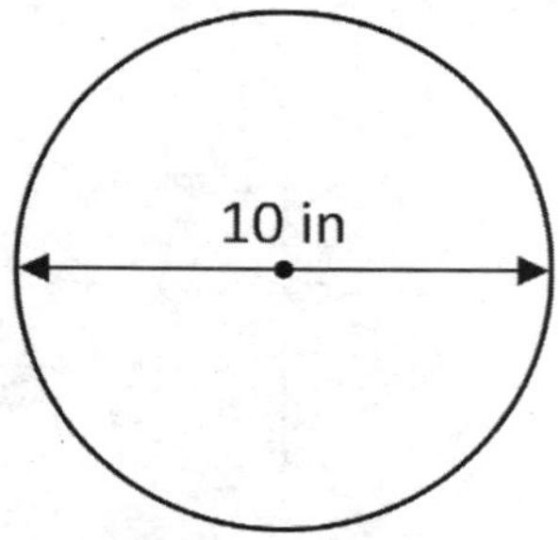

This circle has a diameter of 10 inches. We can use $C = \pi d$ to calculate the circumference.

$$C = \pi d$$
$$C = \pi \cdot 10$$
$$C = 10\pi$$

We could say that the circumference of the circle is 10π inches, or we can express the value as an approximate decimal.

$$C \approx 3.14 \cdot 10$$
$$C \approx 31.4$$

The circumference is about 31.4 inches. We say that it is about 31.4 inches because 3.14 is a rounded form of pi.

The diameter of a circle is twice the radius, so the circumference of a circle can also be found by multiplying the radius by 2 and π. An alternative circumference formula is $C = 2\pi r$, where r represents the radius.

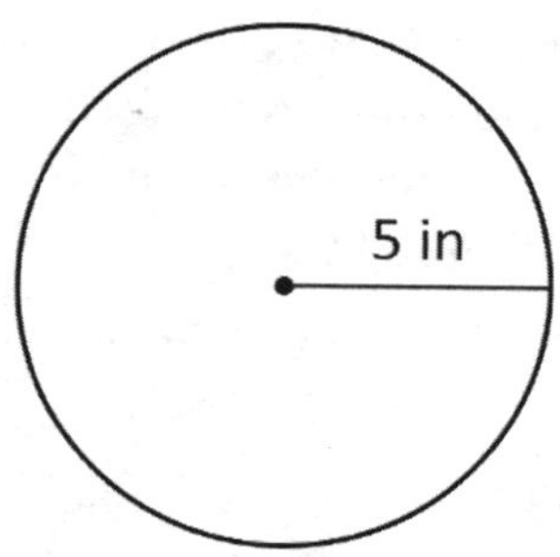

If a circle has a diameter of 10, then the radius is 5. We can use the radius to find the circumference of the circle.

$$C = 2\pi r$$
$$C = 2\pi(5)$$
$$C = 2 \cdot 5 \cdot \pi$$
$$C = 10\pi$$
$$C \approx 10 \cdot 3.14$$
$$C \approx 31.4$$

Both formulas find the circumference of the circle to be 10π inches or about 31.4 inches.

EXAMPLE

A circle has a radius of 6. Which measurement is closest to the circumference of the circle?

a. 113.04 cm
b. 37.68 cm
c. 452.16 cm
d. 18.84 cm

Each answer choice is a decimal, so we will substitute 3.14 for π in the circumference formula to solve.

$$C = 2\pi r$$
$$C \approx 2 \times 3.14 \times 6$$
$$C \approx 12 \times 3.14$$
$$C \approx 37.68$$

The circumference of the circle is about 37.68 centimeters. The correct answer is B.

AREA

The area of a circle can be found by multiplying π by the radius squared.

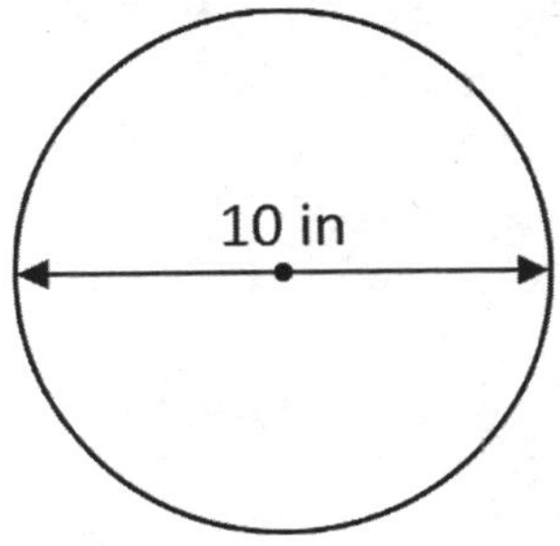

The diameter of this circle is 10 inches, so the radius of the circle is 5 inches. The formula for the area of a circle is $A = \pi r^2$.

$$A = \pi r^2$$
$$A = \pi \cdot 5^2$$
$$A = \pi \cdot 25$$
$$A = 25\pi$$

We can say that the area of the circle is 25π square inches, or we express the area as an approximate decimal by using 3.14 in place of π.

$$A \approx 25 \cdot 3.14$$
$$A \approx 78.5$$

The area of the circle is about 78.5 square inches.

EXAMPLE

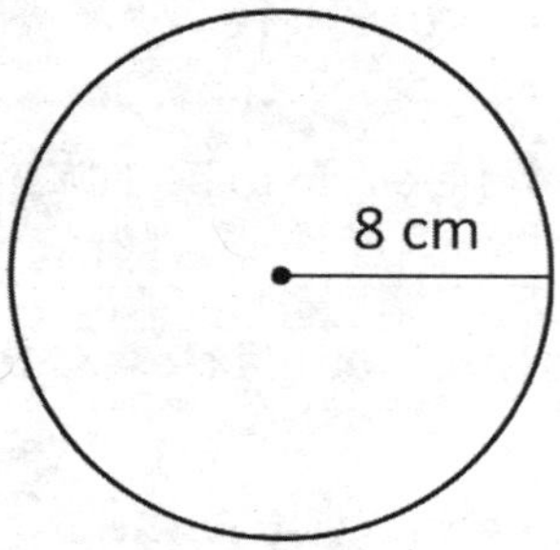

Which measurement is closest to the area of the circle?

a. 25.12 cm^2
b. 50.24 cm^2
c. 200.96 cm^2
d. 204.8 cm^2

Each answer choice is in decimal form, so we will substitute 3.14 for π in the circumference formula to solve.

$$A = \pi r^2$$
$$A \approx 3.14 \times 8^2$$
$$C \approx 3.14 \times 64$$
$$C \approx 200.96$$

The area of the circle is about 200.96 square centimeters. The correct answer is C.

EXAMPLE

Two circles are shown. Circle N has a radius of 5. Circle M has a radius of 3.

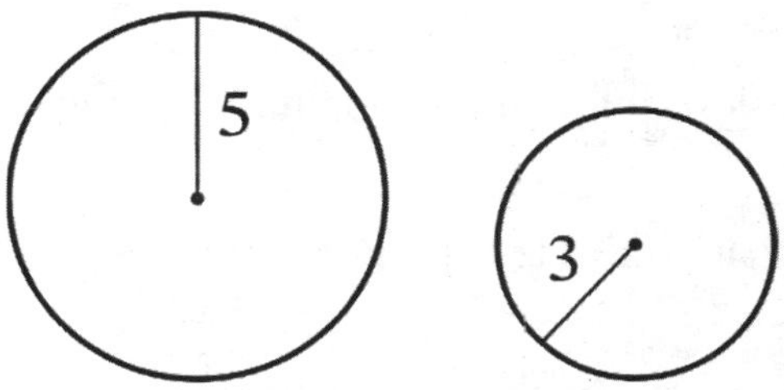

Which measurement is closest to the difference between the area of circle N and circle M, in square units?

a. 50.24 un^2
b. 20.41 un^2
c. 6.28 un^2
d. 12.56 un^2

To solve this problem, find the area of each circle and subtract to find the difference.

Circle M has a radius of 3. We can use the area formula to find the area.

$$A = \pi r^2$$
$$A \approx 3.14 \times 3^2$$
$$A \approx 3.14 \times 9$$
$$A \approx 28.26$$

The area of circle M is about 28.26 square units.

Circle N has a radius of 5.

$$A = \pi r^2$$
$$A \approx 3.14 \times 5^2$$
$$A \approx 3.14 \times 25$$
$$A \approx 78.5$$

The area of circle N is about 78.5 square units.

The difference in the areas of these circles is the difference between 78.5 and 28.26.

$$78.5 - 28.26 = 50.24$$

The difference between these two areas is 50.24 square units. The correct answer is A.

Review Video: Area and Circumference of a Circle
Visit mometrix.com/academy and enter code: 243015

GEOMETRY TERMS

Geometry, or the study of shapes, is filled with unique terminology and vocabulary. It is important to become familiar with this math vocabulary to be able to precisely classify and identify two- and three-dimensional shapes.

The most basic terms include points, lines, line segments, rays, angles, perpendicular lines, and parallel lines.

A **point** is an exact location with no size. This often appears as a dot, and is usually labeled with a letter, such as Point *A*.

Point *A*

A **line** is a straight path that extends in opposite directions. A line does not have a width, and it extends indefinitely in both directions. Lines are labeled with letters representing points on the line, such as $\overleftrightarrow{AB}$.

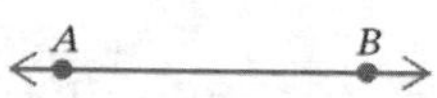

$\overleftrightarrow{AB}$

A **line segment** is a part of a line. A line segment has endpoints, beginning and ending at a point labeled with a letter, such as $\overline{AB}$.

$\overline{AB}$

A **ray** is a part of a line that starts at an endpoint and then extends out indefinitely. Rays are labeled starting with a letter at the endpoint and ending with a letter representing another point on the ray, such as $\overrightarrow{AB}$.

$\overrightarrow{AB}$

An **angle** is formed when two straight lines or rays meet at a common endpoint. The two rays below form an angle.

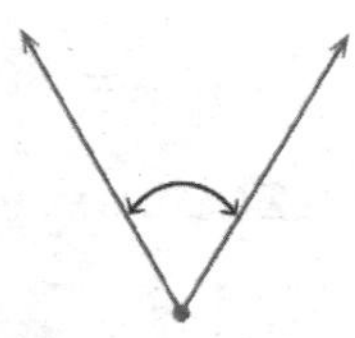

Parallel lines extend side-by-side and never intersect. To help visualize parallel lines, think of train tracks.

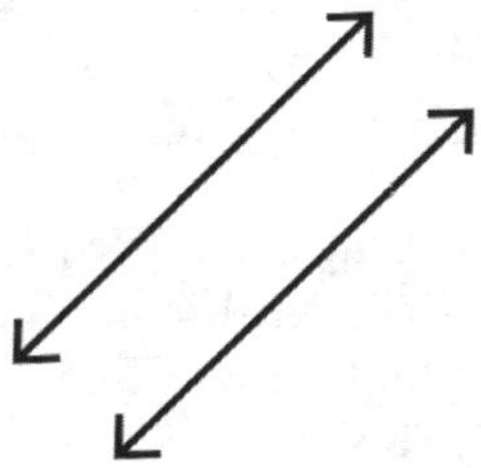

Perpendicular lines intersect to form a right angle. To help visualize perpendicular lines, think of a corner or a T-shape.

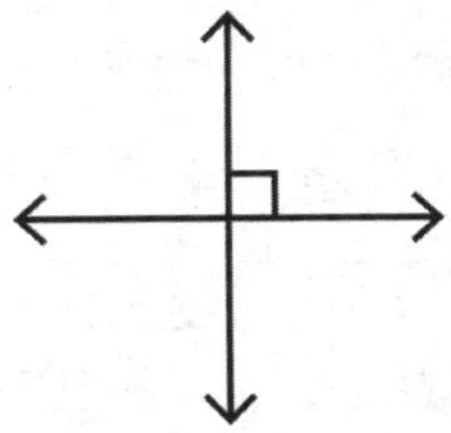

Review Video: Parallel and Perpendicular Lines
Visit mometrix.com/academy and enter code: 815923

Right, Acute, and Obtuse Angles

A **right angle** consists of 90 degrees and forms a corner. Angles that are less than 90 degrees are considered **acute angles**. Angles that are wider than 90 degrees but less than 180 degrees are considered **obtuse angles**.

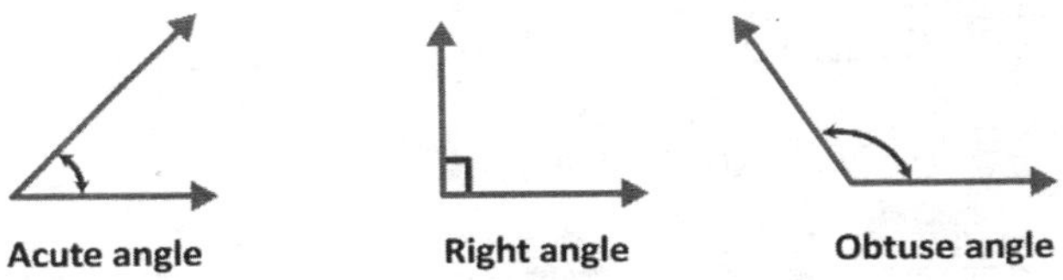

Polygons

A **polygon** is a closed, two-dimensional figure with three or more straight line segments called **sides**. The point at which two sides of a polygon intersect is called the **vertex**. In a polygon, the number of sides is always equal to the number of vertices. A polygon with all sides congruent and all angles equal is called a **regular polygon**. Common polygons are:

$$\begin{aligned}\text{Triangle} &= 3\text{ sides}\\ \text{Quadrilateral} &= 4\text{ sides}\\ \text{Pentagon} &= 5\text{ sides}\\ \text{Hexagon} &= 6\text{ sides}\\ \text{Heptagon} &= 7\text{ sides}\\ \text{Octagon} &= 8\text{ sides}\\ \text{Nonagon} &= 9\text{ sides}\\ \text{Decagon} &= 10\text{ sides}\\ \text{Dodecagon} &= 12\text{ sides}\end{aligned}$$

More generally, an n-gon is a polygon that has n angles and n sides.

Review Video: Intro to Polygons
Visit mometrix.com/academy and enter code: 271869

Congruence

Congruent line segments are the same length, and congruent angles are the same angle measure. Congruent figures are geometric figures that have the same size and shape. All corresponding angles are equal, and all corresponding sides are equal. Congruence is indicated by the symbol $\cong$.

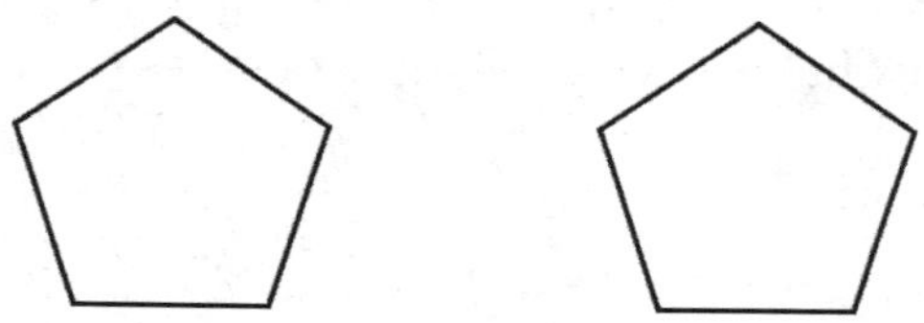

Congruent polygons

Review Video: Congruent Shapes
Visit mometrix.com/academy and enter code: 492281

Coordinate Planes

A **coordinate plane** is a way to graph data by plotting points on a grid. On a coordinate plane, there is an x-axis and a y-axis. The center point is called the **origin**, and its coordinates are (0,0). The x-axis runs horizontally, and the y-axis runs vertically. We use the x- and y-axis to graph ordered pairs. **Ordered pairs** are sets of values that tell us the coordinates of a point. They are written using parentheses and separated by a comma. (3,2) is an example of an ordered pair. In an ordered pair, the first number is the x-value, and the second number is the y-value. In this example, (3,2), $x = 3$ and $y = 2$. We use these values to plot points on a graph. The point (3,2) lies three units to the right of the origin along the x-axis and two units up along the y-axis. The point also lies at the intersection point of the lines $x = 3$ and $y = 2$. Positive values always run to the right along the

x-axis and up along the y-axis. Negative values always run to the left along the x-axis and down along the y-axis.

There are four quadrants in the coordinate plane. Quadrant I is the top left right section, and it has both positive x and y-values. Quadrant II is the top left section, and it has negative x-values and positive y-values. Quadrant III is the bottom left section, and it has both negative x and y-values. Quadrant IV is the bottom right section, and it has positive x-values and negative y-values.

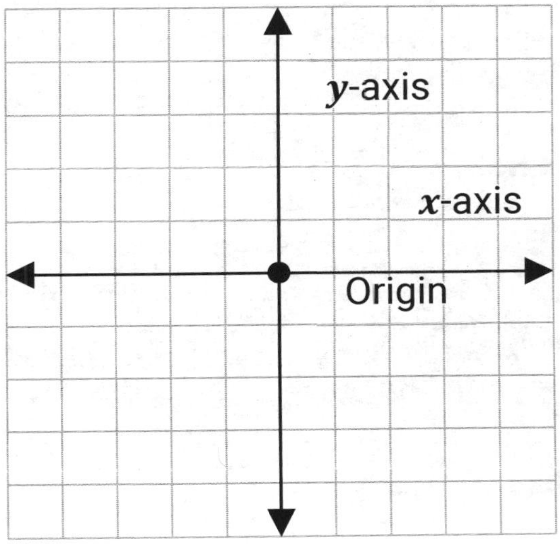

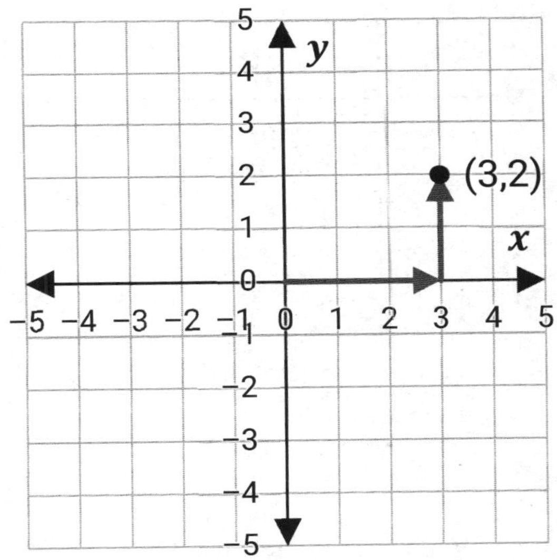

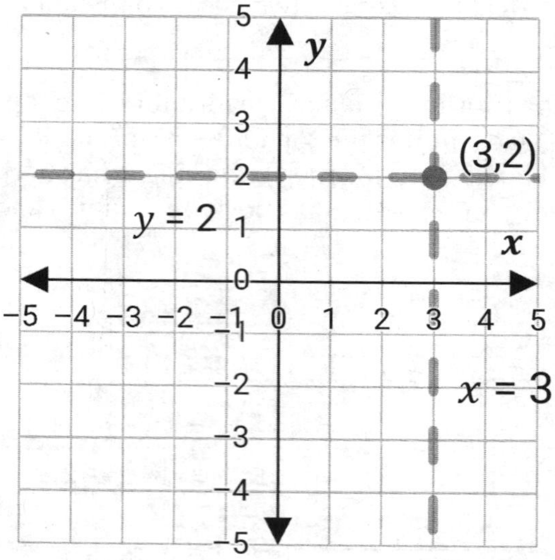

Review Video: Cartesian Coordinate Plane and Graphing
Visit mometrix.com/academy and enter code: 115173

EXAMPLE

Place $(5, -2.5)$ on the coordinate plane.

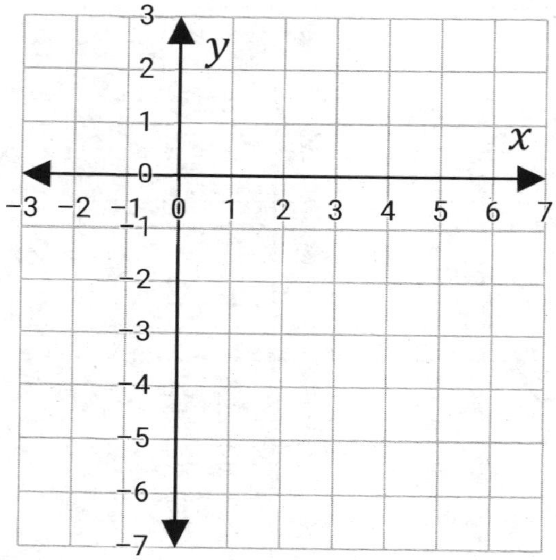

In this problem, we are given the pair $(5, -2.5)$. The x-value in this ordered pair is 5 and the y-value is -2.5.

We will start by finding the x-value, 5, on the coordinate plane. So, we will start at the origin and count 5 units to the right because it is a positive 5.

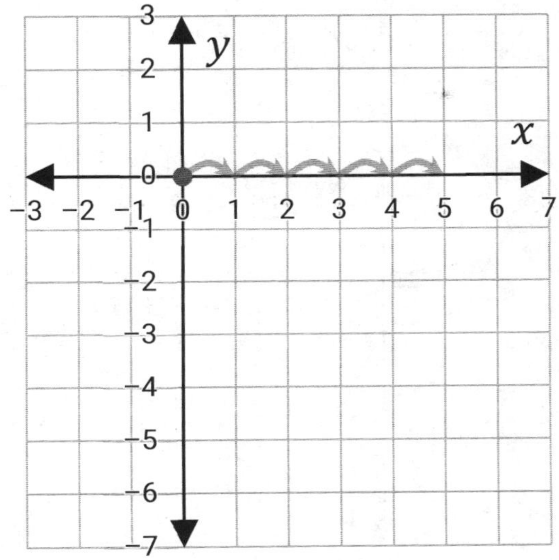

For the ordered pair $(5, -2.5)$, our y-value is -2.5. That means that we will count down 2.5 units. We will count down because it is a negative value.

-2.5 is not labeled on our coordinate plane, but we know that -2.5 is located halfway between -2 and -3. We can also count down 2 units and then a half of a unit. This is where we plot our point.

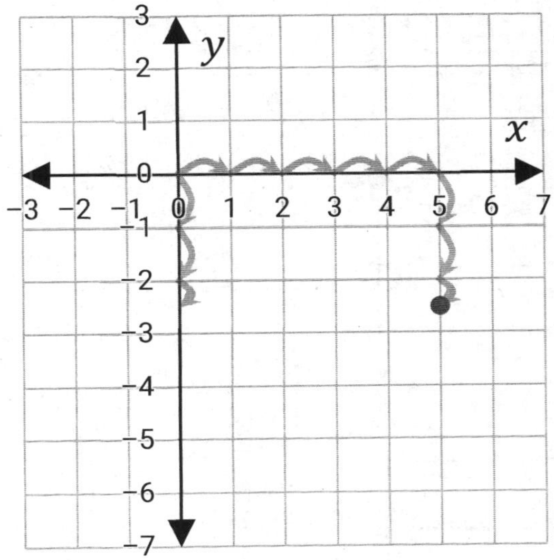

Now, we can double check that our point is placed in the correct location. Let's identify the ordered pair of the plotted point.

First, we will count how many units away from the origin along the x-axis our point is to find the x-value.

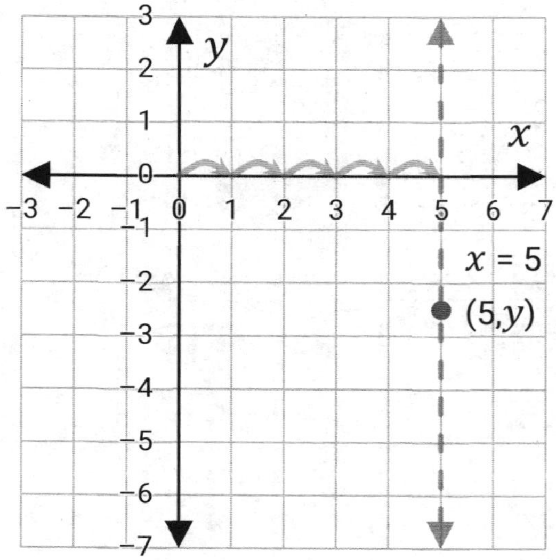

The x-value is 5 units to the right of the origin. Now, we can count how many units away from the origin along the y-axis our point is to find the y-value.

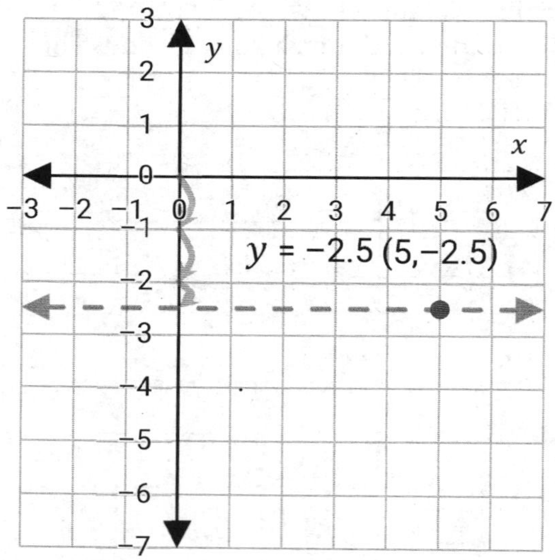

The y-value is 2.5 units below the x-axis, so -2.5 is the y-value. Our point is located at $(5, -2.5)$.

<u>EXAMPLE</u>

Which point best represents the ordered pair $(-3, 1)$ on the coordinate plane?

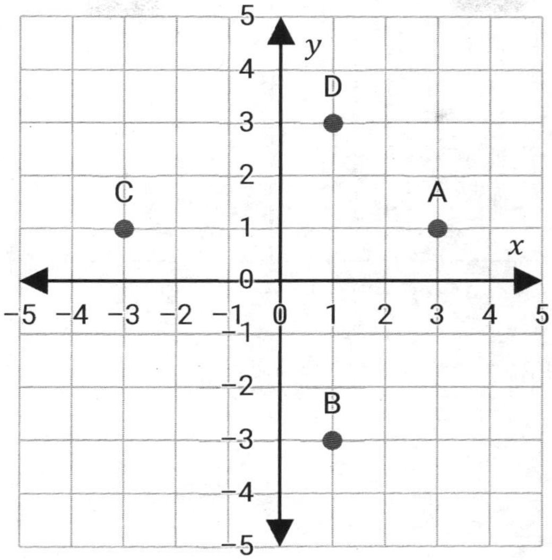

a. Point A
b. Point B
c. Point C
d. Point D

In this problem, we are given four points plotted on a coordinate plane. One of these points represents the ordered pair $(-3,1)$.

The most efficient way to solve this problem is to find the location of $(-3,1)$ and see what point lies in that location.

To find the location of $(-3,1)$, we need to identify which value is the x-value and which is the y-value. In an ordered pair, the first value is the x-value and the second value is the y-value. That means that $x = -3$ and $y = 1$.

So, this location is at the intersection point of $x = -3$ and $y = 1$.

Let's start by finding the location of $x = -3$.

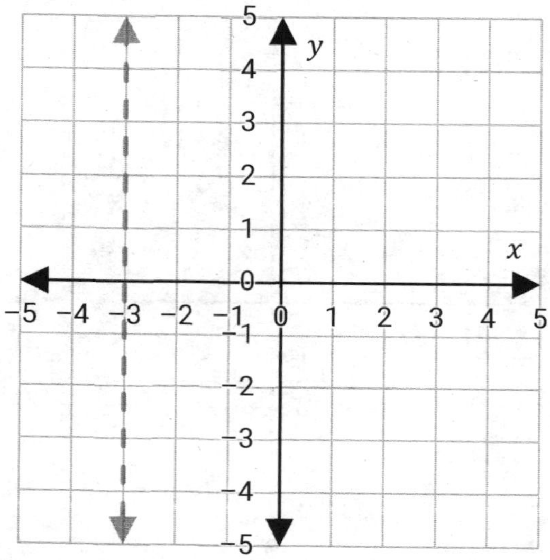

Now, we can find the location of $y = 1$.

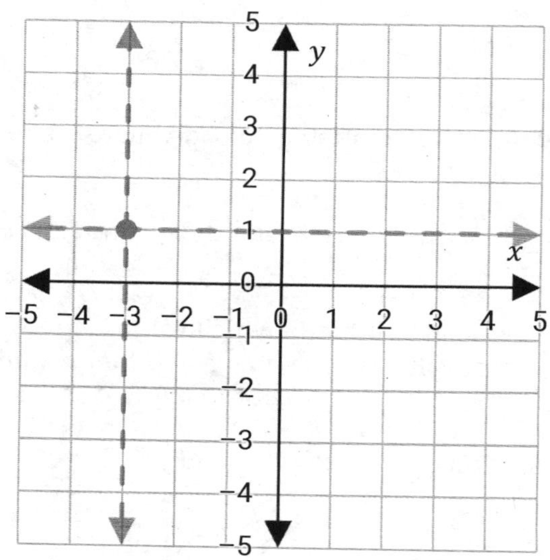

The location of $(-3,1)$ is the point where these two lines cross.

We can also find this point by counting 3 spaces to the left of the origin and up 1 unit from the x-axis.

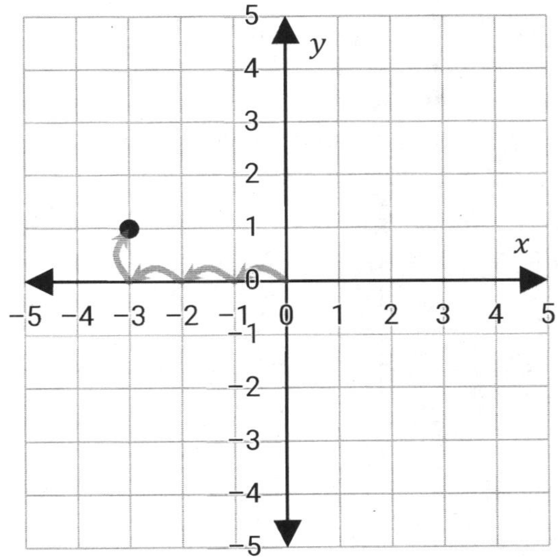

Now that we know the location of $(-3,1)$, we can compare this to our choices. Choice C is the best representation of the ordered pair $(-3,1)$.

The correct answer is C.

EXAMPLE

Which ordered pair describes the point that is located 3 units to the right of the origin and 4 units below the x-axis?

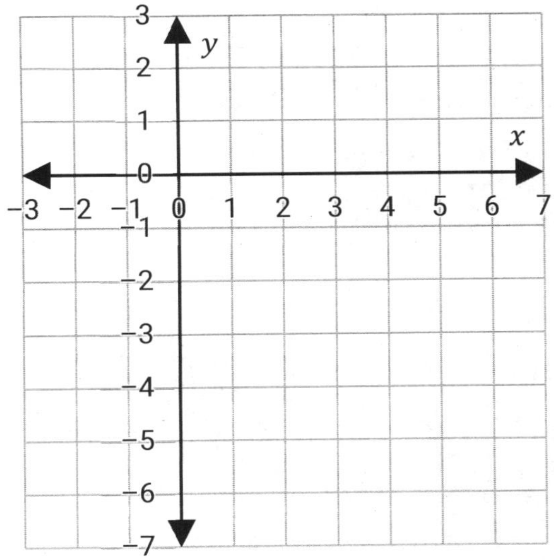

a. $(3,-4)$
b. $(4,3)$
c. $(-3,-4)$
d. $(-3,4)$

In this problem, we are given directions to find a point on a coordinate plane and four options of ordered pairs. To approach this problem, we will follow the directions to locate a point, identify the ordered pair, and match this with the options.

Let's start with following the directions to the location on the coordinate plane.

This point is located 3 units to the right of the origin and 4 units below the x-axis. So, we will start at the origin and count 3 units to the right of the origin.

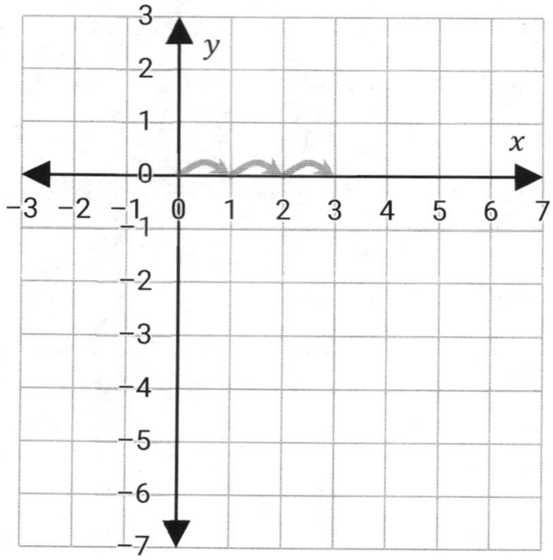

Now, we will count 4 units below the x-axis.

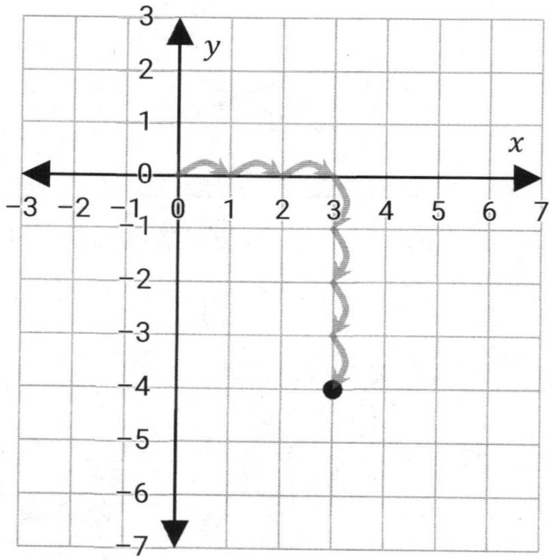

This is our point. Now, what is the ordered pair that best represents this point? Let's find the x- and y-values by identifying the crossing points.

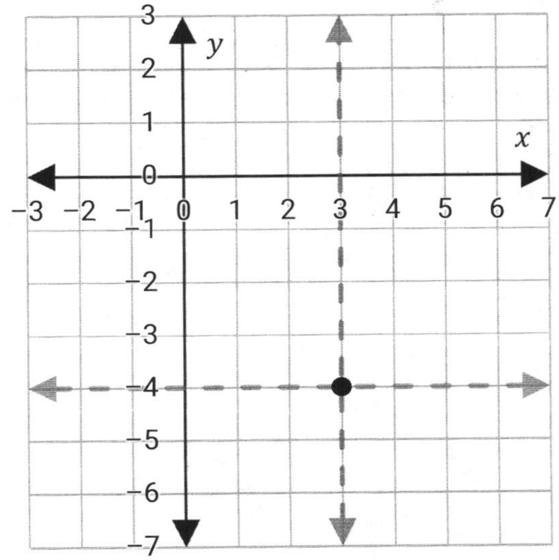

For this point, $x = 3$ and $y = -4$ because the point is 3 units to the right (positive 3) and 4 units down (negative 4). The ordered pair is $(3, -4)$. This matches option A.

The correct answer is A.

Probability, Statistics, Patterns, Functions, and Algebra

Displaying Data

Circle Graphs

Circle graphs, also known as *pie charts*, provide a visual depiction of the relationship of each type of data compared to the whole set of data. The circle graph is divided into sections by drawing radii to create central angles whose percentage of the circle is equal to the individual data's percentage of the whole set. Each 1% of data is equal to 3.6° in the circle graph. Therefore, data represented by a 90° section of the circle graph makes up 25% of the whole. When complete, a circle graph often looks like a pie cut into uneven wedges. The pie chart below shows the data from the frequency table referenced earlier where people were asked their favorite color.

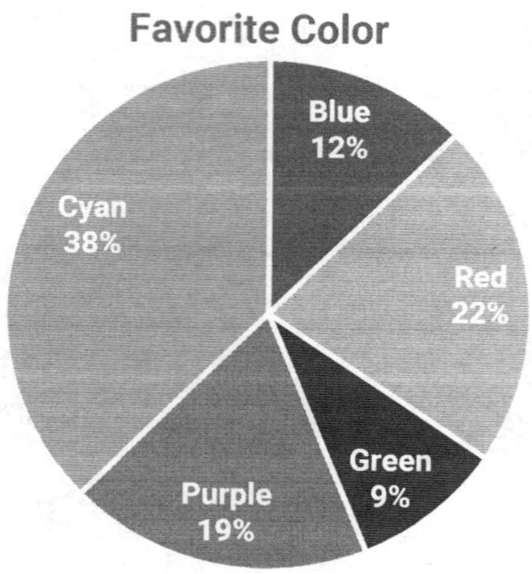

Frequency Tables

Frequency tables show how frequently each unique value appears in a set. A **relative frequency table** is one that shows the proportions of each unique value compared to the entire set. Relative frequencies are given as percentages; however, the total percent for a relative frequency table will not necessarily equal 100 percent due to rounding. An example of a frequency table with relative frequencies is below.

Favorite Color	Frequency	Relative Frequency
Blue	4	13%
Red	7	22%
Green	3	9%
Purple	6	19%
Cyan	12	38%

Review Video: Data Interpretation of Graphs
Visit mometrix.com/academy and enter code: 200439

PICTOGRAPHS

A **pictograph** is a graph, generally in the horizontal orientation, that uses pictures or symbols to represent the data. Each pictograph must have a key that defines the picture or symbol and gives the quantity each picture or symbol represents. Pictures or symbols on a pictograph are not always shown as whole elements. In this case, the fraction of the picture or symbol shown represents the same fraction of the quantity a whole picture or symbol stands for. For example, a row with $3\frac{1}{2}$ ears of corn, where each ear of corn represents 100 stalks of corn in a field, would equal $3\frac{1}{2} \times 100 = 350$ stalks of corn in the field.

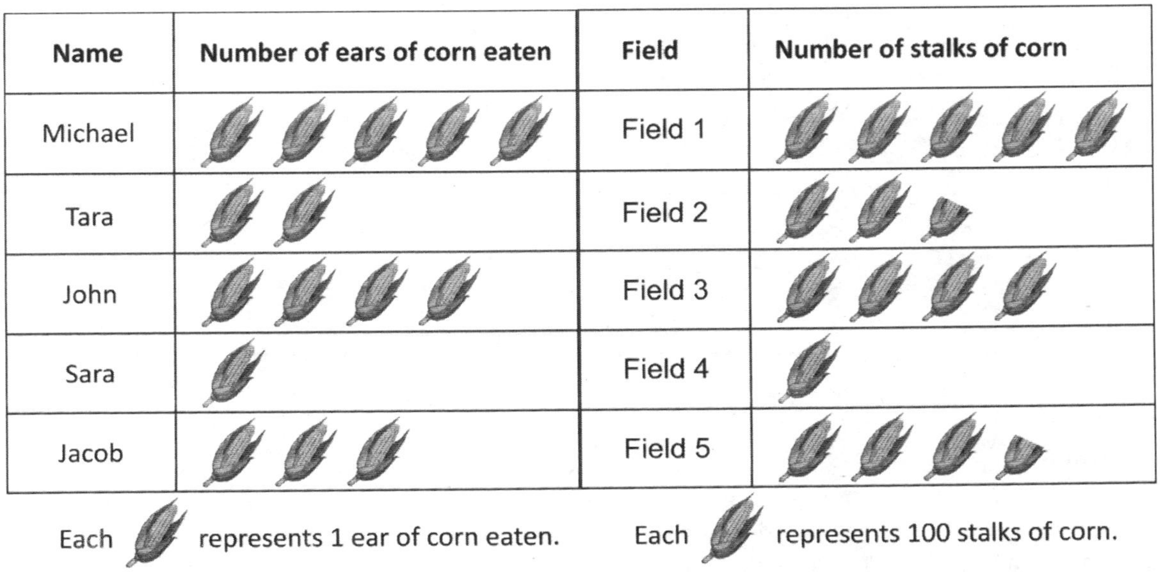

Review Video: Pictographs
Visit mometrix.com/academy and enter code: 147860

LINE PLOTS

A **line plot**, also known as a *dot plot*, has plotted points that are not connected by line segments. In this graph, the horizontal axis lists the different possible values for the data, and the vertical axis lists the number of times the individual value occurs. The values in a line plot are lined up vertically, like a number line, and dots or x's are used to show the frequency of each value, or how many times that value appears in the data. Line plots are used to show how often something happens. Line plots are mostly used when gathering data from multiple trials or surveys. This type of graph is more closely related to a bar graph than a line graph.

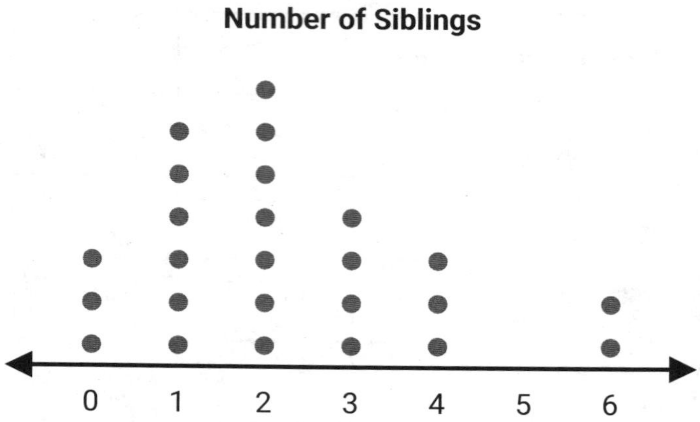

This line plot shows the data from a survey of the 6th graders in a classroom. The survey gathered data about the number of siblings each 6th grader has in their family. The numbers along the bottom represent the number of siblings and the dots represent the number of students. Each dot is equal to one student. Based on this dot plot, you can tell that 7 people said that they have 2 siblings because there are 7 dots above 2.

The data from this line plot can also be written in list form.

6, 6, 4, 4, 4, 3, 3, 3, 3, 2, 2, 2, 2, 2, 2, 2, 1, 1, 1, 1, 1, 1, 0, 0, 0

0, 0, 0, 1, 1, 1, 1, 1, 1, 2, 2, 2, 2, 2, 2, 2, 3, 3, 3, 3, 4, 4, 4, 6, 6

3, 2, 2, 3, 0, 1, 2, 1, 1, 6, 2, 4, 2, 3, 6, 0, 0, 1, 1, 2, 4, 2, 4, 3, 1

As you can see, each value is represented on the line plot. Regardless, there are 2 people who have 6 siblings, 0 people with 5 siblings, 3 people with 4 siblings, 4 people with 3 siblings, 7 people with 2 siblings, 6 people with 1 sibling, and 3 people with 0 siblings.

Review Video: Line Plot
Visit mometrix.com/academy and enter code: 754610

BAR GRAPHS

A **bar graph** is one of the few graphs that can be drawn correctly in two different configurations – both horizontally and vertically. A bar graph is similar to a line plot in the way the data is organized on the graph. Both axes must have their categories defined for the graph to be useful. Rather than placing a single dot to mark the point of the data's value, a bar, or thick line, is drawn from zero to the exact value of the data, whether it is a number, percentage, or other numerical value. Longer bar lengths correspond to greater data values. To read a bar graph, read the labels for the axes to find the units being reported. Then, look where the bars end in relation to the scale given on the corresponding axis and determine the associated value.

The bar chart below represents the responses from our favorite-color survey.

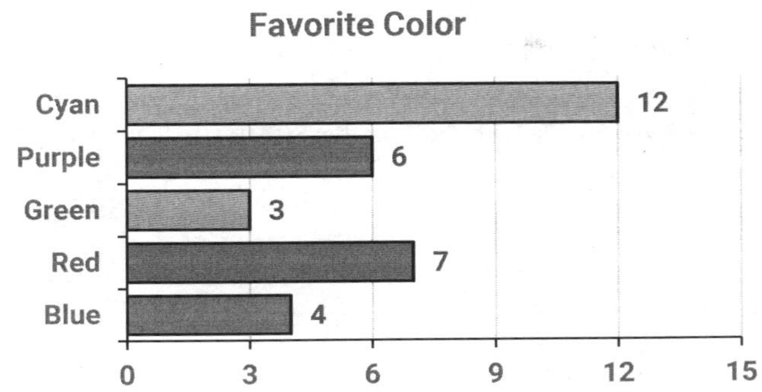

Comparing Data

To compare data, we need to understand measures of center, the spread of data distribution, the shape of data, and how to interpret data from dot plots and box plots.

Measures of Center

The **measures of center** are different methods for estimating or measuring the center of a data set. The center of a data set can be described by the most frequent value in a data set, the value appearing in the middle of a data set arranged from least to greatest, or the value that is the average of that data set. The terms used to describe the center of a data set are mode, median, and mean.

Mode

The **mode** of a data set is the number that shows up most frequently.

Let's say we are given this data set.

$$\{0, 0, 1, 1, 1, 1, 1, 1, 1, 1, 1, 1, 2, 2, 2, 2, 2, 3, 4, 5\}$$

The mode in a data set is the number that repeats the most frequently. If we look at this list of values, we can see that 1 shows up the most often, so the mode of this data set is 1.

Median

The **median** of a data set is the literal middle value in a set of values. If you have a list of values, the median is going to be the value directly in the middle of a list of these values when the values are listed from least to greatest.

Let's say we have a set of data in a list.

$$\{3, 2, 2, 3, 0, 1, 2, 1, 1, 6, 2, 4, 2, 3, 6, 0, 0, 1, 1, 2, 4, 2, 4, 3, 1\}$$

This is a list of values, and we can determine the center, or median value in the data set by lining the values up from least to greatest and finding the middle value.

$$\{0, 0, 0, 1, 1, 1, 1, 1, 1, 2, 2, 2, 2, 2, 2, 2, 3, 3, 3, 3, 4, 4, 4, 6, 6\}$$

Now that we have our data set listed from least to greatest, the median will be the middle number in the set.

12 12

0 0 0 1 1 1 1 1 1 2 2 2 (2) 2 2 2 3 3 3 3 4 4 4 6 6

The center, or median value in this data set is 2, because when you list the values from least to greatest, 2 is the middle number. It is in the middle because it is the same distance from the smallest value to the greatest value and there are the same number of values, 12, on each side.

Finding the median of a data set that has even number of values requires a slightly different approach.

Let's say we are given this data set.

$$\{15, 16, 18, 20, 22, 12, 13, 14, 19, 21, 21, 11, 12, 14\}$$

First, we need to list the values from least to greatest to find the middle.

$$\{11, 12, 12, 13, 14, 14, 15, 16, 18, 19, 20, 21, 21, 22\}$$

Now, we can count to find the middle.

11 12 12 13 14 14 15|16 18 19 20 21 21 22

In this data set, there is not a middle number. Instead, the middle position lies between 15 and 16. So, to find the median value, we will have to find the mean of the two middle numbers, 15 and 16.

To find the mean of these middle values, we will add them together and divide by 2.

$$15 + 16 = 31$$
$$31 \div 2 = 15.5$$

So, the median of this data set is 15.5.

MEAN

The **mean** of a data set is often called the **average**. To find the mean of a data set, add the values in the data set together, and divide the sum by the total number of values.

In school, we are familiar with the mean of data sets because this is the way average grades are calculated. To get a final grade, often teachers will add the grade on each assignment or test together and divide by the total number of assignments or tests.

Let's say you are in a math class and your scores are listed in a data set.

$$\{76, 82, 82, 84, 87, 90, 85, 100, 94, 90\}$$

To find the mean, or average, of your scores, add the values and divide by the number of values. In this data set, if we add all the given grades together, we will get a total of 870. Now, if we divide 870 by the total number of grades, 10, we will get 87. That means that the final grade, the average grade, or the mean of the data set is 87.

Review Video: Mean, Median, and Mode
Visit mometrix.com/academy and enter code: 286207

EXAMPLE

The graph shows the number of students in each 6th grade homeroom class.

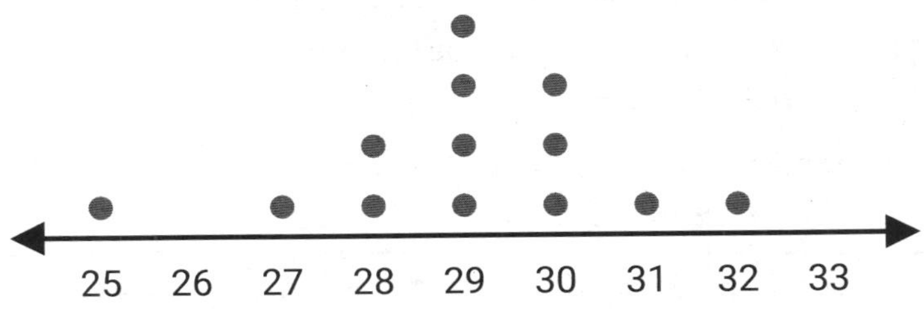

What is the mean number of students in each 6th grade homeroom class?

In this problem, we are given a dot plot that shows the number of students in each 6th grade homeroom class. We need to find the mean number of students in each class.

The mean is the average, and this is found by adding all values and dividing by the number of values

To approach this problem, we need to start by decoding the graph. Let's list the values on the graph. The order that we write the values does not matter, but let's order them from least to greatest.

25, 27, 28, 28, 29, 29, 29, 29, 30, 30, 30, 31, 32

There are a total of 13 dots, so there are 13 homeroom classes. Now we need to add the number of students in all 13 classes.

$$25 + 27 + 28 + 28 + 29 + 29 + 29 + 29 + 30 + 30 + 30 + 31 + 32 = 377$$

So, there are 377 6th grade students. Now, to find the mean, we need to take the total value and divide by the number of values. In other words, divide the number of students by the number of classes.

There are 13 classes, or 13 values, so we need to divide 377 by 13.

377 divided by 13 is 29, so the mean number of students in each class is 29.

EXAMPLE

The table shows the amount of rainfall each day in inches during the rainiest 2 weeks in April.

Rainfall April 1-14

April 1-7	4.0 in	1.2 in	3.5 in	3.8 in	0.0 in	2.4 in	0.0 in
April 8-14	3.1 in	3.5 in	3.4 in	1.0 in	4.5 in	6.0 in	0.2 in

What is the median amount of daily rainfall during these weeks?

In this problem, we are given a table showing the rainfall over 14 days and need to find the median amount of daily rainfall during this time.

The median value is the middle value in a data set. To approach this problem, we need to start by listing the values from least to greatest.

0.0, 0.0, 0.2, 1.0, 1.2, 2.4, 3.1, 3.4, 3.5, 3.5, 3.8, 4.0, 4.5, 6.0

Now that the values are listed from least to greatest, we can find the middle of the data set.

0.0 0.0 0.2 1.0 1.2 2.4 3.1|3.4 3.5 3.5 3.8 4.0 4.5 6.0

The middle of this data set falls in the middle of two numbers. So, to find the median amount of rainfall, we need to find the mean of these two middle values, 3.1 inches and 3.4 inches. To find the mean of these amounts, we need to add the two values and divide by 2.

$$3.1 + 3.4 = 6.5$$
$$6.5 \div 2 = 3.25$$

The median amount of rainfall during these two weeks is 3.25 inches.

ADDITIVE RELATIONSHIPS

An **additive relationship** is a pattern where a value is added to x. For example, the two points (4,6) and (6,8) can be used to represent an additive relationship, since both points have a y-value that comes from 2 being added to the x-value. This pattern can also be described as $x + 2$, where x is the previous number and 2 is added to it. Patterns may be expressed with a series of numbers separated by commas, or in a data table or graph.

x	y
2	4
4	6
6	8
8	10

This data table shows an additive relationship, $x + 2$. When describing an additive relationship, we commonly use the equation $y = x + a$. This additive relationship can be written using the formula $y = x + a$ or $x + a = y$. In this example, x is the starting value, adding 2 is what happens to x, and y

is the ending value. When we use values from the table to replace x and y in our equation, the sentence is true.

Multiplicative Relationships

A **multiplicative relationship** describes a pattern between x and y where x is multiplied by a number to get to y. Looking at the points (3,9) and (9,27), we can see that each x-value is multiplied by 3 to get the y-value. This is also called the **scale factor**.

x	y
3	9
9	27
27	81
81	243

This data table shows the same relationship in table form. This is a multiplicative relationship because the x-value is being multiplied by a number to get a y-value. We describe this multiplicative relationship using the formula $y = ax$, or $ax = y$, where x is the starting value, a is the scale factor, and y is the ending value. In this example, 3 is being multiplied by x to get to y, or y is 3 times as much as x, or x increases by a factor of 3. The equation to describe this relationship is $y = 3x$ or $3x = y$.

Representing Additive and Multiplicative Relationships

Patterns and relationships can be expressed using tables, equations, and graphs. These representations can be used interchangeably. They are different ways to illustrate the same information. In an additive relationship, a number is being added to x to get y. This is expressed using the equation $y = x + a$. This relationship can also be expressed using a table and a graph. Let's look at the equation $y = x + 3$. In this relationship, 3 is added to all x-values, or all y-values are 3 more than x. We can express this using a table.

x	y
1	4
2	5
3	6
4	7

This information can also be described using a graph by using the x- and y-values as coordinate pairs. We can plot each point on a graph to see the pattern graphically.

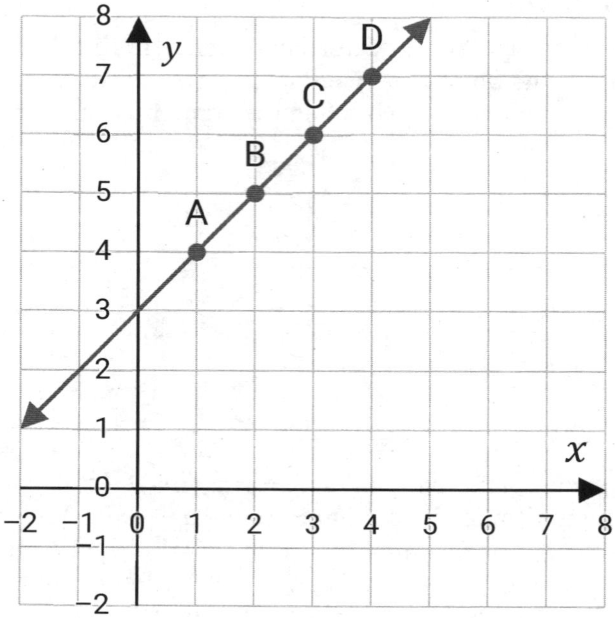

This graph uses the x and y-values from the table to create points. This line illustrates the information in the data table and describes the equation $y = x + 3$.

The equation, table, and graph all describe the same relationship, that y is 3 more than x.

Comparing Relationships and Patterns

We can use tables, graphs, and equations to compare relationships between x and y in additive and multiplicative relationships. To do this, we need to identify a pattern and use that information to compare. You may be given two sets of equations in the form $y = ax$ or $y = x + a$, two data sets, or two graphs, and asked to compare the relationships of x and y. Let's look at two equations and compare.

Equation #1	Equation #2
$y = 5x$	$y = x + 5$

Here we have two equations. You should ask yourself a few questions:

- What is the same in these relationships and how are they different?
- What is happening to x to get y?
- Are these additive or multiplicative relationships?

In this example, both equations have 5 as the a-value. Equation 1 shows a multiplicative relationship where y is 5 times as great as x and equation 2 shows an additive relationship where y is 5 more than x.

Solving Problems with Ratios and Rates

To solve problems using ratios and rates, you will use logic and reasoning to make reasonable predictions. The best way to approach ratio and rate problems is to use tables, models, or equivalence to help you solve the problem. Let's say the ratio of dogs to cats at an animal shelter is 5 to 2. This means that for every 5 dogs there are 2 cats, or for every 2 cats there are 5 dogs. We can use this ratio to solve some problems about the number of dogs and cats at this shelter. Let's say there are 25 dogs at this shelter, and the ratio of dogs to cats is still 5 : 2. We can use the ratio of 5 : 2 to help us find how many cats there are.

Use a model. If the ratio of dogs to cats is 5 to 2, our model may look like this.

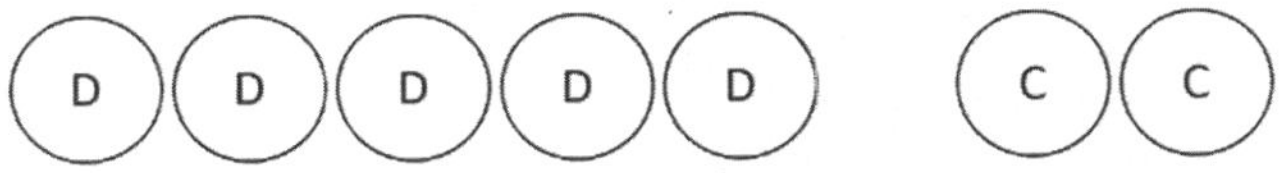

Now, if there are 25 dogs, the ratio needs to stay the same, so we can duplicate our model until we have 25 dogs.

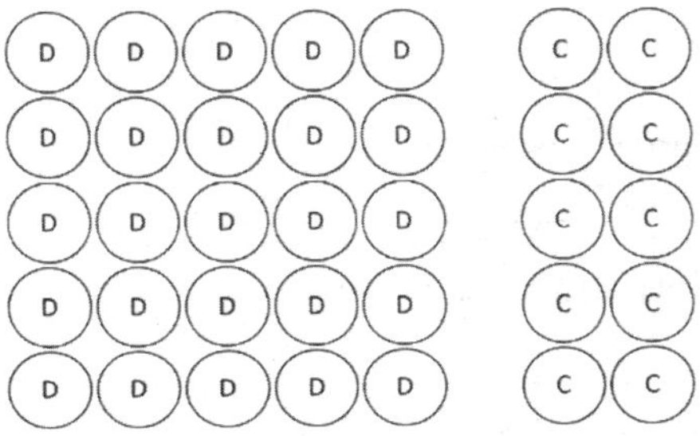

Now, if there are 25 dogs, we can see that there are 10 cats.

We can also use a table to solve this problem. By using a table, we can compare the numbers of dogs and cats. If there are 5 dogs to 2 cats, and there are 25 dogs, our table will look like this.

Dogs	Cats
5	2
25	

Now, we need to find the pattern. It looks like to get from 5 to 25, we multiply by 5. So, if we multiply the value of cats by 5, we will know the number of cats.

Dogs	Cats
5	2
25	10

We can see there are 10 cats.

We can also use equivalent ratios to solve this. We can write the ratio of dogs to cats as a fraction and find an equivalent fraction to solve our problem. In this example we can write the fraction of dogs to cats and in one fraction, the value for cats is missing.

$$\frac{\text{dogs}}{\text{cats}} = \frac{5}{2} = \frac{25}{?}$$

We can find an equivalent fraction my multiplying the numerator and denominator by 5 to find the number of cats.

$$\frac{5}{2} \times \frac{5}{5} = \frac{25}{10} = \frac{\text{dogs}}{\text{cats}}$$

Using each of these methods, the ratio stays the same, 5 : 2, and using any of these strategies, we find that if there are 25 dogs, there are 10 cats.

Example

You are making posters for a school election. You make 3 posters in 1 hour. At this rate, how many posters will you make in 4.5 hours?

In this problem, we are given a rate. You are making posters at a rate of 3 posters per hour. And we need to figure out how many posters you can make in 4.5 hours.

To solve this problem, we can use any of the following strategies: draw a model, draw a table, or use equivalence. Models can take a long time, but if you are feeling stuck, sometimes a picture is the best way to make sense of the information. Tables can also take a little while but can help illustrate patterns. Finding equivalent rates and ratios is likely to be the more efficient way to solve these problems. Let's use equivalence to solve this problem.

So, if you are making 3 posters in 1 hour, the rate you are making posters is 3 posters per hour. This can be written in fraction form:

$$\frac{3\text{ posters}}{1\text{ hour}} = \frac{3}{1}$$

Now that we have a rate, we can find an equivalent rate. We do not know how many posters you will be making, but we know that it will take 4.5 hours.

We can write the new fraction using this information, remembering to keep posters and hours in the same part of the fraction by placing both in the numerator or both in the denominator.

$$\frac{3\text{ posters}}{1\text{ hour}} = \frac{?\text{ posters}}{4.5\text{ hours}}$$

Now that we have our two fractions, we can solve for the missing value. We can see that 1 times 4.5 is 4.5, so if you multiply each value by the same number, we will get an equivalent fraction and that will give us an equivalent rate.

$$\frac{3}{1} \times \frac{4.5}{4.5} = \frac{13.5}{4.5}$$

So, if we make posters at a rate of 3 posters per hour and we work for 4.5 hours, we will make 13.5 posters.

Rates, Ratios, and Proportions

We can represent ratios and rates using proportions and scale factors. A **proportion** is an equation with two equivalent ratios. We use proportions to compare ratios and to solve ratio and rate problems. Suppose a recipe requires 2 cups of sugar and 3 cups of flour. This can be described by the ratio $2 : 3$, or $\frac{2}{3}$. Now, that means that for every 4 cups of sugar, we need 6 cups of flour because these ratios are equivalent. This can be expressed by the following proportion.

$$\frac{2}{3} = \frac{4}{6}$$

Now, what if we were making a recipe with 8 cups of sugar? We can use proportions to help us solve this problem where x is the number of cups of flour needed.

$$\frac{2}{3} = \frac{8}{x}$$

Proportions are written in the form:

$$\frac{a}{b} = \frac{c}{d}$$

They can also be written in the form $ad = cb$ when the equation is rearranged.

$$\begin{aligned} d \times \frac{a}{b} &= \frac{c}{d} \times d \\ b\left(d \times \frac{a}{b}\right) &= c \times b \\ d \times a &= c \times b \\ ad &= cb \end{aligned}$$

This is also known as **cross multiplying**. When we have a proportion, we can cross multiply to solve.

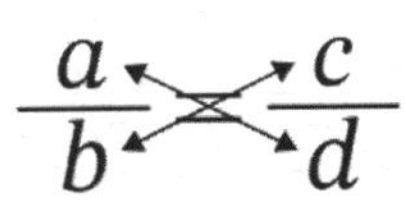

$$ad = cb$$

Now, solve the proportion for the number of cups of flour needed for 8 cups of sugar.

$$\begin{aligned} \frac{2}{3} &= \frac{8}{x} \\ 2 \times x &= 8 \times 3 \\ \frac{2x}{2} &= \frac{24}{2} \\ x &= 12 \end{aligned}$$

So, if we are using 8 cups of sugar, we need 12 cups of flour.

$$\frac{2}{3} = \frac{8}{12}$$

These are equivalent ratios.

> **Review Video: Proportions**
> Visit mometrix.com/academy and enter code: 505355
>
> **Review Video: Cross Multiplying Fractions**
> Visit mometrix.com/academy and enter code: 893904

Independent and Dependent Quantities

When there is a relationship between two quantities, there is an independent quantity and a dependent quantity in the relationship. An **independent quantity** is the quantity that stands alone. This is the value that starts the relationship. A **dependent quantity** is reliant on the other quantity; it is dependent on the independent value. In a mathematical relationship, there is a value, something is done to that value, and then you have an ending value. An additive relationship is an example of a relationship with an independent and a dependent quantity. In an additive relationship, there is a value, something is added to the value, and then you have an ending value. This can be described by the equation $y = x + a$. In this equation, x is the independent quantity. It stands alone; it is the quantity that is being changed. The ending value, the value that is dependent on x, is y; this is the dependent value. The value of y is dependent on the value of x. When looking at independent and dependent quantities in tables, the x-value and the y-value can also be understood as the **input** and the **output**.

Let's look at an algebraic relationship:

You get hired for your first job and make $10 an hour. In this scenario, the relationship is between dollars and hours worked. Which quantity is dependent on the other? The number of dollars you make is dependent on how many hours you work. So, we can say that dollars is the dependent value, the y-value, and hours is the independent value, the x-value.

> **Review Video: Identifying Independent and Dependent Variables**
> Visit mometrix.com/academy and enter code: 627181

Representing Algebraic Relationships

We can describe algebraic relationships using tables and equations. When you are given a table, there is an independent quantity and a dependent quantity. There is a starting value, the value that an operation is done to, and there is an end value, the value that occurs after the operation. We often see algebraic relationships in the form $y = x + b$ or $y = kx$. When subtraction and division are involved, we can see these equations in the form of $y = x + (-b)$, or $y = x - b$, and $y = \frac{x}{k}$. We can use any variable to describe these relationships, but there will be an independent value, the value that the operation is happening to, and a dependent value, the outcome of the operation. We see these relationships often shown in tables; they are sometimes called "in and out tables", where an independent value goes "in", and a dependent value comes "out". When we have a table that shows a relationship, we can write an equation to describe the relationship. In the table, we will have an independent quantity, an operation, and a dependent quantity. Once we can identify those parts, we can write an equation to describe the relationship.

Representing Real-World Algebraic Relationships

Algebraic relationships can be described using tables, graphs, and equations. Algebraic relationships are relationships between independent and dependent variables and appear in real-world situations. It is important to be able to identify equations, tables, and graphs that illustrate real-world algebraic relationships. You may see a scenario that describes a relationship and need to choose the correct graph or table that describes the relationship. You may see an equation that illustrates an algebraic relationship and need to identify a story that the equation best describes. In either type of question, it is important to start by identifying the independent and dependent variables and then identify the pattern. In other words, identify the x-values, the y-values, and the operation. Once you have identified these three main parts of an algebraic relationship, you can convert that meaning to an equation, a table, a graph, or a story.

Example

Elyse bought x stickers from a local artist for $3.25 per sticker. She spent y dollars on stickers. Which equation matches Elyse's situation?

a. $3.25x = y$
b. $y = x + 3.25$
c. $3.25 = x + y$
d. $y = x - 3.25$

In this problem, we are given a situation and a list of equations. We need to choose the equation that matches the situation.

To approach this problem, we need to review the situation and write an equation to match Elyse's situation.

If Elyse bought x stickers for \$3.25, the total number of dollars spent is \$3.25x. If she bought 5 stickers, we would multiply \$3.25 by 5 to get the total, or if she bought 10, we would multiply 10 by \$3.25 to get the total.

One side of our equation will be \$3.25x.

We also know that the total number of dollars spent is y. That means that y is going to be on the other side of our equation.

The equation that matches this story is $y = 3.25x$.

The equation $y = 3.25x$ is equivalent to $3.25x = y$, and this matches one of our choices.

The correct answer is A.

EXAMPLE

The graph shows the average number of sandwiches, y, a restaurant sells per day, x.

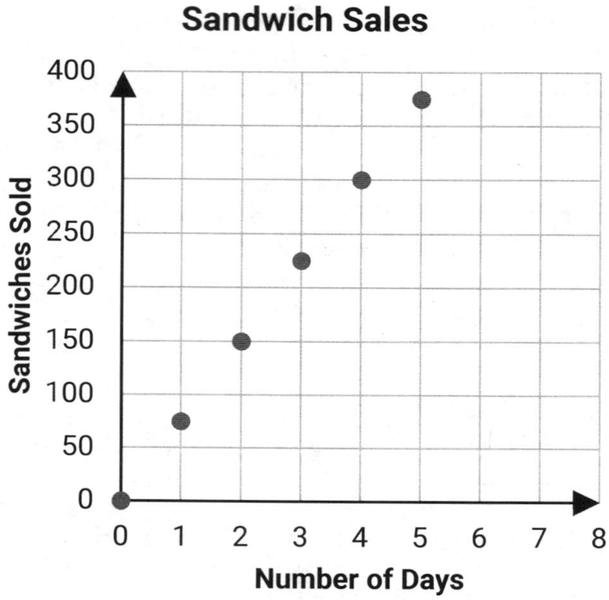

Which equation best represents the relationship between x and y represented by the graph?

a. $y = 75x$
b. $y = 75 + x$
c. $y = 150 + x$
d. $y = 150x$

In this problem, we are given a graph and four equation choices. Examine the graph and select the equation that best represents the relationship between x and y on the graph.

Identify the relationship between x and y on the graph. To do this, we need to first recognize the x- and y-axis and the values of the coordinates.

When we look at this graph, we can see that the number of days is represented along the bottom, the x-axis, and the number of sandwiches is represented along the left side, the y-axis. So, sandwiches are the y-values, and days are the x-values.

Now, we need to list the values that we see on the graph.

We can see that our first point is at (0,0). This means that after zero days, the restaurant sells zero sandwiches.

The next point is at (1,75). This means that after 1 day, the restaurant sells 75 sandwiches.

The next point is at (2,150), followed by (3,225), (4,300), and (5,375).

The best way to examine these values is to make an x and y table and observe the pattern.

x	y
0	0
1	75
2	150
3	225
4	300
5	375

Now that we can observe the values, we can see that the restaurant sells about 75 sandwiches per day because on day 1, they sell 75, and the y-value increases by 75 each day, so the pattern is times 75.

This means that the relationship between the x- and y-values can be represented by the equation $y = 75x$ because the total number of sandwiches, y, can be found by multiplying 75 by the number of days, x.

Our equation, $y = 75x$, matches answer choice A.

The correct answer is A.

EXAMPLE

Tamila is playing a ball game with her brother where they get 3 points for each trick shot they make. Which graph best shows the relationship between the number of trick shots made and the number of points?

a.

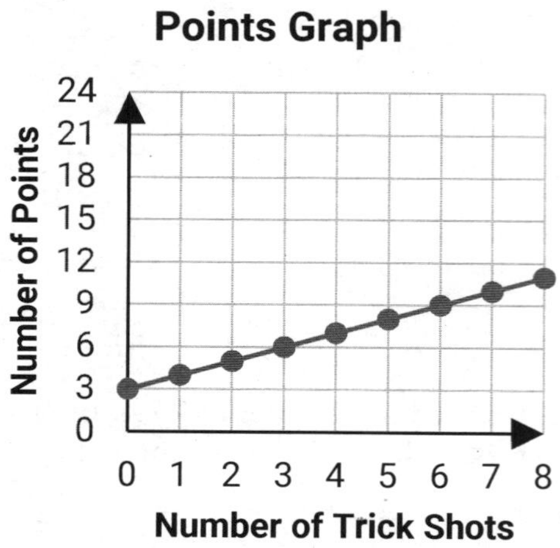

b.

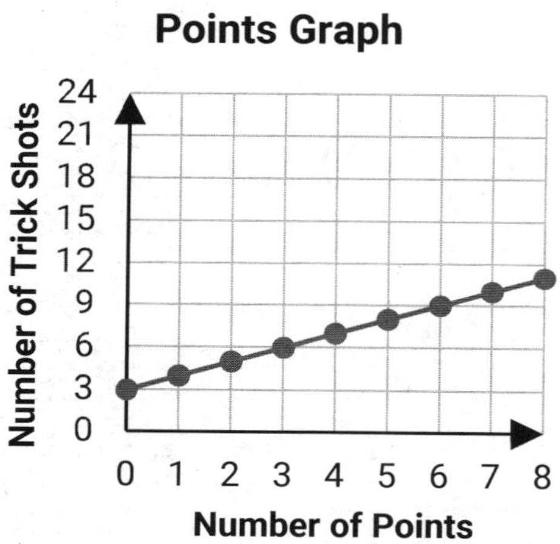

c.

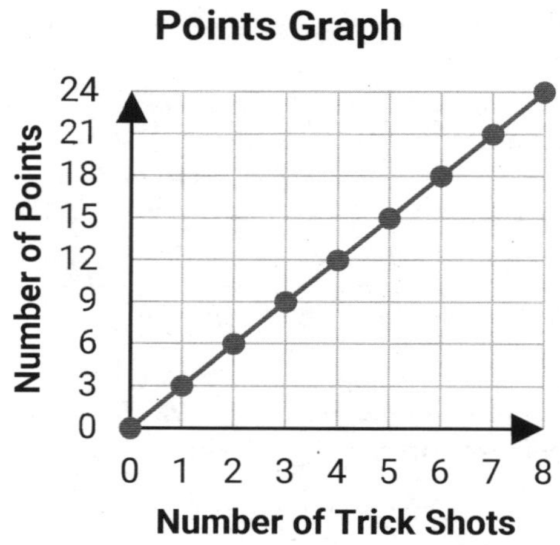

d.

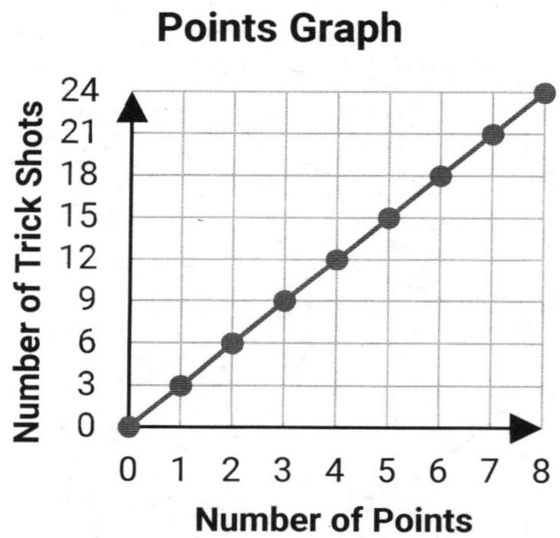

In this problem, we are given a story and four graphs. We need to examine the relationship between trick shots and points and select the graph that best represents the relationship.

In the story, we know that Tamila and her brother are playing a game where they try to make trick shots and they get 3 points for each trick shot made. We should ask ourselves, what is the pattern in this story? There are a few ways to approach this.

One way to approach this is to complete a table. If Tamila makes 0 trick shots, she will have 0 points. If she makes 1 trick shot, she will have 3 points. If she makes 2 trick shots, she will have 6 points. If she makes 3 trick shots, she will have 9 points, and so on. We can include this data in a data table.

x	0	1	2	3	4	5	6	7	8
y	0	3	6	9	12	15	18	21	24

We can also think about the pattern. If Tamila is getting 3 points for each trick shot, we know that this is a multiplication pattern.

Based on the pattern from the story and the table, the equation for this story is $y = 3x$, where y is the total number of points and x is the total number of trick shots made.

Now, we need to examine the graphs and select the graph that best represents this equation and pattern.

If we look at our graph choices, we can see a few main differences.

Choices A and C show the number of trick shots along the x-axis and number of points along the y-axis.

Choices B and D show the number of points along the x-axis and the number of trick shots along the y-axis.

The first difference is in the placement of the x- and y-values.

We can also see a difference in the lines on the graphs. The lines shown in options C and D are steeper than the lines shown in options A and B.

Let's examine these graphs a little more closely.

Choices A and B show a graph that is less steep than choices C and D.

If we observe the data points on graphs A and B, we will see that the data points are (0,3), (1,4), (2,5), (3,6), (4,7), (5,8), (6,9), (7,10), (8,11).

By looking at these data points, we can see that the pattern is adding 3. This would mean that choices A and B represent the pattern $y = x + 3$. This does not match the story.

If we observe the data points on graphs C and D, we will see that the data points are (0,0), (1,3), (2,6), (3,9), (4,12), (5,15), (6,18), (7,21), and (8,24).

By looking at these data points, we can see that the pattern is multiplying by 3 because if you multiply each x-value by 3, you will get the y-value. This would mean that options C and D represent the pattern $y = 3x$. This matches our story.

This means that the correct answer is either C or D. What is the difference between these two graphs? The difference is the x- and y-axis.

In graph C, we can see that the x-axis represents the number of trick shots, and the y-axis represents the number of points.

In graph D, we can see that the x-axis represents the number of points, and the y-axis represents the number of trick shots.

We have already identified the pattern is $y = 3x$ because the total number of points is the number of trick shots made times the number of points for each trick shot, 3. This means that the number of points is represented by the y-values and the y-axis, and the number of trick shots is represented by the x-values and the x-axis.

Graph C correctly represents this information.

The correct answer is C.

Identifying Equivalent Expressions

Expressions Versus Equations

An **expression** includes numbers, variables, or numbers and variables separated with operation signs. Anything that stands alone or could belong on one side of an equal sign, is an expression. $3x + 4$ is an example of an expression. It contains numbers, a variable, and an operation. A single number is also considered an expression. Often, expressions are simplified. $2x + 4x - 1x$ is an example of an expression because there is no equal sign. It cannot be solved; you cannot solve for x in an expression, but it can be simplified. The expression below is simplified.

$$2x + 4x - 1x$$
$$6x - 1x$$
$$5x$$

Each step gives a more simplified version of the same expression. Each step in the simplification gives an equivalent expression.

Identify Equivalent Expressions with Variables

A **variable** is any unknown value represented by a letter or symbol, most commonly x. A **term** is a number or a number multiplied by a variable, like 3, or $3x$. Numerical expressions will include variable terms, and you may be required to identify or generate equivalent expressions that include these variable terms. When you encounter variables, it is important to remember that with each variable, any repetition of that variable is a **like term**. For example, x and y are not like terms because they are different unknown values. Also, x and 4 are not like terms because 4 is a whole number and x is an unknown term. However, x and $3x$ are like terms because they share the same variable. When encountering an expression with like terms, you may be required to simplify or expand the expression to find equivalent expressions.

Simplify the expression $4x + 2x + 7$.

Given the expression $4x + 2x + 7$, you have two like terms. We simplify these terms to find an equivalent expression. We can combine $4x + 2x$ to $6x$ because they are like terms.

So, $4x + 2x + 7$ is equivalent to $6x + 7$.

Expand the expression $4x + 2x + 7$.

Given the same expression $4x + 2x + 7$, we can expand the variable terms to find an equivalent expression. For example, $4x$ can be expanded to $(x + x + x + x)$, and $2x$ can be expanded to $(x + x)$.

So, $4x + 2x + 7$ is equivalent to $(x + x + x + x) + (x + x) + 7$.

When identifying equivalent expressions with variables, like terms can be combined, simplified, or expanded to generate an equivalent expression.

Using the Order of Operations

An **equivalent expression** is part of a set of expressions that have an equivalent value. The order of operations is essential to finding and identifying equivalent expressions. Finding equivalent expressions may require you to simplify or expand an expression. You may simplify the whole expression, or just part of the expression. For example, you may be required to simplify or identify an equivalent expression like $3(2 + 4) - 5$. There are many equivalent expressions that can be generated by this example. These are just a few possibilities.

Simplification

$3(6) - 5$ is an equivalent expression. The part of the expression in parentheses was simplified.

$18 - 5$ is an equivalent expression. The parentheses and multiplication parts of the expression were simplified.

13 is an equivalent expression. All components of the expression have been simplified.

Expansion

$3(2 + 2^2) - 5$ is an equivalent expression. The term 4 has been expanded to include an exponent.

$3(2 + 4) - (5 \times 1)$ is an equivalent expression. The term 5 has been expanded as 5×1.

There are many variations of the same expression. You may be required to simplify or expand an expression to identify equivalence.

Using Exponents

An **exponent** is used to identify a multiple of the same factor. The symbol for an exponent is a small number to the top right of a whole number. The small number shows how many times the whole number should be multiplied by itself. For example, 2^3 is equivalent to $2 \times 2 \times 2$, or 8. When identifying equivalent expressions using exponents, you may be required to simplify exponents, expand exponents, or generate exponents.

Simplification

Given the expression $4^2 + 2 - 3$, you may find an equivalent expression by simplifying the exponent. In this case, the exponential expression is 4^2. This can be simplified by finding the value of 4^2, which is 16. So, an equivalent expression to $4^2 + 2 - 3$ is $16 + 2 - 3$.

Expansion

You may be required to expand an expression including an exponent. Given the expression 4×2^3, you may expand this exponent. In this case, the exponential expression is 2^3. This can be expanded to $2 \times 2 \times 2$. So, an equivalent expression to 4×2^3 is $4 \times (2 \times 2 \times 2)$.

Generate Exponents

You may be required to generate an exponent to identify an equivalent expression. Given the expression $8 + 4 + 36$, you may convert each of these values to an exponential expression. 8 can be rewritten as 2^3, 4 can be rewritten as 2^2, and 36 can be rewritten as 6^2. So, an equivalent expression to $8 + 4 + 36$ is $2^3 + 2^2 + 6^2$.

When identifying equivalent expressions with exponents, these values can be simplified, expanded, or generated to identify equivalent expressions.

Review Video: Exponents
Visit mometrix.com/academy and enter code: 600998

Using Models

We can use models to illustrate and compare expressions to tell if they are **equivalent**. This can be a helpful strategy when starting out comparing expressions. Models are another way to write an expression in expanded form. We can compare expressions using common models, like strip diagrams, hanging models, and tiles. Using models is not the most efficient way to compare expressions and is not recommended to use during testing because it is time consuming. However, models can be helpful when you run out of strategies, or you are just starting out comparing expressions.

Hanging Models

Compare expressions with hanging models.

Hanging models are used to illustrate if two expressions are equivalent. One expression is illustrated on each side of the model to compare. Consider the expressions $3x + 2x$ and $7x - 2x$. These expressions can be compared using a hanging model.

We will start by illustrating one expression on each side of the model.

We can illustrate $3x + 2x$ as:

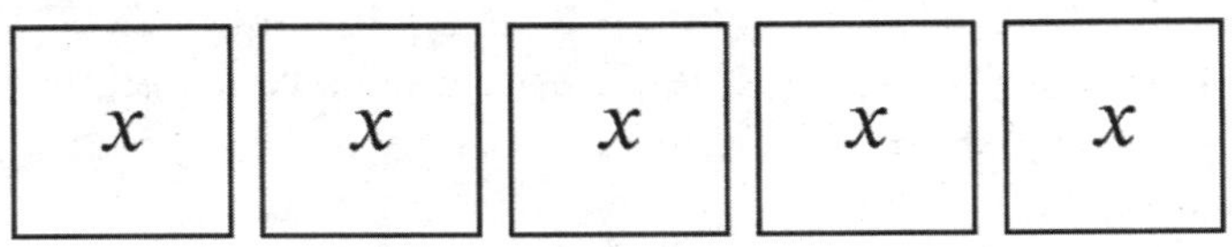

$3x + 2x$

because $3x + 2x$ can be expanded to $(x + x + x) + (x + x)$.

Now, we can model the second expression. We can illustrate $7x - 2x$ as:

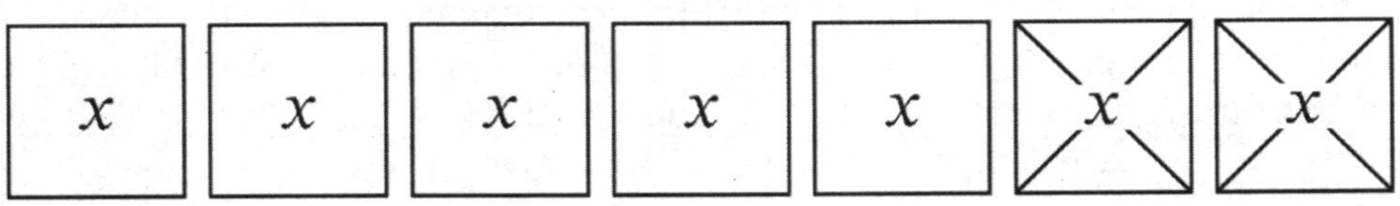

$7x - 2x$

because it can be expanded to $(x + x + x + x + x + x + x) - (x + x)$.

A completed hanging model would look like this.

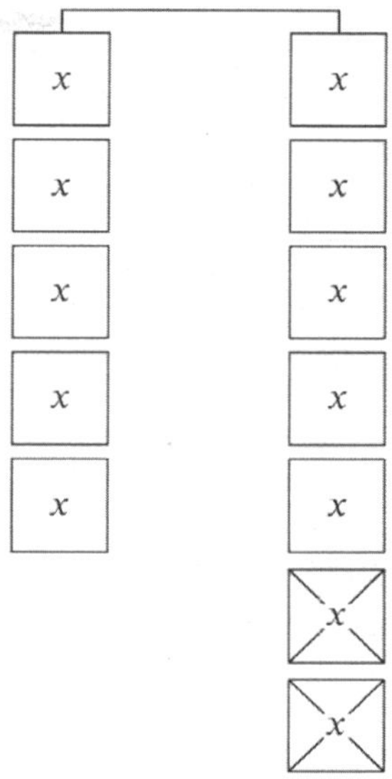

Now that we have a complete hanging model, we can see that each expression is equivalent. Both sides are balanced, since the number of x's on the left side and the number of x's on the right side are equal.

STRIP DIAGRAMS

Compare expressions with strip diagrams.

Strip diagrams can be used to illustrate expressions and make it easy to determine if they are equivalent. Let's use a strip diagram to see if $3x + 5$ and $2x + 7$ are equivalent.

First, we need to illustrate each expression in a strip diagram.

$3x + 5$ can be illustrated as:

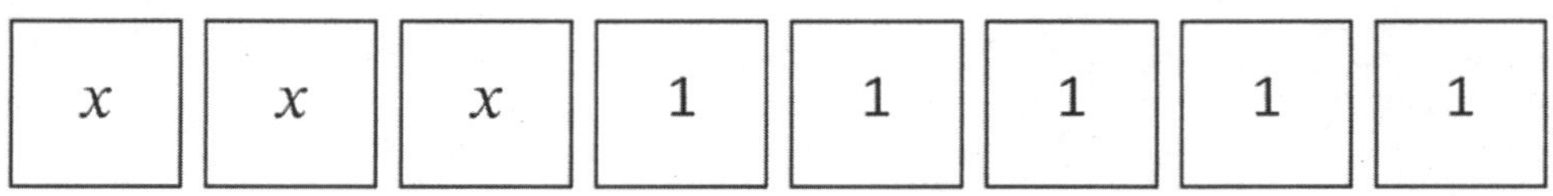

$3x + 5$

The expression $3x + 5$ can be expanded to $x + x + x + 1 + 1 + 1 + 1 + 1$.

$2x + 7$ can be illustrated as:

$2x + 7$

The expression $2x + 7$ can be expanded to $x + x + 1 + 1 + 1 + 1 + 1 + 1 + 1$.

Now that each expression is illustrated by a strip diagram, we can compare. Are these expressions equivalent?

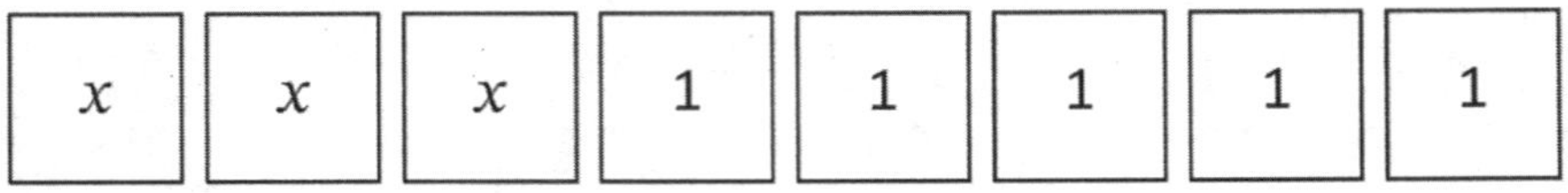

$3x + 5$

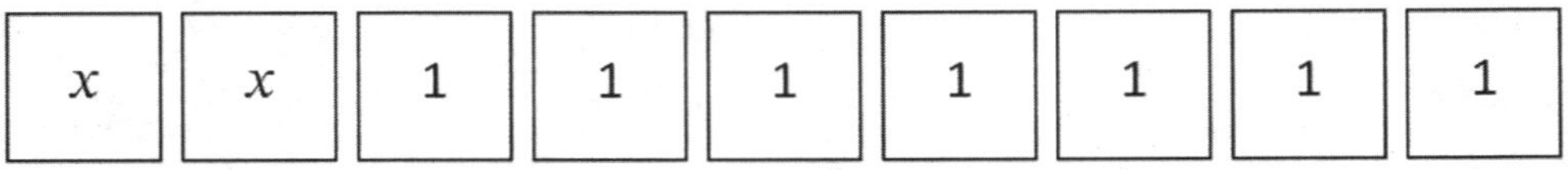

$2x + 7$

No. They each have a different number of x's and a different number of 1's. These expressions are not equivalent.

<u>TILES</u>

Compare expressions using tiles.

Tiles are used to illustrate expressions. In class, you may experience using virtual or physical tiles. They can also be drawn to help compare expressions. Let's use tiles to see if $2(3 + x)$ and $6 + 2x$ are equivalent.

We can start by building an illustration for $2(3 + x)$.

First, we will illustrate the expression $3 + x$.

This can be illustrated with tiles as:

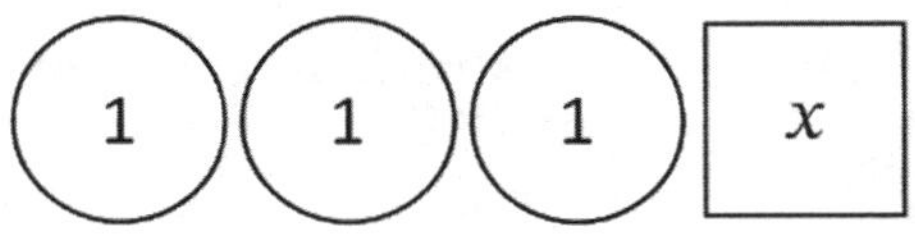

In this expression, $3 + x$ is being multiplied by 2, so let's double that expression.

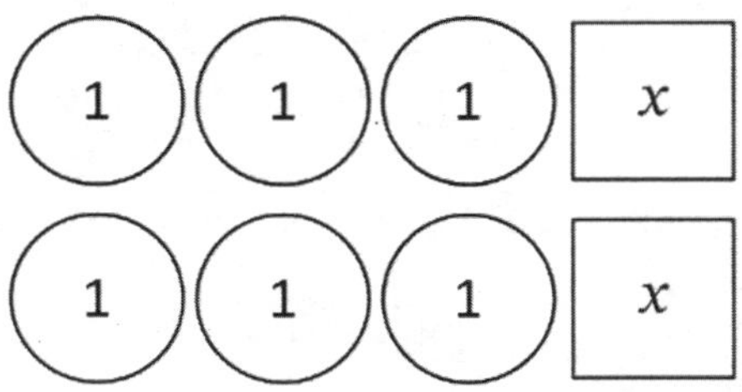

Now that we have one expression illustrated, we can illustrate $6 + 2x$. This can be illustrated with tiles as:

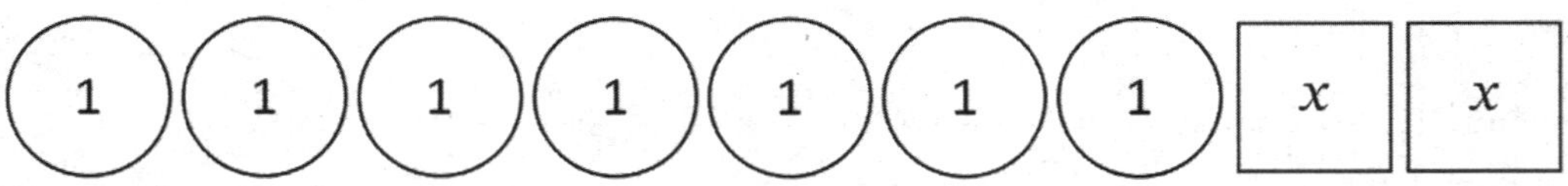

Now we can compare these values. Are these expressions equivalent? Each expression has the same number of x tiles and the same number of 1 tiles. So, they are equivalent.

EQUATIONS

WRITING EQUATIONS TO REPRESENT PROBLEMS

We can use **equations** to represent real-world math problems. When we write equations from problems, we need to understand what information we are provided, and what value is missing. If we can see what we know, and identify what we need to find, we can use numbers and symbols to illustrate any problem. When writing equations, we use variables to stand for the unknown values.

Let's say you are given this story: You get paid \$250 every month from your new job. You have been working there for 2 months and have \$820 in your account. How much money was in your account when you started the job?

In this problem, we know how much money you get per month, we know how many months you have been working, and we know how much money you have now.

What do we not know? We do not know how much money you started with. We are trying to find how much money you had in your account before the 2 months.

We can use d for the number of dollars in your account before you started working.

If we know a total, we can usually assume this can go on one side of our equal sign because we are doing some math and then we end up with \$820.

$$\$820 =$$

Now we have 1 side of our equation. How will we get to \$820? We will start with something and then add 2 months of pay. So, we know we will start with a number and then add to it. We can add this to the other side of the equation.

$$\$820 = d +$$

Now, we started with d and then added 2 payments of \$250. So, we added 2 payments of \$250 to d. We have two options here to show this. We could say that we added \$500 to d.

$$\$820 = d + \$500$$

We can also say that we added $2 \times \$250$ to d.

$$820 = d + 2(250)$$

Because of the associative property, this equation can be written in multiple ways.

$$820 = d + 2(250)$$
$$d + 2(250) = 820$$
$$820 = 2(250) + d$$
$$2(250) + d = 820$$

When writing an equation, it is important to identify what you know and what you do not know. You will use a variable for the unknown value. Then you can start understanding what the problem is saying. Every problem has a starting point, something that happens, and an ending point. When you can identify these things, you can build an equation.

Representing Equations on a Number Line

One-step equations can be represented on a number line. You may be asked to identify a number line that represents an addition, subtraction, multiplication, or division equation. These equations may include a variable. When representing equations on a number line, it is important to identify the starting point, the end point, and what happens in the middle.

In an addition equation, you will have a starting point, add a value, and have an ending point.

$2 + 3 = 5$ can be represented on a number line:

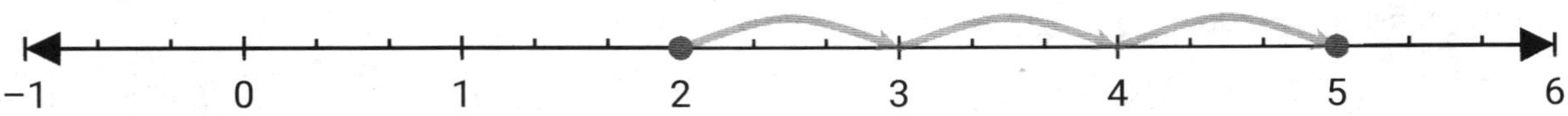

In a subtraction equation, you will have a starting value, a value decreased, and an ending value.

$5 - 2 = 3$ can be represented on a number line:

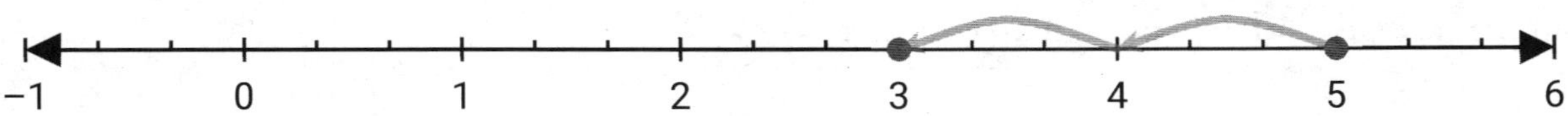

In a multiplication equation, you will start with zero, have a series of equal increases, and have an ending value.

$2 \times 3 = 6$ can be represented on a number line:

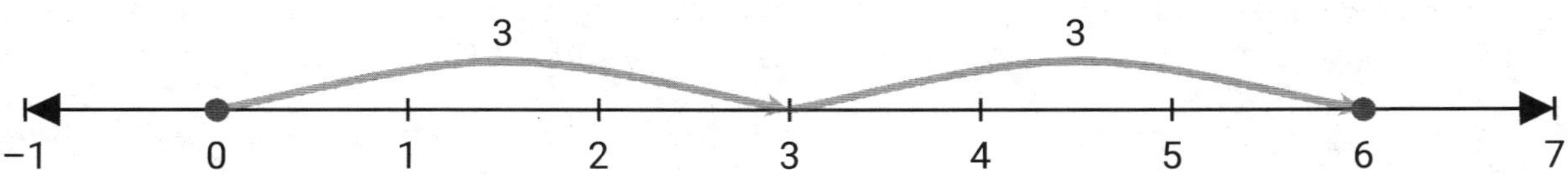

In a division equation, you will have a starting point, a series of regular partitions, an ending point at zero, and a value per partition.

$\frac{6}{2} = 3$ can be represented on a number line:

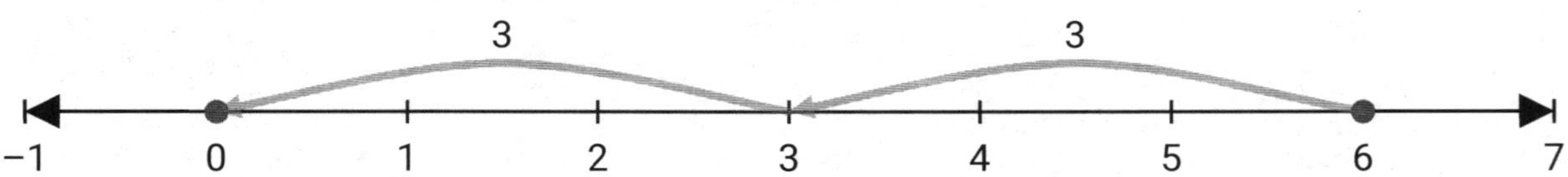

Representing Equations on a Table and Graph

Equations can be represented as a table and as a line on a coordinate place.

Example

The equation $t = 1n$, represents t, the total time in minutes a racecar driver drives for n number of laps. Determine what the 1 in the equation means, and make a table of values that represents this equation and graph them.

The 1 in the equation represents the time the driver takes to complete one lap. This means that every lap takes the driver 1 minute. The variable t represents the y-values on the graph, and the variable n represents the x-values on the graph. The table and graph below show this data:

Number of laps	Time (in minutes)
1	1
2	2
3	3
4	4

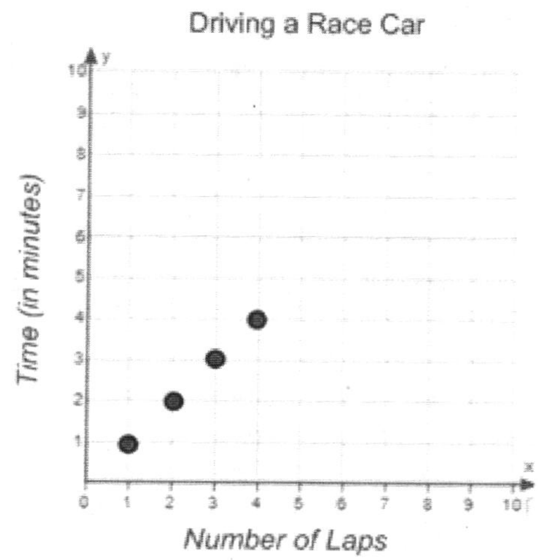

Using Equations to Express Scenarios

Stories and scenarios can be expressed through equations. You can write an equation to match a story or write a story to match an equation. It is important to understand what is going on in an equation, so you can choose a story that makes sense. An addition equation will include adding a value to an existing value and ending with a total. A subtraction equation will include a starting value, an ending value, and a value being taken away. A multiplication equation will usually have a certain number of groups of a value, or a value being replicated a certain number of times, with an ending value. And a division equation will usually have a starting value and that value being broken into segments or groups a certain number of times. Once you identify what is happening in an equation, you can match a story to the problem.

Solve Equations with a Variable

Equations with **variables** include an **unknown value**. When you are solving an equation with a variable, you are finding the value of that unknown quantity. You are finding the value of the variable. Sometimes logic is enough to solve these problems, sometimes you need to complete a series of steps, and sometimes you may need to try different values to check yourself.

Say you are given the equation $-6 + x = 10$, and you are asked what value of x will make this sentence true. There are a few ways to solve this.

The first step to solve this problem is using logic. Do you know this using mental math? Can you solve this problem just by looking at it? Perhaps. If you can use mental math, that is a great place to start. If you use mental math on a test, it is always a good idea to check your answer on paper just to be sure.

The next step to solve an equation is to solve for the variable. Given the equation $-6 + x = 10$, we can solve for x by performing operations to isolate x and get our variable on one side of the equation by itself.

In this example, we want to get x by itself on one side of the equation. We can do this by adding 6 to both sides of our equation.

$$\begin{aligned} -6 + x &= 10 \\ +6 &= +6 \\ x &= 16 \end{aligned}$$

We can do this because if we add, subtract, multiply, or divide the same value on both sides of the equation, the sentence will still be true. For instance, if $2 = 2$, then $2 + 3 = 2 + 3$.

$$\begin{aligned} 2 &= 2 \\ 2 + 3 &= 2 + 3 \end{aligned}$$

Now we know that the solution for $-6 + x = 10$ is $x = 16$. This means that if x equals 16, the sentence will be true.

The last strategy would be to use the values of x to test the solution. In this example, we have 16 as a possible solution, so we can use 16 in place of x to see if the equation is true.

$$\begin{aligned} -6 + x &= 10 \\ -6 + (16) &= 10 \\ 10 &= 10 \end{aligned}$$

When we simplify with 16 as the x-value, we get 10 on both sides of our equal sign, so our sentence is true and 16 is the solution.

EXAMPLE

What is the solution to the equation $-4x = 16$?

a. -4
b. 4
c. 12
d. -12

In this problem, we are given an equation and some possible solutions. We have two strategies to solve this problem. We can solve the equation, or we can use the given values to check to see if the sentence is true.

Let's solving the equation.

The goal of this is to get x by itself on one side of the equation. Right now, x is being multiplied by −4, so we need to do the opposite operation of multiplication, which is division. Divide each side of the equation by −4.

$$\frac{-4x}{-4} = \frac{16}{-4}$$

$\frac{-4}{-4} = 1$, so x is by itself.

$\frac{16}{-4} = -4$ because dividing a positive number by a negative number gives a negative number.

$x = -4$, so choice A is correct.

EXAMPLE

The area of a rectangle is 735 square feet. The base of the rectangle is 49 feet. What is *h*, the height of the rectangle?

In this problem, we are given some measurements of a rectangle and are tasked to find the other measurement. This can be written as an equation with a variable.

In this example, we know the area and we know the base of the rectangle and we need to find the height.

To find the area of a rectangle, multiply the base and the height.

Let's use this information to write an equation we can solve.

$$A = b \times h$$
$$735 = 49 \times h$$

Now, solve for h. We can see that h is being multiplied by 49, so we need to perform the inverse operation on both sides of the equal sign.

$$\frac{735}{49} = \frac{49h}{49}$$
$$735 \div 49 = h$$

You may need to do some long division to find the value of h. The division problem will show that $735 \div 49 = 15$.

So, now we know that $h = 15$.

We can check our answer by using 15 for the value of h.

$$735 = 49h$$
$$735 = 49(15)$$
$$735 = 735$$

This value makes the sentence true, so the height of the rectangle is 15 feet.

DETERMINING IF A VALUE MAKES AN EQUATION TRUE

To determine if a value makes an equation true, we need to use that value in an equation with a variable. You may be given a value for a variable and asked to choose an equation that makes the sentence true. If both sides of an equal sign are the same value, then you can determine that the sentence is true. Let's say you are given the value $x = 3$. What are some possible equations that $x = 3$ would be a solution to? There are an infinite number of possibilities, but some examples would be $2 + x = 5$, $4 - x = 1$, $10x = 30$, and $\frac{12}{x} = 4$. In all these examples, 3 is the solution.

$$2 + x = 5$$
$$2 + 3 = 5$$

$$4 - x = 1$$
$$4 - 3 = 1$$

$$10x = 30$$
$$10(3) = 30$$

$$\frac{12}{x} = 4$$
$$\frac{12}{3} = 4$$

We have to test the value of x in each option to see if the sentence is true and the equation is balanced.

Determining If a Proportional Relationship Exists

Linear relationships can be proportional relationships if the y-intercept is equal to zero. This means that when the two quantities are graphed on the coordinate plane, the result is a straight line through the origin. If given a table, the ratio of y to x must be constant for all values of x and y besides zero for a proportional relationship to exist between the two variables. The value $\frac{y}{x}$ is the constant of proportionality.

Example

For the graphs below, determine whether there exists a proportional relationship between x and y. If a proportional relationship exists, find the constant of proportionality and write an equation for the line.

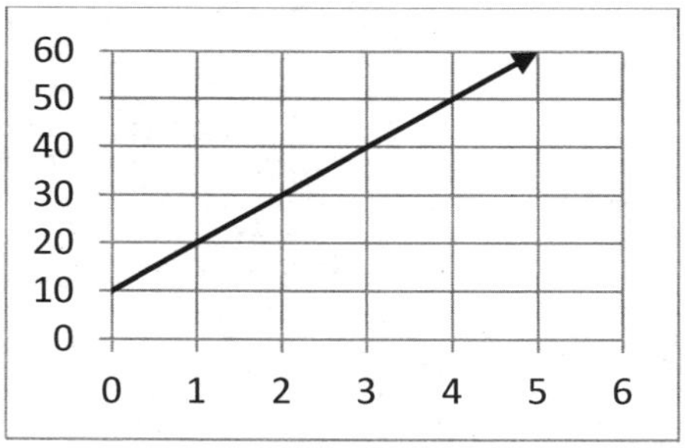

Though the graph of the relationship between x and y is a straight line, it does not pass through the origin. So, though y varies directly as x, the ratio $\frac{y}{x}$ is not constant: for instance, $\frac{20}{1} \neq \frac{30}{2} \neq \frac{40}{3}$..

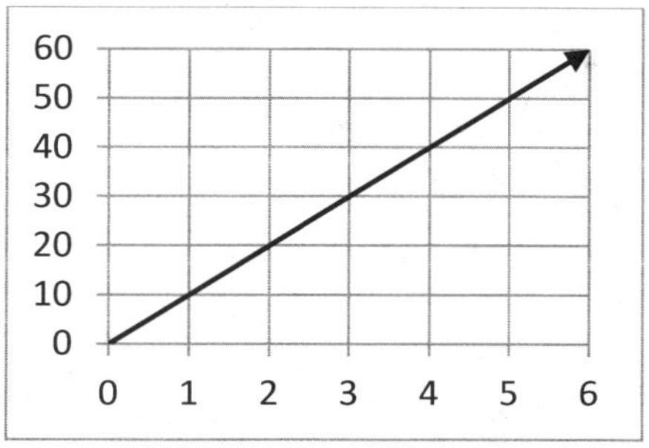

The graph of a proportional relationship is a straight line through the origin.

This graph is a straight line through the origin, so the relationship between x and y is proportional. The constant of proportionality is represented by the ratio $\frac{y}{x}$. This constant is the same as the unit rate. The constant of proportionality is equal to the y-value when $x = 1$. Since the ratio $\frac{y}{x}$ is 10 (see that $\frac{y}{x} = \frac{10}{1} = \frac{20}{2} = \frac{30}{3}$ and so on), or since $y = 10$ when $x = 1$, the constant of proportionality is 10. The relationship between x and y is represented by the equation $y = 10x$.

EXAMPLE

Determine whether there exists a proportional relationship between x and y. If a proportional relationship exists, find the constant of proportionality and write an equation to represent the relationship.

If the ratio of y to x is constant for all values of x and y besides zero, then there is a proportional relationship between the two variables. The value $\frac{y}{x}$ is the constant of proportionality.

x	1	2	3	4
y	5	9	13	17

The ratio of y to x is not constant; therefore, the values in the table do not represent a proportional relationship:

x	1	2	3	4
y	5	9	13	17
$\frac{y}{x}$	$\frac{5}{1} = 5$	$\frac{9}{2} = 4.5$	$\frac{13}{3} = 4.\overline{3}$	$\frac{17}{4} = 4.25$

EXAMPLE

Determine whether there exists a proportional relationship between x and y. If a proportional relationship exists, find the constant of proportionality and write an equation to represent the relationship.

x	1	2	3	4
y	1	4	9	16

If the ratio of y to x is constant for all values of x and y besides zero, then there is a proportional relationship between the two variables. The value $\frac{y}{x}$ is the constant of proportionality.

The ratio of y to x is not constant; therefore, the values in the table do not represent a proportional relationship:

x	1	2	3	4
y	1	4	9	16
$\frac{y}{x}$	$\frac{1}{1} = 1$	$\frac{4}{2} = 2$	$\frac{9}{3} = 3$	$\frac{16}{4} = 4$

EXAMPLE

Determine whether there exists a proportional relationship between x and y. If a proportional relationship exists, find the constant of proportionality and write an equation to represent the relationship.

x	1	2	3	4
y	2.5	5	7.5	10

If the ratio of y to x is constant for all values of x and y besides zero, then there is a proportional relationship between the two variables. The value $\frac{y}{x}$ is the constant of proportionality.

The ratio of y to x is 2.5; therefore, the values in the table represent the proportional relationship modeled by the equation $y = 2.5x$:

x	1	2	3	4
y	2.5	5	7.5	10
$\frac{y}{x}$	$\frac{2.5}{1} = 2.5$	$\frac{5}{2} = 2.5$	$\frac{7.5}{3} = 2.5$	$\frac{10}{4} = 2.5$

INEQUALITIES

WRITING INEQUALITIES TO REPRESENT PROBLEMS

An **inequality** is a math sentence that connects two expressions with a comparison. These expressions are compared using a greater than, $>$, less than, $<$, greater than or equal to, $\geq$, or less than or equal to, $\leq$, sign. These signs are used in inequalities.

There are some stories that can be illustrated by inequalities. In these scenarios, we need to identify what we know, what we do not know, and the comparison. For example, suppose you need to go to the grocery store to buy avocados that are \$0.75 each. You only brought 5 dollars. How many avocados can you buy? This is an example of an inequality because you have a maximum or minimum to meet. You need to get avocados, but you cannot go over the 5-dollar maximum. You can set up an inequality to illustrate this.

We know that avocados are \$0.75 each. We know that you cannot spend more than \$5. You do not know how many avocados you can buy, so this is the unknown.

We can write an inequality using a for avocados.

We cannot go over \$5, so the \$5 must be greater than or equal to the total price of the avocados at a rate of \$0.75 per avocado.

$$5 \geq$$

Now, we want avocados and each one is \$0.75, so the other side of our inequality is \$0.75 times the number of avocados.

$$5 \geq 0.75a$$

This could also be written as

$$0.75a \leq 5$$

Solving Inequalities on a Number Line

Inequalities can be represented on a number line. Inequalities are written using two expressions connected by a greater than, less than, greater than or equal to, or less than or equal to sign. We express solutions to these sentences using number lines and series of arrows, open circles, and closed circles. Inequalities show that a number or term is greater than, less than, greater than or equal to, or less than or equal to another term. You may be asked to draw or identify the number line that represents an inequality, including inequalities with variables.

When representing solutions to an inequality on a number line, we are identifying the number or group of numbers that makes the sentence true.

We can represent the inequality $2 + x > 10$.

In this inequality, x is a number that, when added to 2, is greater than 10. What are the possibilities? x has to be at least 8, because any number less than 8, added to 2, is not greater than 10.

The number must be greater than 8, but not exactly 8, so we will identify 8 on our number line with an open circle.

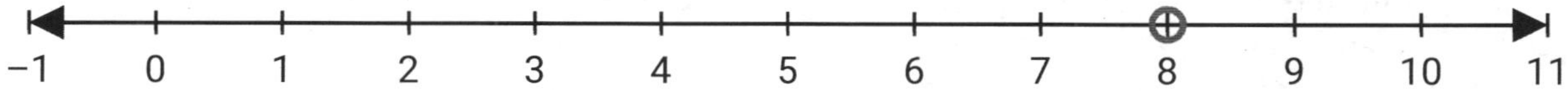

All numbers greater than 8 can be a solution, so we will place an arrow to the right to identify all numbers greater than 8.

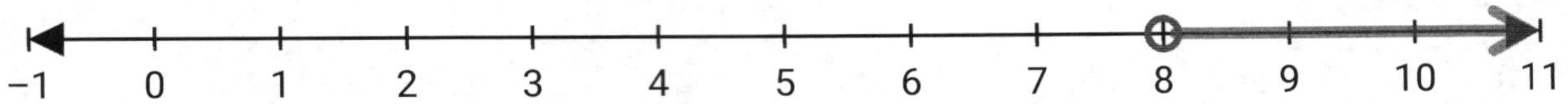

We can represent $2 + x \leq 10$ on a number line.

In this inequality, x is a number that when added to 2 is less than or equal to 10. What are the possibilities? x can be less than 8, and can be exactly 8. 8 would make both sides equal, and that is one option. Because x can be equal to 8, we will represent 8 on the number line with a closed circle.

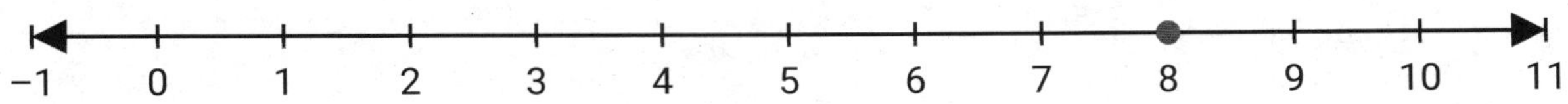

Now, we need to find the other solutions to make the sentence true. What can be added to 2 and be less than 10? Anything less than 8 will make this sentence true. So, we can identify these values by placing an arrow to the left of 8 to identify all values less than 8.

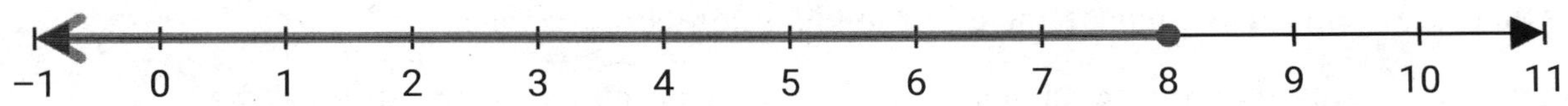

Review Video: Graphing Solutions to Inequalities
Visit mometrix.com/academy and enter code: 391281

USING INEQUALITIES TO EXPRESS SCENARIOS

Real-world scenarios can be expressed through inequalities, and we can also write situations based on an inequality. Inequalities usually use the language, "fewer than," "more than," "no more than," "no less than," "a maximum of," "a minimum of," etc. This language gives us clues that we are dealing with values that are greater than, less than, greater than or equal to, or less than or equal to a quantity.

If it is said a value is no more than 5, that means the value is less than or equal to 5. If there is a value that is more than 10, that means the value is greater than 10. If there is a value that is at least 25, that means the value is greater than or equal to 25. If the value is less or more, you will use greater than or less than. If the value is less or more, but can also be that number, you will use less than or equal to, or greater than or equal to. It takes a little practice and logic to really think about what is happening in the situation.

Solve Inequalities with Variables

Inequalities with a variable include an unknown value and instead of having one single solution, the solution will be a range of values. When we solve inequalities, we use a similar process to solving equations with variables. Sometimes we will be given stories instead of inequalities and will need to write an inequality from a story before solving.

Suppose you are given the inequality $7 + x \geq 4$.

We can solve this using the same strategy we used to solve equations. You want to perform the inverse operation on each side of the inequality so x is by itself.

$$7 + x \geq 4$$
$$7 + x - 7 \geq 4 - 7$$
$$x \geq -3$$

The solution for this inequality is $x \geq -3$. This means that the solutions that make this sentence true are all values that are greater than or equal to −3. Some possible solutions could be −3, −1, 0, 5.5, or 23. Any value that is greater than or equal to −3 is a solution.

Review Video: Solving Inequalities Using All 4 Basic Operations
Visit mometrix.com/academy and enter code: 401111

Example

You have set a personal goal to run more than 10 miles. You run 2.5 miles per day. Which inequality could be used to find the number of days, *d*, you need to run to meet your goal of more than 10 miles?

a. $d < 4$
b. $d > 4$
c. $d > 25$
d. $d < 25$

This problem is asking you to write an inequality that matches the story.

We know that you want to run more than 10 miles, and you run about 2.5 miles per day. You want to know how many days, d, you need to run 2.5 miles to meet your goal of more than 10 miles.

2.5 miles every day for an unknown number of days is a multiplication expression, $2.5d$.

Your goal is to run more than 10 miles, so $2.5d$ must be more than 10.

$$2.5d > 10$$

Now that we have our inequality, we can solve for d, the number of days.

$$\frac{2.5d}{2.5} > \frac{10}{2.5}$$
$$d > 4$$

This matches one of our options, so B is the correct answer.

EXAMPLE

You are building a fence for your dog to run in the backyard. Your dog needs at least 2,100 square feet within the fence. The width of the yard is 17.5 feet. Which inequality shows all the possible lengths, x, that the yard could have to give your dog at least 2,100 square feet?

a. $120 \leq x$
b. $252 \leq x$
c. $252 \geq x$
d. $120 \geq x$

In this example, we are given a story, but no inequality. The first step in solving this inequality is to write an inequality to match the story. We are building a rectangular fence with at least 2,100 square feet of space for your dog to run. The units of square feet indicate this is an area problem. We know that you can find area by multiplying the height and width of the rectangle. In this example, the width of the rectangle is 17.5 feet and we are trying to find the height, x, and the total area is at least 2,100 square feet. We can start our inequality.

$$17.5x\ [\leq, =, \text{or} \geq]\ 2{,}100$$

The story says that the total area needs to be "at least" 2,100 square feet. This means that the fence could have an area of exactly, or more than 2,100 square feet, but not less. So, if we multiply the height and width of the rectangle fence, it needs to be more than or equal to 2,100 square feet. So, $17.5x$ should be greater than or equal to 2,100.

$$17.5x \geq 2{,}100$$

We can solve for x by performing the inverse operation to get x by itself on one side of the inequality. In this case, we would divide each side by 17.5.

$$\frac{17.5x}{17.5} \geq \frac{2{,}100}{17.5}$$
$$x \geq 120$$

D is the correct answer.

DETERMINING IF A VALUE MAKES AN INEQUALITY TRUE

Inequalities include two expressions separated by a comparison and tell a story about a value that is greater than, less than, greater than or equal to, or less than or equal to another expression. When there is a variable in an inequality, we can test numbers to see if they are possible solutions. If you are given a possible value, you can use this value in place of the variable, simplify, and compare. If the given value makes the sentence true, then that value is a possible solution. If the value does not make the sentence true, it is not a solution.

Let's look at the inequality $3x < 30$. What are some possible solutions?

One possible solution is $x = 2$. If $x = 2$, then the sentence is true because $3(2) = 6$ and 6 is less than 30. Another possible solution is $x = -5$. If $x = -5$, the sentence is true because $3(-5) = -15$ and -15 is less than 30.

What about $x = 10$? If $x = 10$, the sentence is not true. $3(10)$ is equal to 30, so $x = 10$ is not a solution to the inequality.

Reading

Word Analysis and Vocabulary

Root Words and Affixes

A **root word** is a word that can be added onto. an **affix** is a prefix or suffix that is added onto a root word. Often, the affixes in the English language come from Latin or Greek origins. A **prefix** is added to the beginning of a root word and a **suffix** is added to the end of a root word. When you look at the meaning of a root word and the meaning of any affixes added to the root word, you can figure out the approximate meaning of the word. For example, the root word "happy" means "to be content." the prefix "un-" means "not." the reader can therefore figure out that "unhappy" means to "not being content."

Common Greek and Latin Root Words

Root	Meaning	Example
auto	self	automobile (a self-propelled vehicle)
geo	earth or ground	geography (study of the earth)
photo	light	photon (a small particle of light)
mis/mit	to send	transmit (to send something to another place)
bene	good	benefactor (a person who uses their resources for another person's good)
man	hand	manual (to do with one's own hands)
vac	empty, void	vacant (the state of being empty)
scrib/script	to write	transcript (a written copy of spoken words)
jur/jus	law	jurisdiction (the area in which a person can make judgements or rules)

Common Prefixes

Prefix	Meaning	Example
dis-	not	disagree (not agree)
im-	not	impossible (not possible)
in-	in, into, not	injustice (an action that is not just)
mis-	wrongly	misspell (to spell wrongly)
non-	not	nonpaid (not paid)
pre-	before	preview (to view before)
sub-	under	submerge (to sink below the surface)
super-	over or greater than	superhuman (greater than a regular human)
trans-	across, through, or change	translate (to write or say in a different language)

Common Suffixes

Suffix	Meaning	Example
-able	can be done	likeable (can be liked)
-er	a person connected with	teacher (a person connected with teaching)
-ful	full of	wonderful (full of wonder)
-it/ity	state of	activity (state of being active)
-ive	cause to, tend to, or doing	creative (a person who tends to make new things or think of new ideas)
-logy	study of	biology (study of life)
-ment	the result	payment (the result of being paid)
-ness	state of being	darkness (being dark)
-y	characterized by	cloudy (characterized by clouds)

Example

Determine the meaning of the word "misconception" based on its root and affixes.

The word "misconception" is made up of three sections: a root, a prefix, and a suffix. to figure out the meaning of the word, you need to analyze these parts of the word individually. The root *concept* means "idea." It comes from the Latin word *conceptus* meaning "something conceived. There are two affixes in the word. The prefix *mis-* means "not" or "bad." the suffix *-tion* means "action" or "process." Put these meanings together and the word "misconception" means "the act of having a bad idea" or "misunderstanding."

Studying roots and affixes is important because it allows you to decode words that you might not otherwise understand with relative ease.

Synonyms and Antonyms

When you understand how words relate to each other, you will discover more in a passage. This is explained by understanding **synonyms**, which are words that mean the same thing, and **antonyms**, which are words that mean the opposite of one another. As an example, *dry* and *arid* are synonyms, and *dry* and *wet* are antonyms.

Review Video: Synonyms and Antonyms
Visit mometrix.com/academy and enter code: 105612

Example

Read the following sentence from the *Secret Garden* by Frances Hodgson Burnett and determine the meaning of the word *pattering* based on context clues.

> "I like you! I like you!" she cried out, *pattering* down the walk; and she chirped and tried to whistle, which last she did not know how to do in the least.

In the example sentence, the words 'down the walk' show that the character is moving on a sidewalk. The reader knows that the character is crying out and trying to chirp and whistle while moving, so the character cannot be completely out of breath. The character is also trying to reach the person or thing that she is crying out to. from these context clues, the reader can guess that the word *pattering* means to walk quickly.

Example

Using context clues, determine the meaning of the word *pestilent* in the following excerpt from *Rip Van Winkle* by Washington Irving

> In fact, he declared it was of no use to work on his farm; it was the most *pestilent* little piece of ground in the whole country; everything about it went wrong, and would go wrong in spite of him.

In the example, the word *pestilent* is used to describe the ground. The character states that it was of no use to work on his farm and that everything about it went wrong. This indicates that the ground was difficult to work with, since the character had trouble with the ground no matter what he tried ('and would go wrong in spite of him'). The reader can assume, from these observations, that the word *pestilent* means troublesome, annoying, or not allowing anything to grow, since this example is about the ground on a farm.

Example

Read the following sentences and determine the meaning of the word *reluctant* based on context clues:

> Sam was *reluctant* to be in the play, so he told the director that he was too busy to rehearse and didn't go to tryouts. He felt too shy to get up on a stage.

In this example sentence, the words "too busy" show that Sam made an excuse about why he couldn't be in the school play. The sentence also says that he "didn't go to tryouts." the second example sentence has other clues. It says, "He felt too shy to get up on stage." These clues give the reader hints about what the word *reluctant* means. It means "not willing."

Definition Within a Text

An author may **define** a word in the text. For example, an author may write, "The company did not have sufficient capital, that is, available money, to continue operating." The author defined "capital" as "available money." Authors will use words and phrases, such as "that is," "or," "meaning," and "which is," to let the reader know that they are defining the word.

Analogy

Analogies are used to **compare relationships**. For example, the analogy "restaurant is to eating as store is to shopping." A restaurant is a place where you eat, and a store is a place where you shop. The analogy compares locations and the things people do at those locations. **Analogies** can also be used to show the meaning of unfamiliar words. For example, consider the analogy "author is to writing as artisan is to crafting." *Artisan* may be an unfamiliar word to some. However, this analogy begins with "author is to writing." An author writes to create books, articles, and poems. The first part of the analogy pairs a person's job title with the action that their job requires. Based on this, a reader can conclude that an artisan is someone who crafts things.

Examples that Clarify Meaning

An author may use a word and then give examples that reveal its meaning. Consider this text: "Those who do not know sign language can communicate with people who are deaf or hard of hearing by using gestures. These may include pointing their fingers to indicate which direction to look or go or holding up a hand to indicate stopping." The author of this text has used the word *gestures* and then followed it with examples. This shows a reader who is unfamiliar with the word that gestures are hand motions. Readers can find examples by looking for signal words like "for example," "for instance," "like," and "such as."

Using Context to Determine the Meanings of Words

Readers of all levels will encounter words that they have either never seen or that they have seen before but still don't know what it means. The best way to define a word in **context** is to look for nearby words that can assist in learning the meaning of the word.

Context Clues

Context clues are hints about the meaning of a word. They are the words or phrases in the sentence or sentences before and after a new or unfamiliar word. **Context clues** give the reader an idea about what a word means. A context clue may also contain words that help define the new word or an example of what the new word means. A context clue in the form of an example may contain the words including 'such as', a dash, or a colon before stated information.

Using context clues to figure out meaning can be helpful when learning a new set of vocabulary words or reading a difficult text. The dictionary definition of a word can always be looked up to double-check intended meaning.

Review Video: Reading Comprehension: Using Context Clues
Visit mometrix.com/academy and enter code: 613660

Substitution *to Find Meaning*

One way to find out if you have figured out the correct meaning of a new word is to **substitute** the meaning for the word. Using the example for *reluctant*, if the reader substituted in "not willing," the sentence would read

> Sam was "not willing" to be in the play, so he told the director that he was too busy to rehearse and didn't go to tryouts. He felt to shy to get up on a stage.

This is a way for the reader to confirm that they have used the context clues in the sentence correctly.

Multiple-Meaning Words

A multiple-meaning word has different definitions, depending on the contextual use of the word. A multiple-meaning word is also called a **homonym**. A homonym is defined as a word that has more than one meaning, but is spelled and pronounced the same for all of them. For example, look at the word *leaves* in the following two sentences:

1. Michelle *leaves* the building at 5 o'clock every day.
2. The *leaves* fell off the oak tree in September.

In the first sentence, *leaves* means exits. in the second sentence, *leaves* refers to parts of a tree. By looking at the rest of each sentence, the reader can understand which definition of the multiple-meaning word the author is referring to.

Similar Words

Homophones are words that are pronounced the same, but may be spelled differently. an example of two homophones would be *heir* (someone due to inherit an estate) and *air* (the invisible substance people breathe).

Homographs are words that are spelled the same, but may be pronounced differently. an example of a homograph is the word *row*, which is pronounced one way when used to mean a horizontal grouping and is pronounced another way when used to mean an argument.

Dictionary

A print or digital dictionary can be used to find out many things about a word. A dictionary will show the correct pronunciation of a word, provide its meaning, and identify what part of speech the word is. It will also tell how the word was derived—that is, what words it came from originally. A dictionary will have a **pronunciation guide** for each word that shows how to sound it out and where its syllables start and end. It will use symbols to indicate sounds, and will also use sample sounds (the "a" in "bad," for instance). A dictionary lists all of the meanings of a word and the parts of speech the word can be used as.

> **example** \ ig-'zam-pəl\ noun
> 1. something that shows what a group of things is like
> 2. a model that should be either copied or avoided
> 3. a punishment meant to serve as a warning to others

EXAMPLE:

Julia used her dictionary to check the various meanings of the word *clear*. She found this entry:

> **clear** (klîr) adjective
> 1. obvious.
> 2. easily seen through
> 3. free from flaw or blemish
> 4. free from guilt; untroubled
> 5. out of the way
> 6. to tidy *v*
> 7. to free *v*
> 8. to earn *v*

Identify which definition of *clear* is used in the following sentence:

> Janet stood *clear* of the crowd pushing to get through the door.

The correct answer is meaning 5: "out of the way." If you substitute that definition for the word, the sentence makes sense. Meanings 1, 2, 3, and 4 do not fit with the context of the sentence. Meanings 6, 7, and 8 are verbs and "clear" as it is used in the sample is an adjective. When considering which meaning is being used, always check for context clues in the sentence or in the sentences before or after the sentence in which the word is used. Dictionaries also tell you how to pronounce words and often the derivation of the word, although that is not given here.

THESAURUS

A **thesaurus** is a reference book that gives **synonyms** of words. It is different from a dictionary because a thesaurus does not give definitions. A thesaurus can be helpful in finding the meaning of an unfamiliar word when reading. If the meaning of a synonym is known, then the meaning of the unfamiliar word will be known. Another time in which a thesaurus can be helpful is when writing. Using a thesaurus helps authors to vary their word choice.

GLOSSARY

A **glossary** is a **list of terms and their definitions** that can be found **at the back** of certain types of books, such as textbooks or reference books. A glossary does not have the definitions of all words, like a dictionary, but instead gives the definitions of the important terms within that particular book which are either uncommon or newly introduced. One may use a glossary when reading a book about economics or a chapter in a science textbook, for example, to define some of the technical terms within the text.

Denotative and Connotative Meanings

The **denotative meaning** of a word is the exact dictionary definition of the word. The **connotative meaning** of a word is the emotion conveyed by the use of the word in context. The word may have associated meaning in addition to its dictionary definition. For example, the word *home* is defined in the dictionary as a place where a person or people live. When a reader sees the word in the following context: "Marisol walked briskly *home*, where the smell of fresh-baked apple pie wafted through the warm kitchen," the reader will associate the meaning of the word with coziness and a feeling of well-being. The connotative meaning of a word in a passage can be found by looking at the context clues.

Example

Determine the connotative meaning of the word *ancient* in the following sentence.

> Amy pulled an *ancient* calculator out of the desk, and sat down to figure out how to use it.

In the example, the word 'ancient' literally means very old. The connotative meaning of the word ancient suggests that the calculator does not work as well as more modern versions. in technology, ancient is relative to what is currently being used. For example, a computer may be out of date in a couple years, whereas an ancient society may date back several thousand years.

Literal and Figurative Language

Literal and Figurative Language

Many types of text use both **literal language**, which means just what it says, and **figurative language**, which allows the writer to expand the way in which he or she uses language. When an author uses figurative language, she connects things in an exaggerated and non-literal way in order to create a memorable image, which helps to describe a situation in a new way for the reader.

Review Video: Figurative Language
Visit mometrix.com/academy and enter code: 584902

Simile

- Shows similarity between two ideas or objects, using the words "**like**" or "**as**"
- For example, an author might write "The princess is as beautiful as a rose" to compare the appearance of a woman to a beautiful flower.

Metaphor

- Puts one idea in place of another to draw a parallel between the two ideas.
- For example, an author might write "Her room was a pigsty," to compare a person's bedroom to a dirty spot where pigs sleep.

Symbolism

- Using one object to stand for something else.
- For example, an author may include a flag flying high throughout a story to show pride in the characters' country and to represent the idea of patriotism.

HYPERBOLE

- An extreme exaggeration of an idea.
- For example, a character might say "I'm starving to death!" to show that they are really hungry. Most of the time a character who says this is not literally going to die from hunger, they are just ready for a snack.

IRONY

- Uses sarcasm or humor (usually with an emphasis on the opposite) to show difference from literal meaning.
- For example, if a character says "Well today must be my lucky day!" after they left their homework on the kitchen table, they are being ironic. The irony used here helps show that it is definitely *not* the character's lucky day.

PERSONIFICATION

- Gives life or human characteristics to an inanimate object
- For example, if an author writes "The trees whispered to each other across the wide blue sky," they are using personification to help the reader imagine the scene. Trees are not human beings, so they do not whisper, but the image created in the reader stands out more than a literal description would.

EXAMPLE

Based on current knowledge, identify whether metaphor, simile, or hyperbole is used in this sentence:

> The chiming bell was a beacon of hope for the downtrodden villagers.

A **metaphor** is used in this sentence to draw a parallel between "the chiming bell" and "a beacon of hope." the bell is being compared to something else in the sentence, which indicates the use of metaphor or simile, but the reader knows that the sentence does not contain a simile, because the words like and as are not used to show the comparison. The sentence also does not contain an exaggeration of facts, so the reader can see that hyperbole is not used.

EXAMPLE

Discuss the kind of figurative language used in the following poem by the Scottish poet Robert Burns:

> O my luve's like a red, red rose
> That's newly sprung in June;
> O my luve's like the melodie
> That's sweetly played in tune.

The poet uses **similes** to create an image in this poem. The two similes here occur when the speaker says that his love is "**like** a red, red rose" and that she is also "**like** the melodie." These are examples of similes because they use the comparing word 'like' to compare two things. They are not metaphors because metaphors do not use the comparing words 'like' or 'as.' the poem paints an image of the speaker's love by comparing her to a red rose that has newly sprung and a melody that is sweetly played.

EXAMPLE

Read the following excerpt from "The Raven" by Edgar Allan Poe, identify the metaphor, and discuss how it impacts the text:

> And the raven, never flitting, still is sitting, still is sitting
> On the pallid bust of Pallas just above my chamber door;
> And his eyes have all the seeming of a demon's that is dreaming

One **metaphor** in the excerpt from "The Raven" by Edgar Allan Poe is: "And his eyes have all the seeming of a demon's that is dreaming"

The metaphor compares the raven's eyes with a demon, which shows that the speaker thinks there is evil in the bird. The metaphor helps contribute to the overall tone of the poem and the reader's understanding of how the speaker views the bird.

EXAMPLE

Read the excerpt from a poem by William Blake and describe what form of figurative language it uses.

> The wild winds weep,
> And the night is a-cold;
> Come hither, sleep,
> And my griefs unfold.

This poem contains several examples of **personification**. in the poem, the speaker says "The wild winds weep," thereby giving the winds the human characteristic of weeping. Later it says "Come hither, sleep," which is another use of personification asking that sleep to go somewhere as though it were a person. The poem gives the winds and sleep human characteristics. This is the definition of personification. It is not an example of simile because there is no comparison using the words "as" or "like." It is not a metaphor because there is no comparison between two things sharing a similar quality. and it is not an example of hyperbole because there is no exaggeration. The poem does contain some alliteration, however; the repetition of the letter "w" in "wild winds weep" qualifies as alliteration, which is another literary technique.

Author's Purpose and Craft

Author's Purpose

The author's purpose his or her reason for writing the text. As the readers read a text, they should always try to figure out the author's purpose for writing as this will help them to better understand the message that the author is trying to convey.

Informational Texts

- Inform the reader on a topic that they previously knew nothing about, such as many non-fiction texts.
- For example, an informative paper on early Native American Indian tribes would detail where Native American Indians lived, what types of foods they ate, how they bartered for goods, and other aspects of their culture.

Persuasive Texts

- Influence the reader to think a certain way about a topic, calling them to action or pointing them toward resources that would help them to learn more about the topic.
- A **proposition and support** paper would be an example of this, where an author gives their opinion and then tries to convince the reader to see something from their point of view.
- For example, an author may try to persuade the reader that waterparks are the best place to go in the summer when it is hot outside. The author would present information about waterparks and explain why they are good places to visit.

Expressive Texts

- Express the author or speaker's opinion or emotions about a topic. Generally, expressive texts include descriptive words to clearly show the reader how the author or speaker feels.
- For example, the author of a poem may think that compassion is an important quality in a person, and they may write a poem in which the speaker discusses how compassion is what binds all people together.

Entertaining Texts

- Entertain the reader, such as in most fictional texts.
- For example, Wilson Rawls, the author of *Where the Red Fern Grows* entertains his readers with the adventures of a young boy named Billy and his two hound dogs, Old Dan and Little Ann.
- Entertaining texts can be either fiction or non-fiction, but are usually stories such as a fairy tale or fictional piece of writing. Entertaining texts usually follow a chronological order.

Authors usually write to entertain, to inform, or to persuade their readers. The organization structure or pattern they use is related to what the author's purpose is. It is important to choose the pattern that best presents the information, as not all patterns will work for every piece of writing.

Review Video: Understanding the Author's Intent
Visit mometrix.com/academy and enter code: 511819

EXAMPLE

Read the following sentence. State the author's point in writing the sentence, whether it is to inform, persuade, express an opinion, or entertain:

> The rollercoaster reached a peak and paused for a second, before gliding down the other side of the hill with a roar.

The purpose of the sentence is to entertain the reader. The author does not state his or her opinion on the topic, and the sentence doesn't inform the reader about an important topic. The sentence does not persuade the reader to accept a certain point of view, and is instead meant to entertain the reader by giving them the feeling they might get from riding an exciting roller coaster.

Notice that the text describes an event, rather than an issue or conflict. The event is part of a larger tale, where a series of events occur to form an entire story. The reader may notice that the author uses descriptive words to present the setting, such as gliding and roar. The reader can better picture a story when the setting is clearly presented.

EXAMPLE

Read the following sentence and state the author's point in writing the sentence, whether it is to inform, entertain, persuade, or state an opinion:

> The new student handbook makes it against the rules to wear roller skates inside the school buildings.

The purpose of this sentence is to inform the reader. The sentence does not state an opinion on the topic, nor is it meant to entertain the reader. The sentence also does not persuade the reader to accept a certain point of view. The sentence gives information to the reader that they need to know in order to avoid breaking the rules.

EXAMPLE

Read the following sentence from the *City of Ember* by Jeanne DuPrau and state the author's purpose in writing the sentence: whether it is to inform, entertain, persuade, or state an opinion:

> Lina looked out at the lighted streets spreading away in every direction, the streets she knew so well. She loved her city, worn out and crumbling though it was

The purpose of the sentence is to entertain the reader. The sentence does not tell the reader important information about a specific topic, it is simply used as part of a greater fictional story meant for entertainment. The sentence does not persuade the reader to accept a certain point of view, nor does it state an opinion.

When an author wishes to persuade the reader to accept a certain point of view, evidence is used to back-up a claim. If the author wants to state an opinion, that opinion is included within the text. Sentences that are meant to inform contain facts that the reader needs to know and are not often found in fictional stories.

Rhetorical Devices vs Logical Fallacies

Writers of persuasive and argumentative texts will often use strategies that may help them persuade the reader to agree with their claims. These strategies may be used to convince the reader on a logical or emotional level. The writer may also use them to prove his or her own credibility, or reliability. These strategies are called **rhetorical devices**. However, writers make statements that seem like rhetorical devices, but are not actually logical. They may sound persuasive, but they are unreasonable and may leave out part of the truth or try to prove a weak argument. These are called **logical fallacies**.

Types of Texts

Literary Genres

Literature contains many different **genres**, which are categories that texts can be divided into. Genres are used to group types of writing together for purposes of study, reading, or simple organization. Some common literary genres are

- **Realistic fiction** -A story that could actually happen and reflects life in a realistic way.
- **Adventure stories** -Short, mostly fictional stories that follow characters as they go on an adventure or quest.
- **Historical fiction** -Often strays from historical reality in order to tell a story and make a true historical event more interesting to the reader.
- **Mysteries** -Fiction stories about solving crimes or revealing secrets.
- **Humor** –Stories, mostly fictional, full of fun and excitement meant to entertain readers. Can be seen in stories from all genres.
- **Myth** -A legend or traditional narrative, often based on a historical event. The story reveals something about human behavior or the natural world, and often involves actions of gods.

Poetry

Poet Versus Speaker

The author of a poem is called a **poet**. Many poems are written in first person, which means the **stanzas** (groups of lines) include words like "I" and "me." However, the poet is not always the **speaker** of the poem. In a novel, the author can create characters with different points of view. The characters can argue or have different roles to play in telling the story. Similarly, a poet may write a poem from a different point of view or even include more than one voice. The speaker is the voice of the poem, and is not always the same person as the poet him or herself. The reader or listener should know that the person telling the story is a character, and not always a real person.

For example, this excerpt from a poem by Dr. Seuss reads:

> When you think things are bad,
> when you feel sour and blue,
> when you start to get mad...
> you should do what I do!
> Just tell yourself, Duckie,
> you're really quite lucky!
> Some people are much more...
> oh, ever so much more...
> oh, muchly much-much more
> unlucky than you!

Even though one line has the word "I" in it, the poem is not from the perspective of Dr. Seuss. He is the author of the poem, but not the speaker. The person saying "I" is a character, just like in a story.

Sensory Language in Poetry

Sensory language is when the author uses descriptive words and specific details that appeal to a reader's senses (sight, touch, taste, hearing, smell, emotion). For example, the author can use scents that the reader is familiar with to help them imagine what the setting of the poem smells and feels like. This use of sensory language is also called **imagery**.

Rhyme in Poetry

Poets use rhymes to help readers understand poems. Words **rhyme** when they sound similar to each other, especially when the similar sound is at the end of the words, like *cat* and *hat*, or *roar* and *soar*. Rhyming words usually have endings that are spelled the same way, but sometimes they are spelled differently, like *wait* and *hate* or *bear* and *snare*.

Famous poet Shel Silverstein uses rhyme in many of his poems. For example, in his poem "Listen to the Mustn'ts", the last word of the first- and second-lines rhyme with each other, and the last word of the third- and fourth-line rhyme with each other.

> Listen to Mustn'ts, child, listen to the Don'ts.
> Listen to the Shouldn'ts, the Impossibles, the Won'ts.
> Listen to the Never Haves, then listen close to me.
> Anything can happen, child, Anything can be.

The pattern of the rhymes in this poem forms a **rhyme scheme**. Sometimes poets use a rhyme scheme that makes every other line of the poem rhyme instead.

Line Breaks in Poetry

Line breaks are used to end a line of poetry. Poets use **line breaks** to control the **length** of **each line**. The length of lines in a poem can impact the poem's meaning and the **speed** at which the poem is read. **Long** lines are usually read more **quickly**, while **short** lines cause the reader to briefly pause and look to the next line, so their reading is **slowed**. These effects often contribute to the reader's experience when reading the poem, so poets aim to make the effects match the tone of their message in the poem.

Drama

Dramas are texts that are written to be performed by people reading the lines or acting the stories out. They can also be presented as monologues (one character speaks), dialogues (two character speak to each other), or pantomimes (body movements are used instead of spoken words). Dramatic texts are called plays or **scripts**, and they are written differently than other texts.

Text Structure in Drama

Plays are divided into **acts** (large units) and **scenes** (small sections inside acts) instead of chapters. There are also **stage directions**, which are instructions from the playwright about where items go, where actors should move, and what the characters should be doing during the scene. Stage directions are usually in italics to set them apart from other parts of the play. When it is time for a character in a play to speak, there will be **character tag** on the left side of the page which shows the name of the character (all letters of the name are capitalized) followed by a colon.

Here is an example of how a page from a play might look:

Title of Play

Act Number

Scene Number

The setting of the scene is being described here. The reader is being introduced to the characters and the things happening around them. Characters will enter speak to one another during the scene.

CHARACTER 1:

I am speaking. These are words I say. *(stage directions)* I am still speaking.

CHARACTER 2 *enters and does something.*

CHARACTER 2:

Now I am speaking. This is my dialogue.

DIALOGUE AND STAGE DIRECTIONS

Dialogue refers to what the characters say in a play when they are talking to each other, talking to themselves, or even talking to the audience. The type of speech, word choice, and accent a character uses is specific to the role he is playing. For example, a person cast to play a cowboy would have certain words in his vocabulary that a character from a big city in the North would not have.

A playwright also uses stage directions to make the play flow smoothly. Character interaction helps the viewer to understand the mood of the scene. If two characters are confrontational, the viewer is aware that there is some type of conflict occurring. Stage directions create order when all the characters are on stage together.

INFORMATIONAL TEXTS

Informational texts, also called instructional or expository texts, are compositions written to inform the reader about a specific topic. An informational essay can inform readers in a variety of ways, such as giving them instructions, telling them facts about the topic, or teaching them why something happens. Informational texts should be logical, meaning that they should present information in an order that the reader can easily understand, and they should include the right amount of information so the writer successfully informs his or her audience of new information.

Informational texts should also focus on a **controlling idea**. In the introduction of an informational text, there may be a sentence or two that clearly state the essay's controlling idea. This sentence, or sentences, is called a **thesis statement**. The controlling idea should be clear throughout the composition. By emphasizing the controlling idea in the introduction, body, and conclusion, the writer can ensure that the controlling idea is clear. One way to make sure that the controlling idea is emphasized is to think about the purpose of each part of the essay. The introduction prepares the reader by telling them what the rest of the essay is about, so the controlling idea should be **introduced** in this section. The body tells the reader the information the writer wants to tell the audience, so this **explains** the controlling idea and facts about it to the reader. The conclusion is used to **remind** the reader of how the information in the body is related and **restates** the controlling idea one final time.

Review Video: Informational Text
Visit mometrix.com/academy and enter code: 924964

Structures or Organizational Patterns in Informational Texts

Informational text can be **descriptive**, meaning that it gives information that can be experienced through the five senses, or it answers the questions what, who, when, where, and why. One common method of organizing informational text is to put it in a certain sequence, or order. **Chronological** texts include events in the order that they occurred, from start to finish. **How-to**, or **instructional**, texts organize information into a series of instructions in the order in which the steps should be followed. **Comparison-contrast** structures of informational text describe different ideas to their readers by pointing out how things or ideas are similar and how they are different. **Cause and effect** structures of informational text describe events that occurred and the causes or reasons for those events. **Problem and solution** structures of informational texts introduce and describe problems and offer one or more solutions for each problem described.

Structural Features of Informational Text

Texts which intend to inform the reader about a topic are often accompanied by visual aids or graphics. Some common examples are listed below.

- **Forewords** appear before the actual text. Usually, forewords are not written by the author of the text. They are written by a different person who is well-respected in a related field of work or study. The author of the foreword usually provides some information about the texts and explains why they support the text.
- **Prefaces** are written to provide the reader with supporting information that was not included in the text. This information may help the reader better understand the text or may show the reader why the topic of the text is important or interesting to the author.
- **Introductions** usually appear as the first paragraph in a text. An introduction is used to catch the reader's attention and let the audience know what the text is about and how the topic will be covered by the text.
- **Insets and sidebars** show additional information related to the text in boxes or on the sides of the page. Insets can contain pictures or text, and sometimes have different colored backgrounds or font types to make them stand out from the text.
- **Visual aids** include features like diagrams, graphs, and charts. These can help the user think about information in a different way. They do this by visually presenting the relationship between the information in the text.
- **Bullet points** list items separately, making facts and ideas easier to see and understand.
- **Numbers** can also be used to list separate items. Usually, numbers are used to show that the items are part of a sequence. For example, in a list of instructions, each instruction may be numbered to show the reader the order in which each instruction should be completed.
- **References** are the sources of the information the author included in the text. In most works, the references will all be listed after the last page of the main text. These may be included on a page titled "Bibliography," "Works Cited," or, simply, "References." Reviewing the author's sources and reviewing their credibility can show the reader whether the work itself is credible, unbiased, and accurate.

- **Acknowledgements** appear near the end of books, after the main text and any resources that the author has included for the reader. The acknowledgements section is used by authors to thank the people that helped them create the work. People who encouraged the author, assisted the author with writing and editing, or made it possible for the work to be published are usually named in the acknowledgements section.

Argumentative Texts

Identifying the Claim

In a persuasive or argumentative text, the author is writing in order to make and support a claim. A claim is similar to the key idea of an informational text. However, a claim can be argued, which means that some readers may not agree with it. The author of the text will need to use the body of the text to support the claim and show readers why they should agree with it. To identify the claim of a text, first identify the topic. Then, read the introduction text to see what the author writes about the topic.

The claim should be clearly stated in the introduction. However, if the claim is still not clear, read the body to see what kind of evidence the author uses to support the claim. The way that the author gives and applies evidence may also show what the claim of the text is.

Call to Action

Another strategy is to look for a call to action in the text. A call to action is a statement that instructs the reader to do something after reading the text. Often, the call to action will tell the reader to do something that shows that he or she agrees with the author's claim. For example, if an author's claim is that reading is better than watching a movie, the author may include a call to action that says "Turn off the TV and dig in to a new book today!" By including this statement, the author is telling the readers to show their agreement by choosing to read rather than watch a movie.

Identifying How the Author Supports a Claim

In a persuasive or argumentative text, the author must use information to support his or her claim. This information is called evidence. Below are common types of evidence an author may use to support a claim:

- **Facts:** Authors may use facts that show that their claim is true. For example, a claim that fish are better pets than dogs can be supported by the fact that fish cannot make a mess inside a house.
- **Personal Anecdotes:** A personal anecdote is a story from a person's own experience. Authors can use personal anecdotes to tell stories that show why their claim is true. For example, an author can support the claim that people should wear elbow pads when riding a bike can be supported by sharing a story about their experience of scraping their elbow after falling off of a bicycle.
- **Statistics:** Statistics are observations that are based on a collection of data. Statistics can show trends or preferences among members of a group. An author can use statistics to support a claim by sharing the statistic says is likely to happen or be true for many people.
- **Examples:** Authors may give examples of events or experiences that suggest that their claim is true. For example, an author may claim that people should exercise because it will make them healthier. The author could give an example of how exercise can improve a person's health in order to support this claim.

- **Quotes:** An author can support a claim by using quotes from other people or texts. If the person or text makes a statement that shows that the author's claim is true, the author can include that quote in his or her text. When authors include quotes in their work, they must always tell the reader where the quote came from.

The author must use enough evidence to support the claim. If the evidence does not fully support the claim in the text, then the author must continue working to find evidence for the claim. The evidence used to support a claim must also be believable and come from a reliable source.

Identifying the Intended Audience

Authors of persuasive and argumentative texts want to convince others to agree with a claim or take a certain action. Because of this, they will often write to a specific audience. Often, the target audience will include people who disagree with the author's claim. The author's desire is to give these people information that will lead them to change their minds or actions.

Strategies for Identifying the Intended Audience

One way to identify the intended audience of a persuasive or argumentative text is to first identify the author's claim. Then, consider who would disagree with the author's claim. This group of people is likely the group that the author wants to persuade.

Another way to identify the audience is to look for clues in the text. Sometimes, authors will clearly state which people are included in the intended audience. For example, imagine that an author includes the statement, "Teachers should reward their students every time they make a good grade on a test." This shows that the text is written to persuade teachers who do not already reward their students for good test grades. Similarly, a call to action may show who the target audience is by instructing the members of the audience to take a certain action.

Argumentative Writing

In argumentative writing, the writer expresses a belief or opinion that he or she wants to lead readers to agree with. When writing an argumentative composition, the writer should first identify the **topic** his or her opinion is about. The topic may be serious or fun, as long as there is one clear topic in the composition. The next step is for the writer to determine his or her opinion on the topic and determine why he or she holds that opinion. In order to persuade others to agree with their opinion, the writer must be able to give readers reasons to support the opinion. If the writer does not know why he or she has an opinion, it will be difficult to convince readers to agree. In addition to having reasons that support their opinion, writers should prepare examples that support each of these reasons in order to strengthen their composition.

Once the writer has determined his or her topic, opinion, and reasons for having the opinion, he or she is ready to begin writing an argumentative essay. In the introduction, the writer should capture the reader's interest, introduce the topic, and reveal his or her opinion about the topic. In the body of the composition, the writer should remind the reader of the opinion and give his or her reasons for holding the opinion. If the writer has any examples, facts, or other information that supports his or her opinion or reasons for believing it, these should also be included in the body. Writers may also use a body paragraph to mention opposing opinions or beliefs and explain why they disagree with them. As in other compositions, the conclusion should remind the reader of the essay's topic and purpose, as well as remind the reader how the opinion has been explained and supported. The conclusion should also invite the reader to continue thinking about the topic and writer's opinion.

This can be done through questions or statements that lead readers to consider whether or not they agree with the author's opinion or what their own opinions are.

Review Video: Argumentative Writing
Visit mometrix.com/academy and enter code: 561544

Informative vs. Persuasive Writing

Informative writing, also called explanatory or expository writing, is written to show that something is true or factual, while **persuasive** writing is written to lead the reader to agree with something that may or may not be true or factual. While persuasive text is written to **persuade** readers to agree with the author's position, informative text simply **provides information** to readers. Informative writing **informs** readers about why or how something is as it is. This can include offering new information, explaining how a process works, or describing a concept for readers.

Main Ideas and Supporting Details

Informational Text

Controlling Idea

The controlling idea, also called the main idea or thesis, of a passage is usually located in the first paragraph or two of text. Having the controlling idea near the beginning of the passage allows the author to grab the reader's attention and let them know what the rest of the passage will discuss.

To find the controlling idea in a passage, there are questions the reader can ask while reading: What is this passage about? What does the author want the reader to know about the topic? The supporting details will provide evidence that the controlling idea is correct and are found in the body of a passage. The supporting details often provide examples of the controlling idea.

For example, a passage may contain the controlling idea: "Ellis Island was an entry-point to America for many immigrants during the Industrial Revolution." A supporting detail for the controlling idea may be "Immigrants were examined for contagious diseases at Ellis Island before being granted entry to America."

Review Video: Thesis Statements
Visit mometrix.com/academy and enter code: 691033

Example

Determine the controlling idea the following sentence tells the reader and indicate what details support the controlling idea:

> Her breath billowed out in clouds of white and disappeared into the quiet air.

The controlling idea is what the author wants the reader to understand about the text. Details help to explain or support that controlling idea. A controlling idea usually states the point of an entire essay, article, or book, but can be simply stated in one sentence. The controlling idea in the sentence above is that a girl is outside in the cold. Details to support this statement include the word 'her,' showing that the character is a girl, and 'clouds of white,' which indicate that the air is cold. in order to conclude that the girl is out in the cold, the reader needs to understand that breath can be seen when the air is cold.

Supporting Details

Authors use supporting details to provide evidence and backing for the main point. All texts contain details, but they are only classified as supporting details when they serve to reinforce some larger point. Supporting details are most commonly found in informative and persuasive texts. in some cases, they will be clearly indicated with words like **for example** or **for instance**, or they will begin with words like **first**, **second**, and **last**. However, these special words are not a requirement. As a reader, it is important to consider whether the author's supporting details really back up his or her main point. Supporting details can be factual and correct but still not relevant to the author's point. Sometimes, supporting details can seem important but they might not support the controlling idea in the story well because they are based on opinion that cannot be proven.

Example

Decide whether the following sentence is the main point or a supporting point of a text, and state where the information would be placed in an outline:

> One type of horseback riding, bareback horseback riding, involves sitting on a moving horse without a saddle and grasping the horse's mane.

This sentence is a supporting point, with the main point of the entire text likely about horseback riding in general. As a supporting point, this sentence would go further down in an outline, next to any numeral after numeral I. This sentence can be followed by additional sub-points that further explain the concept of bareback horseback riding. When a supporting point is used to clarify a main point or topic, the supporting point helps to break the topic down into smaller pieces.

Key Ideas and Supporting Details

Identifying **key ideas** helps the reader see what a text or story is mostly about. They are the **most important ideas** in a text, and everything else in the text builds around and supports them. Every piece of writing has key ideas. The **supporting details** in a story, such as the characters, events, and settings, will work together to reveal the key ideas. The details are not key ideas, themselves. They make the key ideas clear and show the reader the author's purpose for writing the text.

Point of View

Point of View

The point of view of a text is the perspective from which it is told. Every literary text has a narrator or person who tells the story. The two main points of view that authors most often use are first person and third person.

First Person

- Tells a story through the eyes of one character.
- Uses the pronouns 'I,' 'me,' 'we,' and 'my.'
- The reader gets only one side of the story, without any other angles on what may have happened in the text

Second Person

- Second person is an uncommon point of view in literature that uses the pronoun 'you.' Second person is usually reserved for speaking directly to someone, often when giving instructions.
- Examples might include: "Go get me a fork" or "will you wash the dishes?"

Third Person

- Tells a story about a character or group of characters from an outside viewpoint.
- Uses the words 'her', 'his,' 'they,' or a name to talk about a character or characters.
- A common way to show action in a story which allows the author to easily and realistically tell a story from more than one person's viewpoint.
- Gives readers a more complete view of a story as it is told from many different perspectives.

Different Forms of Third Person

When an author writes in third-person point of view, there are a couple of options to choose from:

- **Third person omniscient** - There is an all-knowing narrator telling the story as well as interpreting events, and relating thoughts of the characters.
- **Third person limited** - The author writes in the third person, but does so from only one character's point of view. There are two different variations of this type of narration: the narrator can either stay with the same character throughout or cycle through different characters over the course of the story.

Elements of Story

Setting

The setting is the **time** and **place** in which a story **takes place**. The setting of a story may stay the same for the entire story or change as events in the story unfold. For example, an entire story may take place in one room or cross continents as the reader follows the characters along on a trail of events.

The setting of a story is described by the author in terms of what it looks like, how the character feels, and anything else that is happening at that location at the time. For example, a character may be caught on a doorstep on a cold, rainy day. The character may feel frustrated as they shiver in the doorway, waiting for the heavy rain to let up a bit.

Shaping a Character with Setting Or Plot

The setting of a story shapes character because it helps to define the situation that a character finds herself in. A character is limited to the setting of a story. For example, if a story takes place in a cold environment filled with snow and ice, this is certain to impact what actions a character can and will take. Frequently, the setting changes the way characters behave based on time. For example, the character of a woman who is a single mother in 1920 would be seen and behave very differently than a single mother in 2020.

Example

Read the excerpt and determine how the setting influences the character in this excerpt.

> She had swum too far out. The waves were higher than she thought. She was struggling hard to get to shore. She wondered if she would make it. She thought of her childhood. Had she been right to run away from home, she wondered? Just then, a lifeguard grabbed her and helped her to shore.

The setting of the ocean and the high waves creates a conflict in the character. She is worried. She thinks about her childhood and her parents. She doesn't know if she will make it to shore. This is how the setting affects the character in this excerpt. without the high waves and the struggle, she would not become so worried and start to think about her past. She probably would not have questioned herself. This is an example of how a setting influences a character. If the waves had not been high, there probably would not have been a struggle or any self-searching of the swimmer's past.

Historical and Cultural Setting

Historical context influences literature in a number of ways. The style of the author's writing can be impacted by the historical period during which it was written (e.g., Dickens wrote at a time when authors were paid by the word; this is why his novels are so long). Obviously, the setting of the book includes its historical context. in addition, dialect may be a function of the historical period of the book. When a reader understands the historical context of a particular book, he or she can have a deeper understanding of the novel. Knowing about the time period during which the author wrote, as well as the time period discussed in the novel, helps the reader understand some of the author's choices, including character motivations.

Patterns Related to Settings

The setting of a story can allow the reader to draw on personal experience about where the story takes place. If a story takes place on a farm, the reader will likely picture a rural, peaceful setting, which may go along with (or be in contrast to) the actual plot of the story. For example, a reader would not expect a scary story to occur on a farm on a sunny day. Conversely, a reader may view a dark subway as a dangerous place, while the plot of a story set there may be based on a very calm series of events. When an author is crafting a story, they need to consider what the audience may already think about a particular setting in order to properly present the events of a story for greatest impact.

Style, Voice, Tone, and Mood

Style, tone, and mood all play an important role in the development of a story. The reader's impression of a story can vary based on the style, tone, and mood established by the author.

- **Style** refers to the way an author uses words, phrases, and sentence structure. The style of the text can change depending on whether the author uses short, choppy sentences, long, elaborate sentences, formal language, or informal language.
- **Voice** refers to the characteristics of a text that show the author's personality and distinguish the author from other writers. An author's voice may be recognized through the way they use words or the way they organize and present their thoughts. Voice is specific to each writer, and it can be as specific and unique as personality.
- **Tone** refers to the attitude of the writer toward the subject matter. The tone can change throughout the text or stay the same. There are many ways to describe the tone of the text, such as light, playful, questioning, humorous, serious, solemn, or tense. The reader can identify the tone by paying attention to the author's word choice.
- **Mood** refers to the overall feeling conveyed by a setting. For example, a story may be dark in terms of setting, characters, and events that occur. If a story is presented in a picturesque countryside location where the characters are content and the style of speaking is elaborate, the reader will have a different impression of the story than if the setting is in a rundown house with a pale, unhappy caretaker that rarely speaks.

Review Video: Style, Tone, and Mood
Visit mometrix.com/academy and enter code: 416961

IMAGERY

Imagery is the use of **descriptive language** to add life or feeling to a work of literature. Many authors add literary and sound devices to create vivid pictures in the minds of their readers. Most of the time, imagery is thought to be one of the best ways to help readers fully understand and remember a work.

The most common forms of imagery are those that appeal to the sense of sight and sound. Imagery that appeals to the sense of sight, or **visual imagery**, helps the reader picture an event in their mind, usually by including specific details in the text that are not strictly necessary for the purpose of the story, but allow the reader to more easily "see" the scene. Some common forms of figurative language can help create visual imagery.

Review Video: Sensory Language
Visit mometrix.com/academy and enter code: 177314

PLOT

The storyline of any text is also called a **plot**. The characters and events in the story determine what the plot will be. Readers may find a **plot line** useful as they try to put the events in the text in order and determine the relationships between events.

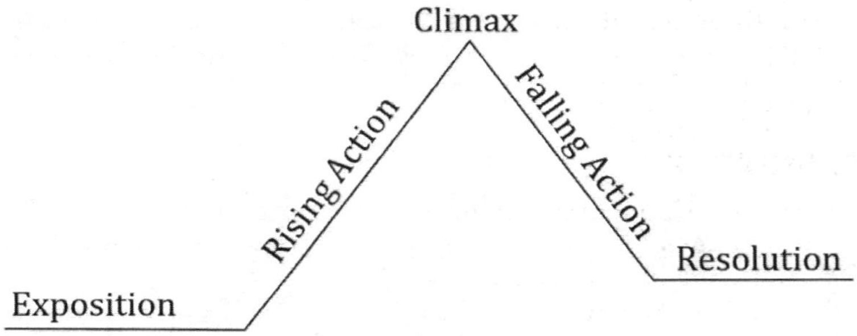

Review Video: Plot Line
Visit mometrix.com/academy and enter code: 944011

Every plot will begin with **exposition**, which introduces the characters and the setting of the story. The plot will continue to develop as new ideas and events centered on the main conflict in the story are revealed, which is called the **rising action**. The action in the story will rise until a **climax** is reached within the conflict. The climax can also be referred to as the turning point in the story, since the climax is where each character makes an important decision. After the climax, the action starts to wind down during the **falling action**. At this point, the characters begin to follow the paths they chose in during climax. The events of the story reach **resolution** in some way by the end of the story. Some conflicts are left open-ended, so that the reader is left to decide what really happened at the end of the story. Keep in mind that not all resolutions are happy or peaceful.

EXAMPLE

Read the following plot and analyze what event is missing from the plot sequence.

> Martin's family decided to go camping at the local park over the weekend. They packed all the camping necessities and drove to the park. Thick sheets of rain poured down all day, so they were stuck in their tent.

Martin and his family forgot to check the weather forecast before they left for their camping trip. to fill in the missing detail, the author may write: "Martin and his family checked the forecast and saw that it was going to rain, but decided to go camping anyway." the flow of the story is broken up by the sudden realization that it is raining, something that could be prevented by adding in the missing detail.

When details are missing from a plot sequence, the audience has trouble following the action in a story. By adding in additional details, the point of each step in a story can be made clearer to the audience.

Conflict

An important part of analyzing the plot of a passage is identifying the **main conflict**. There will likely be many smaller conflicts in the story, but there will be one main problem that influences the characters and events. to identify the main conflict, first look at who the main character is. Now ask yourself what they want. They may want to something to happen or not happen, another character to do or not do something, or to confront or avoid a problem, among other things. Once you know what they want, now ask yourself what is standing in the character's way. It may be a person, an event, or something less tangible like the passing of time. Combining what the main character wants and why they do not currently have leaves the reader with a summary of the main conflict.

Review Video: Conflict
Visit mometrix.com/academy and enter code: 559550

Example

Read the following sentence from the *Call of the Wild* by Jack London and describe the main conflict in the sentence. Explain how the conflict may be resolved.

> The breaking down of discipline likewise affected the dogs in their relations with one another.

Based on the information in the sentence, an event has caused the dogs, the characters in the story, to not follow their regular routine. The sentence indicates that there has been a breaking down of discipline which is affecting how the dogs relate to each other. in order to solve this conflict, discipline needs to be restored. However, in order to return to previous relations between the dogs, any problems that are in the way of conflict resolution need to be taken care of. The word *likewise* means *also*, which tells the reader that other parts of the story are being affected besides the relations between the dogs.

Example

Read the following sentence and explain the main conflict between the two characters:

> Joe stared angrily at Jamie's retreating back as Jamie raced away down the field with Joe's soccer ball.

The main conflict in the sentence is that Jamie has Joe's soccer ball. There may be additional conflicts between the two characters, but none are evident from the evidence shown in the sentence. in any story, a conflict may be minor and only affect part of the story, or be the main focus, taking an entire story to solve a conflict between characters. in the context of the sentence, it is not clear whether or not the entire story will revolve around Jamie taking Joe's soccer ball.

RESOLUTION

The term **resolution** usually indicates the result of a conflict in a story. Conflict between characters, within a character, or against an external element is necessary in order to have a plot for a story. without conflict, no events would occur to form the story. A conflict will come to a climax, and then conclude in some way. The resolution of a problem may be open-ended, end tragically, or end in a way that is good for everyone involved. The problem resolution typically occurs near the end of a story, after the climax has happened. A problem may be resolved by the characters involved within the conflict or by an external event; an upcoming resolution may be foreshadowed in the text, or may be completely unexpected by the reader. If the resolution is completely unexpected, it is considered to be a **twist** in the story.

NON-LINEAR PLOT DEVELOPMENT

Some texts contain a **non-linear plot**, which means the plot is not told in chronological order, or is not told from "beginning to end" in one straight line. There are several devices that authors can use to make their plot non-linear, including:

- **Foreshadowing:** the author gives the reader hints early on in a work about something that will become clearer (or more important) later on.
- **Flashback:** the author shows the reader an event that happened in the past to explain something about the present.
- **Subplot:** a side story, usually about a supporting character, is told along with the main story. Sometimes subplots occur within flashbacks.
- **Parallel plot:** two stories are told alongside each other, often narrated by two different characters in alternating chapters. The events in the stories usually end up overlapping or coming together at some point, most often the climax of the text.

CHARACTERS

CHARACTER TRAIT

The traits of a character may include how they act and physical characteristics; a character trait is a behavior or physical characteristic that is unique to a specific character. For example, a character may be outgoing, which means he or she likes to talk a lot, or they may have bright red hair. These are both character traits.

An author uses character traits to describe a character in a story and help the reader to learn more about how the character acts and what they look like. By comparing the character traits in a story, the reader can see similarities and differences between characters. The author includes character traits to help the reader understand why a character may act a certain way in the story. For example, a character who is shy may not want to talk with a lot of people in a new classroom, but a character who is outgoing may want to talk with many people.

An author typically provides many details about a character so that the reader can learn more about the character's traits, motivations, relationships, and any conflicts they may have in the story. The traits of a character may include how they act and how they look. Characters are often motivated by things that have already happened in their life or how they feel about a topic. The author will often give the reader enough information about the character so that the reader can figure out why the character responds to a situation in a certain way. The author will also often give details about the relationships between characters and points they may conflict on. For example, a character may be good friends with another character; however, the two characters may disagree on where to play outside if one character likes being near the water and the other character does not.

Example

Read the following description of a character and decide, logically, whether the character is likely to go hiking outdoors:

> Jeremy lived in a high-rise in Chicago. He was studious, and not very athletic. Jeremy preferred to stay indoors and read a book, rather than enjoy outdoor weather.

Based on the description of the character's traits, preferences, and personality, he is not likely to go hiking outdoors. The description indicates that the character prefers reading, rather than enjoying outdoor weather. In addition, the character lives in a tall building in the middle of a large city, in order for him to enjoy the outdoors, he would have to travel away from where he lives. The character is not likely to change his preferences. A situation may lead the character to go hiking, but he is not likely to initiate the action on his own. A description of a character that is likely to go hiking outdoors may include a preference for outdoor activity and living near trails.

Character Relationships

A relationship is the way one character acts with another character in a story. The characters are often called **major characters** if they have a main part in the story and **minor characters** if they have a smaller part. There are many different kinds of relationships. For example, two children in a story may be friends, but they could be angry with each other, competing with each other, or helping each other. An author may tell the reader what kind of relationship the characters have. An author might give hints about a relationship. For example, the author may show one child making fun of the other child, which would suggest that the two children do not have a friendly relationship. The author might show one child teaching the other child how to read, which would suggest that the two children have a friendly relationship.

Example

Read the following sentences and describe the relationship Jill and Anna have:

> Jill came over to Anna and asked if she wanted an apple. "Sure, I'd love one. Thanks," Anna answered. Anna took a bite of the apple and started to chew it. Her chewing was so loud that they both started to laugh.

The author does not tell what the relationship between Jill and Anna is. The reader must figure it out from their actions. These actions are the clues the author gives. Jill asks Anna if she wants an apple. Anna says yes and starts to eat it. Her chewing is very loud. Both Jill and Anna start to laugh. They seem to like each other. Jill seems generous to Anna because she gives Anna an apple. They laugh together, and friends often laugh together. The reader can use personal experience to decide that it seems as though Jill and Anna are friends.

Character Changes and Responses

Characters can change in a multitude of ways throughout a story; however, there are main aspects of a character that change. A character's identifying **characteristics**, such as personality or behavior traits, may change as the result of a prominent event in the story, current **motivations**, and conflicts. As **conflicts** change or are resolved, a character may no longer be motivated by striving toward a goal that was previously important to them. Furthermore, a character's development may also lead them to make **different choices**, which can **impact the plot**. As the plot of a story moves along, characters can constantly change in relation to events that occur. Relationships between characters and the points of view of characters may change throughout a story as well.

Each story will have many different types of characters and each of these characters will have a different relationship with other characters. Stories usually have a protagonist, antagonist, and a variety of other characters including round, flat, and stock characters.

PROTAGONIST

The main character in a drama, movie, novel, or other fictional text. The author portrays the protagonist in a way that the audience is most like to identify with themselves. The protagonist is generally undertaking some type of personal challenge throughout the story. The author writes the story so that the reader becomes aware of the protagonist's emotions and is generally able to empathize with the personal challenge.

ANTAGONIST

The character that actively opposes the protagonist by trying to prevent them from succeeding. The antagonist is usually presented in such a way as to make the audience dislike them, and want them to fail at stopping the protagonist. The protagonist and antagonist oppose each other, so their relationship is almost always one of dislike.

FLAT CHARACTERS

Does not have any substantial changes throughout the story. They stay the same despite the conflict, and do not learn any lessons. They are usually minor characters that might interact with the main character in some way.

ROUND CHARACTERS

Major characters in the story that will be more fully developed than other minor characters. They will usually encounter some type of conflict that they must overcome, and usually learn a lesson about life or themselves along the way.

STOCK CHARACTERS

Often get their characteristics and mannerisms from stereotypes of people that are widely recognized. These types of characters are often repeated and well-known. Readers should be aware that stereotypes are rarely accurate in reality, and are generally intended to be humorous or dramatic. Some examples are evil stepmothers, unintelligent blondes, rude athletes, and loyal servants.

Themes

THEME

The **theme** of a story is the lesson that it teaches, or the message the author wants to get across. The theme is linked to the characters, the setting, and the events in a story. A passage can have two or more themes that convey its overall idea.

The theme of a story is not the same as the topic of a story. The topic is what the story is about, but the theme is what a reader is meant to learn. When readers are discussing theme, they can determine both theme topics as well as theme statements.

Theme topics are broad ideas that apply to the text. Examples are:

- Love
- The importance of friendship
- Good vs. evil
- The circle of life

Themes may also be complete statements written in sentence form. Examples are:

- Acts of courage can bring positive changes to the world.
- True friendship can withstand the hardest challenges.

Some themes are fairly common. These themes are called **universal themes** and they suggest things about life, society, and human nature.

Themes are very rarely stated in the text. Instead, the reader has to **infer** the theme by reading closely and thinking carefully about what the author is saying.

Themes are an important part of literature because they serve the purpose of teaching the reader or listener a truth about life. The theme is developed by how a character or characters respond to their situations and challenges.

EXAMPLE

Explain why "Take care of what you care about" accurately describes the theme of the following excerpt.

> Luca collected baseball cards. But Luca wasn't very careful with them. He left them around the house. His dog liked to chew. Luca and his friend Bart were looking at his collection. Then, they went outside. When Luca got home, he saw his dog chewing on his cards. They were ruined.

This excerpt tells the story of a boy who is careless with his baseball cards and leaves them lying around. His dog ends up chewing them and ruining them. The lesson is that if you care about something, you need to take care of it. This is the point of the story. The theme is the lesson that a story teaches. Some stories have more than one theme, but this is not really true of this excerpt. The reader needs to figure out the theme based on what happens in the story. Sometimes, as in the case of fables, the theme is stated directly in the text. However, this is not usually the case.

EXAMPLE

Read the following passage and explain why "It is better not to run away" describes the story's theme.

> Ivan made fun of Sasha. So Sasha was scared of him. If he saw Ivan coming, Sasha hid. Then Sasha changed. He stopped hiding from Ivan. If Ivan laughed at him, Sasha laughed right back. He wasn't afraid anymore. Soon, Ivan stopped making fun of Sasha. This made Sasha feel happier.

The theme "It is better not to run away" fits what happens in the story. Sasha is scared of Ivan and hides from him. But then Sasha stops hiding and laughs back at Ivan, and after that he is not afraid anymore. For him it was better not to run away, but to stay and face his fears. in the end Sasha is happier. He solved his problem. This is the theme that the story teaches through the events of the story. Sasha and the reader learn that something good happened when Sasha did not hide or run away. This is the message of this passage. The reader needs to figure out the theme from what happens in a story.

Organizational Patterns of Texts

Organizational Patterns

When writing there are a variety of ways that an author can choose to organize their text. It is important for them to choose the pattern that best presents their information, as not all patterns will work for every piece of writing. Some examples are:

Advantage/Disadvantage

The author chooses a topic or concept and addresses both the advantages and disadvantages (or pros and cons) of the subject. in this type of text, the author is not trying to persuade their audience to choose a side, but rather, to inform the reader of all the possible positive and negative effects.

Cause and Effect

The author will write about relationship between two events that occur, where the second event occurs as a result of the first.

For example, a text may discuss a school policy stating that when a student is late to school too many times, they receive a detention. Later in the text, we might see a student repeatedly arriving late to school, after which he is given a detention. in this example, the **cause** is the student being late to school, and the **effect** is the student receiving a detention.

Classification

The author chooses a topic and divides it into smaller parts or groups in order to discuss them individually. These types of texts address how parts work within a whole, or what characteristics can be used to classify a given subject or concept.

Chronological Order

the author organizes the progression of events based upon when they occurred and what was included in each step of the story. By organizing the text in this way, the author presents all necessary information about the six questions readers can ask to help themselves understand the text: who, what, when, where, why, and how.

Compare and Contrast

The author will show similarities and differences between items or events.

For example, the author may write about cats and dogs. They might start by giving a brief description of the two. Then they will want to point out all of the similarities, such as; they both have tails, and both are kept as pets. Next, they will explain the differences, such as; dogs are canines, while cats are felines. They will try to provide as much detail as possible about both the similarities and the differences.

Definition

Authors introduce a concept or word and then explain or describe it. This type of text often included examples that will help the reader gain understanding of what is presumably a new concept for them.

Order of Importance

The author puts the information in the text in order of what is most important. Order of importance can be either increasing or decreasing, depending on how the writer wants to structure the work.

Problem and Solution

The author presents some information as a problem and then discusses a solution or attempted solution to that problem. In problem and solution, there is generally one main problem, but that one problem may have several possible solutions.

For example, suppose Billy wants a new video game but does not have the money. There are several possible solutions to this. He might try asking his mom to buy it for him. If that does not work, he could offer to do small jobs to earn enough money to buy it. A third possibility might be to wait until his birthday and ask for it then.

Identifying Organizational Strategies

Example

Explain which organization pattern would be the best choice for this writer and why.

> Sara is writing a report on sea turtles. She has researched the various dangers that they face: their predators, the difficulties they encounter in their life cycle starting with their birth, their migration to the ocean, and the dangers that await them as they mature. She is unsure of how to organize her report.

A cause and effect order would seem to be the best idea for Sara because she would be able to identify the causes and effects of the dangers that sea turtles encounter. She could organize the report so that each paragraph deals with a different threat, using headings to identify what would be in each section. A chart would also be useful because it puts the same information in a clear format so that readers would be able to refer to it. She might also consider using a video showing baby turtles migrating towards the open sea, which would give her audience an even greater understanding of the turtles' plight.

Example

Identify the text structure that is used in the following sentences:

> Madison and her brother Jake used to live on a wind-torn island in the Chesapeake Bay. Last year they moved to Baltimore, a city in Maryland. Next summer they plan to visit the island where they grew up.

Chronological order is used as a text structure in the example sentences, as they are organized according to the passage of time. Note that each sentence refers to a point in time. The first sentence refers to where the siblings lived in the past. The second sentence refers to the siblings' move to Baltimore last year. The final sentence refers to what the siblings plan to do in the future. By referring to a specific place in time, the reader can see what occurred in the story during that time period. an author will often use flashback to indicate what happened in the past, and foreshadowing to give the reader a glimpse of what may occur in the future.

Example

Identify the text structure that is used in the following sentences:

> Three cousins lived in the same small town. One day the cousins decided to journey together to enter a singing contest across the country. The cousins won the contest and made their hometown fans proud.

The information in the story can be organized according to the passage of time, called chronological order. The story will start based in the cousins' hometown, to give some background on where the cousins come from. Subsequent events in the story will occur over time based on the cousins' motivations due to their background. The story will end by referring back to how far the cousins have come from their small-town roots.

Graphic Features in Texts

Print and Graphic Features

An author may show information in a chart, a graph, in paragraph format, or as a list. Information may also be shown in a picture or a diagram. The way an author chooses to show information is often based on the purpose of the text and the audience that the text is meant to reach.

A reader may be asked to answer questions based on the graphic by itself, how the graphic relates to the text, or how the text would best be shown in a graphic form. Some common examples of graphics are cause and effect organizers, circle graphs, bar graphs, illustrations, and diagrams.

Cause and Effect Graphic Organizers

Cause-and-effect graphic organizers are often used to map the **elements of a story**. A reader might read a story about a string of events and then be asked to correctly fill in either the **cause** or **effect** of an event in the story.

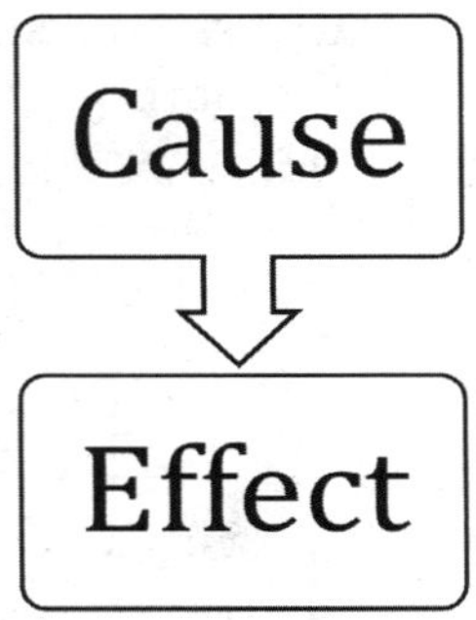

Example

Read the following excerpt from *Ramona Quimby, Age 8* by Beverly Cleary and decide what the cause of the hectic morning at the Quimby house is.

> With all four members of the family leaving at different times in different directions, mornings were flurried in the Quimby household.

A **cause and effect** graphic organizer for this excerpt might look something like this:

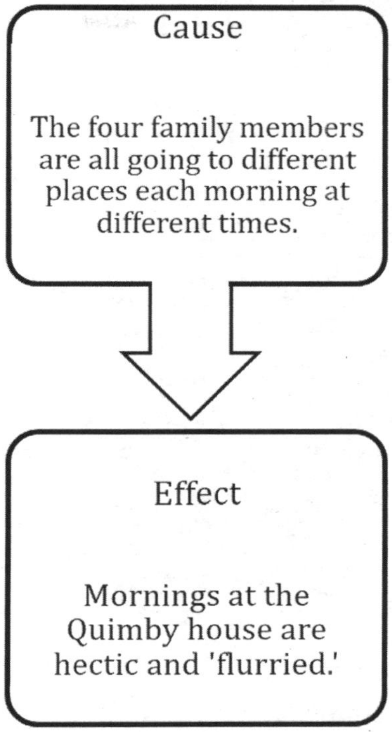

Line Graphs

Line graphs are used for measuring general **trends over time**. For example, this line graph shows an overall upward trend in the amount of candy bars sold for four weeks.

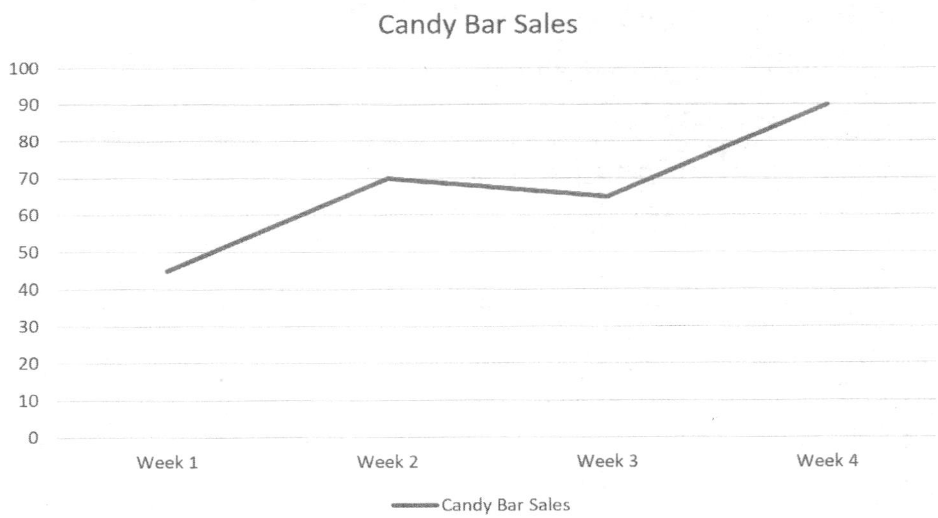

Circle Graphs

Circle graphs, also called pie charts, are often used to represent information that can be shown as **parts of a whole**. For example, this graph shows the results of people being asked about their favorite color:

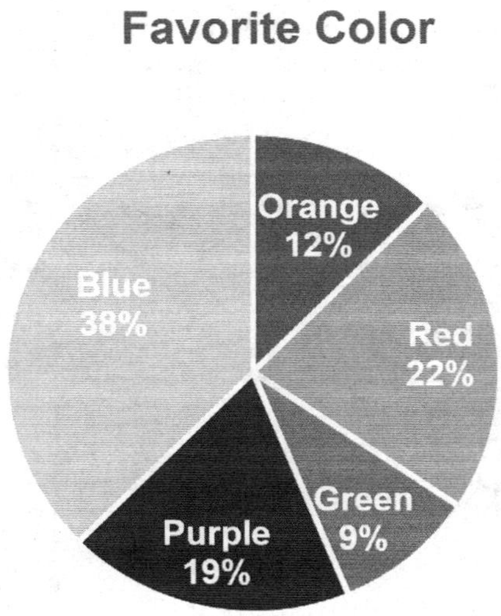

Bar Graphs

Bar graphs are used to show information about **numbers**. For example, this graph is a different way of representing the same results as those in the circle graph.

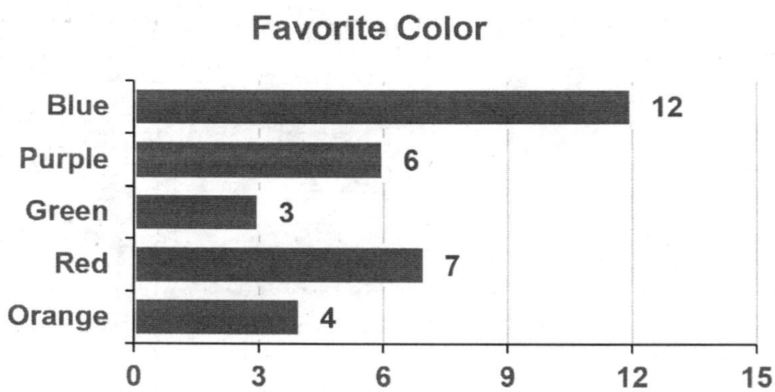

Illustrations and Photographs

Authors may choose to include **illustrations** or **photographs** (or both) with their texts. These two image types both show something from the text or give more information about the text.

Illustrations are drawings of an object. They may be based on reality, or they may represent an artist's abstract idea. For example, this is an illustration of a 1903 automobile:

Photographs are pictures of objects. They are generally extremely realistic, and most often show an object as it actually existed at that moment in time. For example, this is a photograph of a 1917 automobile:

Both illustrations and photographs give the reader another way to relate to and understand the text. The reader may be asked how the image relates to the text, what type of caption the image should be given, or why the author chose to include the image with the text.

Diagrams

Diagrams are used to show information in a visual way. There are many different types of diagrams, including:

Diagrams that show the parts of an object, how they work together, or how they should be put together. This is an example of a diagram which shows how gears turn together

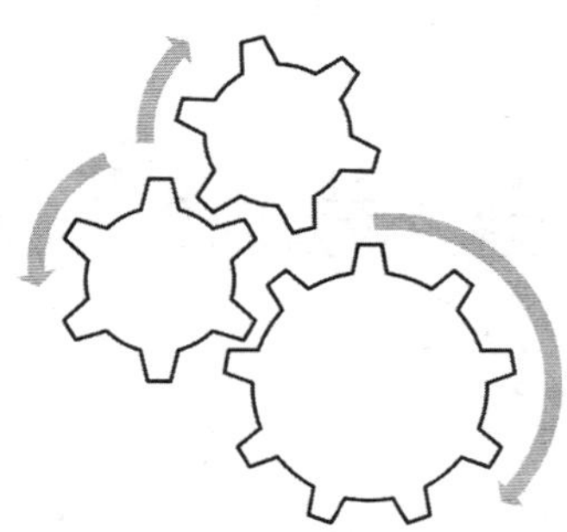

Diagrams that show how information is related are called **Venn Diagrams**. These are ways to visually see the way in which two different ideas overlap. This is an example of a Venn Diagram comparing cats and dogs:

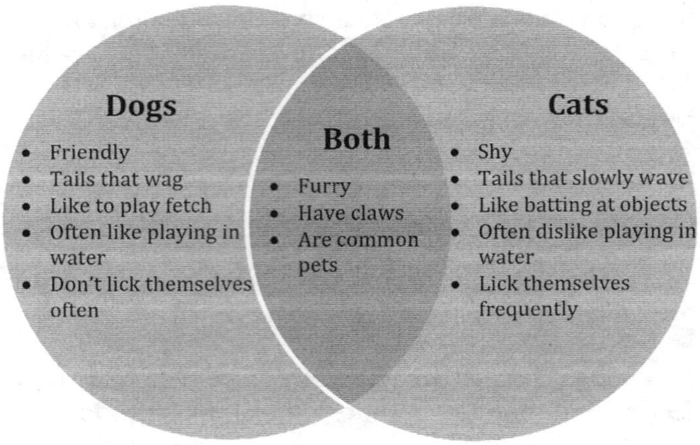

Paraphrasing and Summarizing

Paraphrasing and Summarizing

Paraphrasing and summarizing are two ways readers can work to understand what they read. Both involve reading a text and recalling the main points in an accurate way, but they differ in several ways.

How to Paraphrase	How to Summarize
State the message in the text in the reader's own words, while keeping the original meaning of the text Take all of the original ideas and word them in a way that the reader can better understand Put what the reader has read into their own words, rephrasing what the author has written	State main points of the text clearly and to-the-point. Take information and state it simply, in a much shorter form. Put information in a short form that keeps the main points of the whole text. Do not include many details, just the main idea of the text

Paraphrasing is often done for individual ideas, while summarizing is done for an entire block of text or ideas. Often times, a summary can be done in just one sentence, boiling down the author's words into just main idea.

Review Video: Summarizing Text
Visit mometrix.com/academy and enter code: 172903

Paraphrasing the Main Point of a Sentence

Paraphrase the main point of the following two sentences:

> Emmanuel went swimming in the lake by his house, where the water reached a depth of twenty feet in the middle. He did not venture out more than six feet into the water, however.

When paraphrasing a couple sentences or an entire paragraph, always include the main point of the text being reviewed, this is what the reader needs to know about the text. in the example, the reader needs to know that Emmanuel went swimming in the lake, but not more than six feet out. A paraphrase of the text may include: Emmanuel went swimming six feet out in the lake by his house. That is the main point that the audience needs to know.

Recall that a paraphrase is stating the author's ideas in the reader's own words. A summary typically involves including the main points of a longer text, such as a novel or full story.

Example

Read the following paragraph and then give a one sentence summary statement:

> When choosing a pet, people need to think about what type of home they can offer the animal. For example, a small apartment might not be a good fit for a large dog, but could be a comfortable home for a kitten. A house that has a big yard would be great for a puppy, but a rabbit does not need a large yard.

In order to summarize, one has to identify the main idea and any supporting ideas in the author's work. The summary is an overview of the author's paragraph and will tell what it is about without getting into any of the details. The summary needs to be broad enough to cover all of the information in the author's paragraph. Here is a possible summary statement for the above paragraph:

> People need to consider a number of factors, particularly the available space they have, when choosing a pet.

Example

Read the following sentences and then paraphrase the material:

> Phillipe is debating which elective he should take next year. He is considering choir, band, and soccer. He is making a list of pros and cons to talk about it with his mom so that he is sure to make the right choice.

When paraphrasing information, one needs to read carefully and pay attention to details, then put the material away and write or tell it in their own words. One does not want to look at the material while paraphrasing to avoid plagiarizing by accident. Here is one example of a way to paraphrase the sentences:

> Phillipe has to choose a new elective for his schedule. His choices are choir, band, and soccer. He wants to make the right choice, so he's making a list of pros and cons and planning to talk to his mom.

Summarizing Literature to Support Comprehension

When reading literature, especially demanding works, summarizing helps readers identify important information and organize it in their minds. They can also identify themes, problems, and solutions, and can sequence the story. Readers can summarize before, during, and after they read. They should use their own words, as they do when describing a personal event or giving directions. Previewing a text's organization before reading by examining the book cover, table of contents, and illustrations also aids summarizing. So does making notes of key words and ideas in a graphic organizer while reading. Graphic organizers are another useful method; readers skim the text to determine main ideas and then narrow the list with the aid of the organizer. Unimportant details should be omitted in summaries. Summaries can include description, problem-solution, comparison-contrast, sequence, main ideas, and cause-and-effect.

Drawing Conclusions and Making Inferences

Making Inferences and Conclusions

An **inference** is a **conclusion** or generalization that the reader makes based on the information provided within a text. Certain facts are included to help a reader come to a specific conclusion. It is what the story may hint about, and what a reader can conclude as a result of what the author says in the passage. It is also the best guess that a reader can make based on what happened or was said or in a story. A good inference is based on or supported by details in the passage.

Readers may come to their own conclusion about a topic, or the author may state a conclusion at the end of a story. When readers are in the middle of a story, they can predict what will happen at the end of it based on the events that have occurred so far and the typical characteristics that have been presented by the author up to that point. A reader needs to consider all of the information that an author has presented, including the main point and supporting points, to make logical conclusions and inferences about the story.

For instance, if a passage says that Joan is holding her mouth and moaning, you might conclude, or **infer,** that she has a sore mouth or a toothache. You cannot be sure of this, but it is the best conclusion that you can reach using the information at hand. Inferences are considered **implicit information**. They are not found directly in a passage, but they can be supported by explicit information from the passage.

Review Video: Inference
Visit mometrix.com/academy and enter code: 379203

Finding Explicit Information

Explicit information is the term for information that is **directly stated** in a story or passage. It is what **the author tells you**. It is not information that is hinted at or that you have to make a conclusion about. Explicit information can be facts or details about an event, something or someone. There is usually a lot of explicit information in a story and this information is often used to make an inference or draw a conclusion. to answer questions that ask about explicit information, simply reread the story until you find the answer. in fiction, details about characters, events, and setting are often explicit.

Example

Read the following excerpt and tell what information is explicit.

> From his bed, Steve could see the moon begin to rise and the stars twinkle. He could hear the nurses as they walked down the long hall, their footsteps echoing in the quiet.

The explicit information in the excerpt is all about Steve and what he could see and hear. The passage says that he could see the moon begin to rise and the stars twinkle from his bed. It also says that he could hear the nurses walking down the hall. This is explicit information. The author is describing what Steve can see and hear. There is nothing that is hinted at in the excerpt except that Steve seems to be in a hospital. However, that conclusion is not explicit information. The author does not say this directly, so it is implicit information.

EXAMPLE

Read the following excerpt and tell what you can conclude about why Vicki got a cold.

> Hi Nance,
>
> Richard and I went camping last weekend. A bear ate all our food while we were sleeping. and it was cold and rainy the last night. We have both caught colds. Next time we go camping we are going to bring warmer clothes and extra food for the bears.
>
> Love, Vicki

You can conclude that Vicki got a cold because it was cold and rainy on the last night of her camping trip. She also talks about bringing warmer clothes the next time she goes camping, which further suggests that she was cold. However, the fact that a bear ate her food would have little to do with her getting sick, so that is not the reason she got a cold. It is logical to conclude that she got a cold because of the weather and not having warmer clothes. It is the best inference that you can make from the letter. Inferences are the best guesses that a reader can make based on the information in a passage.

EXAMPLE

Read the following sentence. Draw a conclusion based upon the information presented:

> The hilltop was covered in low-lying clouds of grey, and a moist silence hung in the air as if the sky had drawn in a breath and paused.

The reader can conclude, or infer, based on the information in the sentence, that it is about to rain on the hilltop. The words used in the sentence give the reader clues to draw this conclusion. For example, the words low-lying clouds of grey indicate that rainclouds are present. A moist silence often occurs just before a storm. Based on the reader's own experience and the words presented in the sentence, the reader can conclude that the storm is about to break. Authors will often only present a certain amount of detail to the reader, and the reader needs to fill in the blanks. an author will give the reader just enough information to come to a logical conclusion without having to directly state that conclusion in the story.

IMPLICIT INFORMATION

Implicit information is information that is **not directly stated** in a text, but can be inferred from something that the author explicitly states. For instance, the author may say "Seth buys a new TV, laptop, and home theater system every year." from this the reader could infer several things. For instance, Seth probably likes electronics and has a lot of spending money.

EXAMPLE

Draw a conclusion based on the implicit information in the following sentence from the *Adventures of Tom Sawyer* by Mark Twain:

> He had discovered a great law of human action, without knowing it—namely, that in order to make a man or a boy covet a thing, it is only necessary to make the thing difficult to attain.

The reader can clearly see from the sentence that the character did not set out to learn something, but through an action, the character learned that people will want what is hard to attain. Although it's not explicitly stated, the reader can draw the conclusion that the character gained the experience of coveting (or desiring) something that was hard to get.

Making Predictions

When you read a story, you should look for clues to make a prediction about what will happen. At the end of the story, you may even think about what will happen next to the main character, and use the clues in the story to make a prediction. You can also use personal experience to help make a prediction.

Suppose there is a story about a boy going swimming, and he swims too far out. Suppose the story says the boy can't get back to shore and starts to yell. Suppose the lifeguard comes and helps him. Suppose the story stops after the boy goes back in the water again. The reader might make the prediction that the boy won't swim as far out this time. This may not be true, but it is the most likely thing to happen.

Example

Describe what prediction can be made based on the following sentences:

> When Glen is sick, his mother keeps him home from school. He stays in bed all day and takes medicine. Glen woke up this morning with a sore throat. His head was hot, and he felt achy.

The story says that Glen's mother keeps him home when he is sick and that Glen spends the day in bed when he is sick. The story says that Glen woke up this morning with a sore throat. His head was hot, and he felt achy. The reader can figure out that Glen was sick. Because Glen's mother always keeps him home when he is sick, the reader can predict that Glen will be staying home from school and spending the day in bed.

You can also use text features find information to make predictions and verify conclusions determined about different texts. Using key words as clues, looking for bold print words, looking for sentences that include captions, and words that are written in italics are a few features that can be used to help understand and make predictions about a text.

Using Structure and Genre to Make Predictions

The structure and genre of a story can also help readers make predictions. Most stories follow the same structure. They have an exposition, rising action, a climax, falling action, and a resolution. Because most stories follow this structure, readers can predict that each of these parts will occur in the story. For example, rising action usually begins after the conflict of the story is introduced. This means that if characters have not faced any conflict, the reader can predict that something will go wrong for the characters. Likewise, stories in the same genre may contain similar events. For example, in a mystery, the characters work to solve a crime or explain a strange event. So, when reading a mystery, the reader can predict that the conflict will be a crime or event that the characters must learn more about.

Facts and Opinions

Writers and readers must always be aware of the difference between fact and opinion. A **fact** can be tested and proven to be true. An **opinion**, on the other hand, is someone's personal thoughts or feelings. Opinions are often not changed by information. If an author writes that a newborn elephant is about five times taller than a newborn giraffe, then he or she is stating a fact. If the author writes that giraffes are more interesting than elephants, then he or she is giving an opinion because this cannot be proven to be true or false. Opinions are often supported by facts. For instance, the author might use a comparison between the way that giraffes eat and the way elephants eat as evidence of how giraffes are more interesting. An opinion supported by facts tends to be more convincing. On the other hand, when authors support their opinions with other opinions, readers should seriously think about and read the argument carefully to see whether it is logical and trustworthy.

Review Video: Distinguishing Fact and Opinion
Visit mometrix.com/academy and enter code: 870899

Analyzing Ideas Within and Between Selections

Making Connections to Enhance Comprehension

Reading involves thinking. For good comprehension, readers make text-to-self, text-to-text, and text-to-world connections. Making connections helps readers understand text better and predict what might occur next based on what they already know, such as how characters in the story feel or what happened in another text. Readers can make connections before, during, and after reading. Venn diagrams and other graphic organizers can help readers visualize connections.

Text-to-Self

Reading while looking for connections with the reader's life and experiences makes literature more personally relevant and meaningful to readers. Sentences showing text-to-self connections may begin with these examples:

- This reminds me of a time when...
- I understand how the character feels because...
- The setting makes me think of...
- I experienced this same thing when...

Text-to-Text

Reading while looking for connections to other texts helps the reader learn to identify the way authors use genre, setting, characters, plot elements, literary structure and devices, and themes to create meaning. Sentences showing text-to-text connections may begin with these examples:

- The character in this story reminds me of the character in...
- These two stories are alike because...
- The conflict in this story is similar to the conflict in...
- The relationship between the friends in this story is different than the relationship in...

Text-to-World

Reading while looking for connections to the world helps the reader begin to see literature as a reflection of real life and notice patterns in history and current events. Sentences showing text-to-world connections may begin with these examples:

- The event in this story sounds like the event in history when...
- The actions of this character sound like...
- This is like what happened in real life when...
- I heard about this on the news when...

Synthesizing a Text With Existing Knowledge

Synthesizing is similar to summarizing but it takes it one step further. Synthesizing involves taking the main points of a text and comparing it with existing knowledge to create a new idea, perspective, or way of thinking.

Another term for knowledge that you already have is **schema**. The plural form of this word is **schemata**. Schemata contain all the ideas you have about something. Synthesizing is all about how schemata change over time with the introduction of new information.

Example

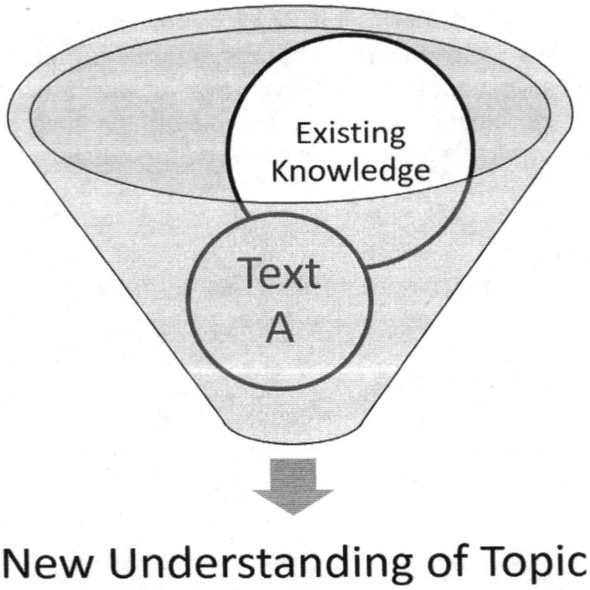

Using self-questioning strategies can help readers synthesize texts with their schemata to increase or change their understanding of topics. These questions include

- What do I already know about this topic?
- Is any of this new information?
- Has my perspective changed now that I've read this?
- What do I understand now that I didn't before?
- What are the main ideas of this text?
- How do the parts of the text fit together to create meaning?
- Are there any text-to-text, text-to-self, or text-to-world connections here?

Synthesizing Texts Without Existing Knowledge

If the reader is completely unfamiliar with the topic, they will have no background knowledge. in this case, instead of using existing knowledge, synthesizing may instead be done by combining the ideas provided in two or three different texts. The reader must make connections between the texts, determine how the ideas fit together, and gather evidence to support the new perspective.

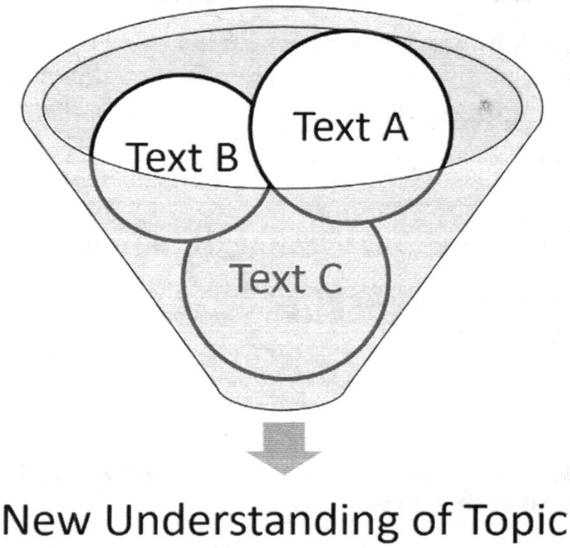

Using self-questioning strategies can help readers synthesize texts to increase their understanding of topics. in this case, readers are creating new schemata as they read. Common questions include:

- What do these texts have in common?
- What is different between these texts?
- What new information have I learned?
- What do I understand now that I didn't before?
- How do these texts relate to one another?
- If I think of these texts as parts of one whole, what meaning do they create together?
- What predictions can I make about this topic?

Mathematics Practice Test

1. Antonio wants to buy a roll of border to finish an art project. At four different shops, he found four different borders he liked. He wants to use the widest of the borders. The list shows the width, in inches, of the borders he found.

$$1\frac{7}{10}, 1.72, 1\frac{3}{4}, 1.695$$

Which roll of border should Antonio buy if he wants to buy the widest border?

a. $1\frac{7}{10}$
b. 1.72
c. $1\frac{3}{4}$
d. 1.695

2. Daniella wrote a decimal and a fraction which were equivalent to each other. Which pair of numbers could be the pair Daniella wrote?

a. $0.625, \frac{7}{8}$
b. $0.375, \frac{3}{8}$
c. $0.75, \frac{7}{5}$
d. $0.45, \frac{4}{5}$

3. Glenda poured salt into three salt shakers from a box that contained 21 ounces of salt. She poured $\frac{1}{7}$ ounces of salt into one shaker. She poured $\frac{1}{3}$ into the second shaker, and she poured $\frac{3}{7}$ into the last shaker. How many ounces of salt are left in the original box?

a. 19 ounces
b. 2 ounces
c. 0 ounces
d. 11 ounces

4. Ms. Henderson shops for new clothing for her young son. She buys two pairs of pants at $24.99 each, and three shirts at $17.99 each. How much does Ms. Henderson spend on her son's clothing?

a. $102.95
b. $103.95
c. $103.96
d. $102.96

5. Enrique used a formula to find the total cost, in dollars, for repairs he and his helper, Jenny, made to a furnace. The expression below shows the formula he used, with 4.25 being the number of hours he worked on the furnace and 2.60 being the number of hours Jenny worked on the furnace.

$$20 + 35(4.25 + 2.60) + 47$$

What is the total cost for repairing the furnace?

a. $277.00
b. $303.25
c. $306.75
d. $2,4042.00

6. One morning at Jim's café, 25 people ordered juice, 10 ordered milk, and 50 ordered coffee with breakfast. Which ratio best compares the number of people who ordered milk to the number of people who ordered juice?

a. 5 to 7
b. 5 to 2
c. 2 to 7
d. 2 to 5

7. At the middle school Vanessa attends, there are 240 Grade 6 students, 210 Grade 7 students, and 200 Grade 8 students. Which ratio best compares the number of students in Grade 8 to the number of students in Grade 6 at Vanessa's school?

a. 5:6
b. 5:11
c. 6:5
d. 7:8

8. A display at the bottom of the laptop computer Erica was using showed that the battery had a 70% charge. Which decimal is equivalent to 70%?

a. 0.07
b. 70.0
c. 7.0
d. 0.7

9. The drawing shows a chart used to record completed Math assignments. A checkmark is used to show which assignments are finished.

Math Assignment

✓	✓	✓	✓	✓
✓	✓	✓	✓	✓
✓	✓	✓		
✓	✓			

Which of the following shows the percentage of Math assignments in the chart which are finished?

a. 15%
b. 25%
c. 55%
d. 75%

10. Harold learned that 6 out of 10 students at his school live within two miles of the school. If 240 students attend Grade 6 at his school, about how many of these students should Harold expect to live within two miles of the school?

a. 24
b. 40
c. 144
d. 180

11. A unit of liquid measure in the English System of Measure is the gill. The table, shown here, gives conversions from gills to fluid ounces.

Conversion Table

Gills	Fluid Ounces
2	8
4	16
5	20
6	24
10	40

Which equation best describes the relationship between gills, *g*, and fluid ounces, *f*?

a. $f = 8g - 8$
b. $f = 2g + 4$
c. $f = 4g$
d. $4f = g$

12. The table below shows changes in the area of several trapezoids as the lengths of the bases, b_1 and b_2, remain the same and the height, *h*, changes.

Trapezoids

b_1 (in feet)	b_2 (in feet)	h (in feet)	A (in square feet)
5	7	2	12
5	7	4	24
5	7	6	36
5	7	8	48

Which formula best represents the relationship between *A*, the areas of these trapezoids, and *h*, their heights?

a. $A = 5h$
b. $A = 6h$
c. $A = 7h$
d. $A = 12h$

13. This table shows lengths, widths, and areas of four rectangles. In each rectangle, the length remains 40 meters, but the width changes.

Rectangles

Length	40 meters	40 meters	40 meters	40 meters
Width	20 meters	30 meters	40 meters	50 meters
Perimeter	120 meters	140 meters	160 meters	180 meters

Which formula best represents the relationship between *P*, the perimeters of these rectangles, and *w*, their widths?

a. $P = w + 80$
b. $P = 2w + 80$
c. $P = 2(2w + 40)$
d. $P = 10(w + 40)$

14. Thomas drew a polygon with vertices: *A*, *B*, *C*, and *D*. He measured the angles formed and recorded the information shown here.

$m\angle A = 80°, m\angle B = 80°, m\angle C = 120°, m\angle D = 80°?$

Which angle measures are congruent?

a. $m\angle A$ and $m\angle C$ only
b. $m\angle C$ and $m\angle D$ only
c. $m\angle A$, $m\angle B$, and $m\angle C$
d. $m\angle A$, $m\angle B$, and $m\angle D$

15. Which set of figures are congruent?

a. 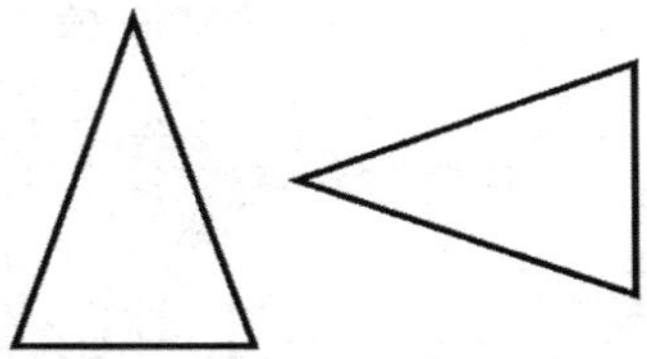

b. 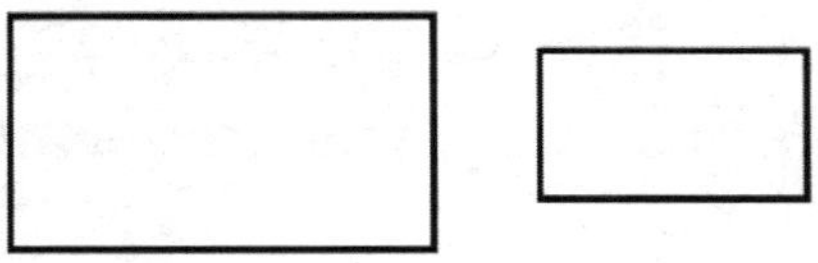

c. 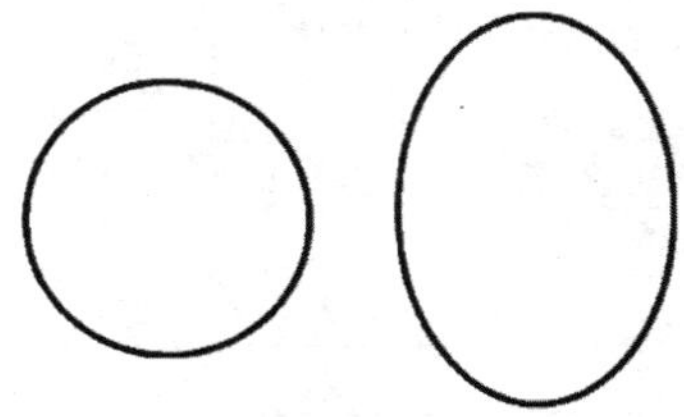

d. 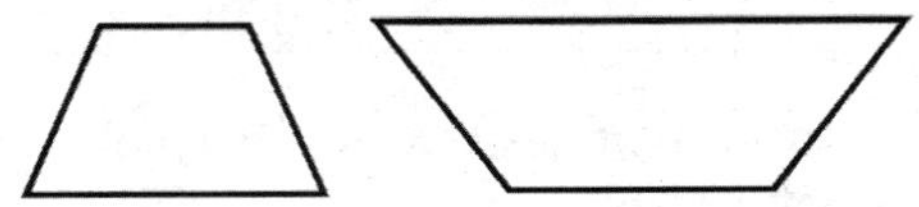

16. Ellen measured $\angle R$ in the parallelogram shown here and found it to be 35°. She knows that $\angle R$ and $\angle T$ are congruent.

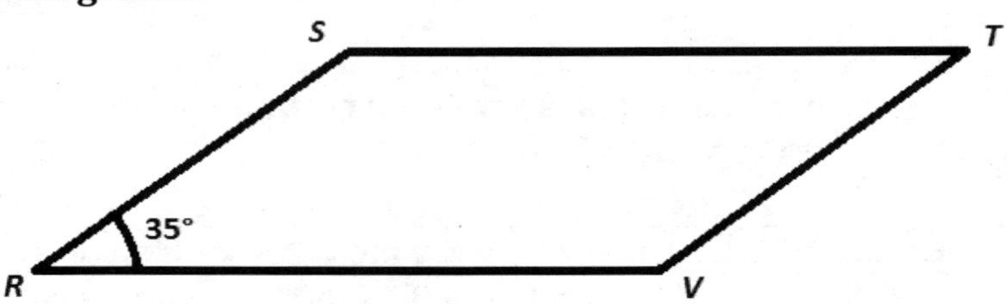

What is the measure of $\angle T$?

a. 215°
b. 145°
c. 70°
d. 35°

17. What is the solution to the inequality:

$$x + 8 \leq 56$$

a. $x \geq 64$
b. $x \leq 48$
c. $x \geq 48$
d. $x \leq 64$

18. Put the following integers in order from greatest to least:

-52, 16, -12, 14, 8, -5, 0

a. -52, 16, -12, 14, 8, -5, 0
b. 0, -5, 8, -12, 14, 16, -52
c. 0, -5, -12, -52, 8, 14, 16
d. 16, 14, 8, 0, -5, -12, -52

19. Jessica wrote down the times required for five girls to run a race. The times are shown in this list.

25.1 seconds, 24.9 seconds, 25.2 seconds, 24.8 seconds, 25.0 seconds

What is the total time for all five runners?

a. 1 minute and 5 seconds
b. 1 minute and 25 seconds
c. 2 minutes and 5 seconds
d. 2 minutes and 25 seconds

20. This drawing shows an equilateral triangle and a ruler.

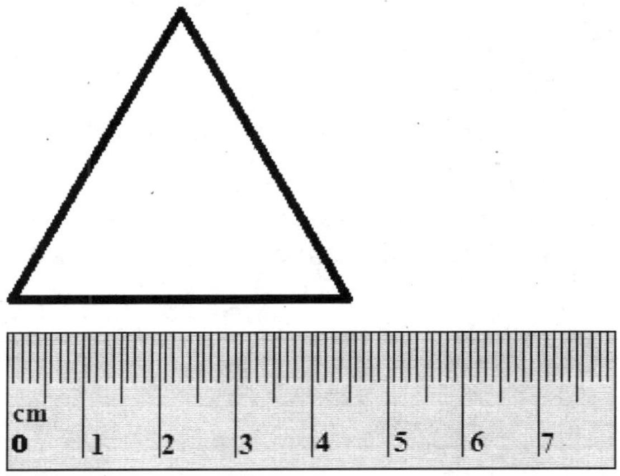

Which is closest to the perimeter of the triangle?

a. 4.5 centimeters
b. 9.0 centimeters
c. 13.5 centimeters
d. 20.3 centimeters

21. Arrange the following rational numbers from least to greatest:

$$\frac{4}{5}, \frac{9}{12}, 0.56, 1.6, 1\frac{3}{8}, 85\%, \frac{1}{2}$$

a. $\frac{1}{2}, 0.56, \frac{9}{12}, \frac{4}{5}, 85\%, 1\frac{3}{8}, 1.6$
b. $0.56, \frac{1}{2}, \frac{9}{12}, \frac{4}{5}, 85\%, 1\frac{3}{8}, 1.6$
c. $\frac{1}{2}, 0.56, \frac{9}{12}, \frac{4}{5}, 85\%, 1.6, 1\frac{3}{8}$
d. $\frac{1}{2}, 0.56, \frac{4}{5}, \frac{9}{12}, 85\%, 1.6, 1\frac{3}{8}$

22.If a=-2, b=-5, c=8, and d=4, evaluate the expression below.

$$\boldsymbol{a^2 + (2b - c) \times d}$$

Write your answer on the provided griddable answer sheet.

–	0	0
+	1	1
	2	2
	3	3
	4	4
	5	5
	6	6
	7	7
	8	8
	9	9

23. A mathematics test has a 4:2 ratio of data analysis problems to algebra problems. If the test has 18 algebra problems, how many data analysis problems are on the test?

a. 24
b. 28
c. 36
d. 38

24. Stephen researched the topic of solar-powered lights for his science project. He exposed 10 new solar lights to five hours of sunlight. He recorded the number of minutes each light continued to shine after dark in the list below.

63, 67, 73, 75, 80, 91, 63, 72, 79, 87

Which of these numbers is the mean of the number of minutes in Stephen's list?

a. 28
b. 63
c. 74
d. 75

25. Grade 6 students at Fairview Middle School were asked to name their favorite of six school subjects. The circle graph below represents the data.

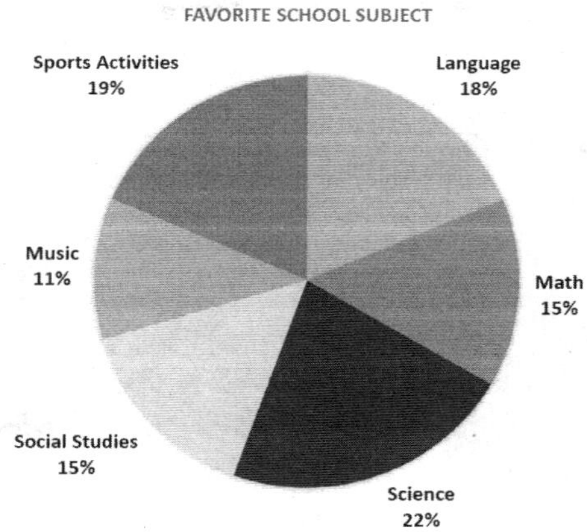

Which graph best represents the data in the plot?

a.

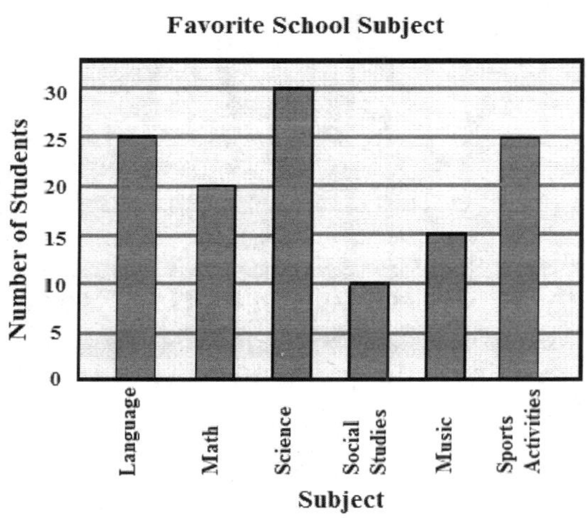

b.

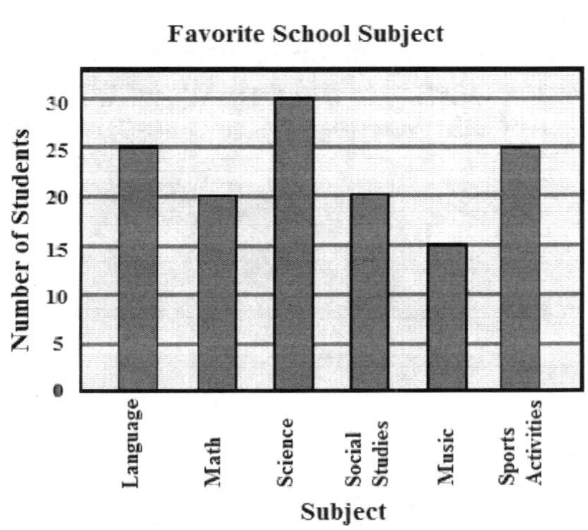

c.

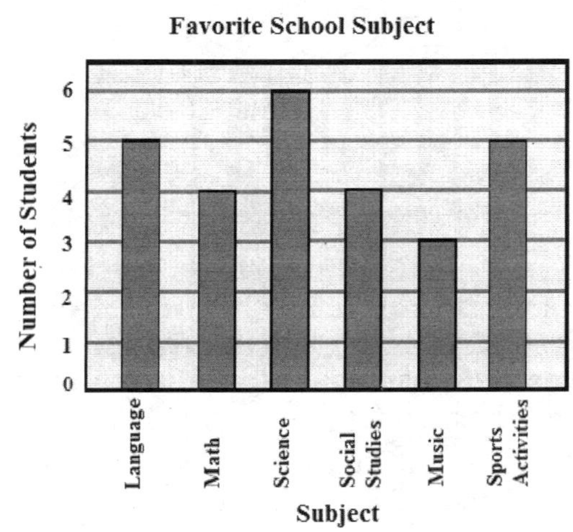

d.

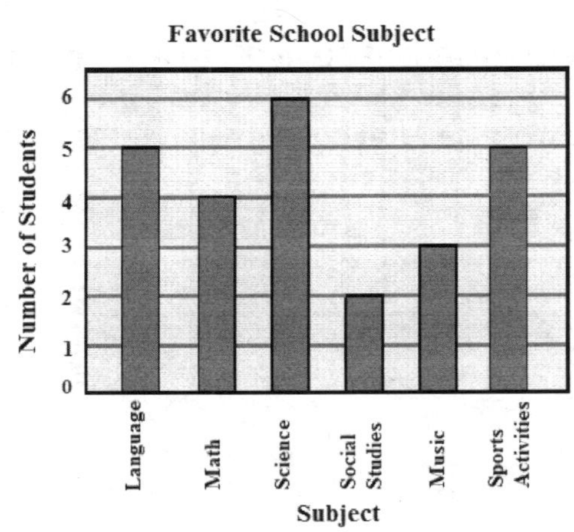

26. Sammie had $120 he had earned doing chores for people in his neighborhood. When school started, he spent $50 for shirts, $30 for jeans, and $40 for school supplies. Which graph best represents how Sammy spent his $120?

a.

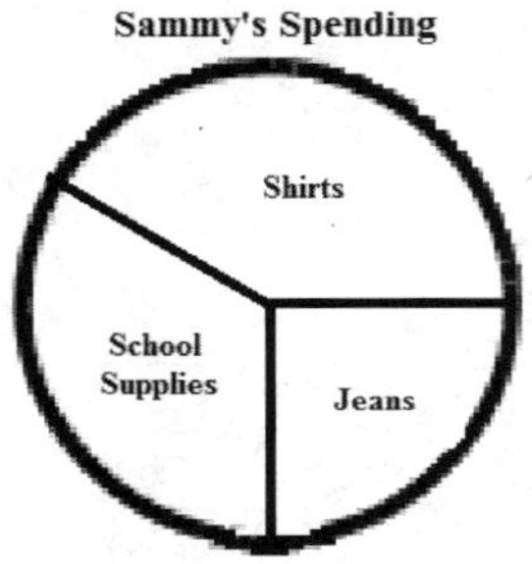

c.

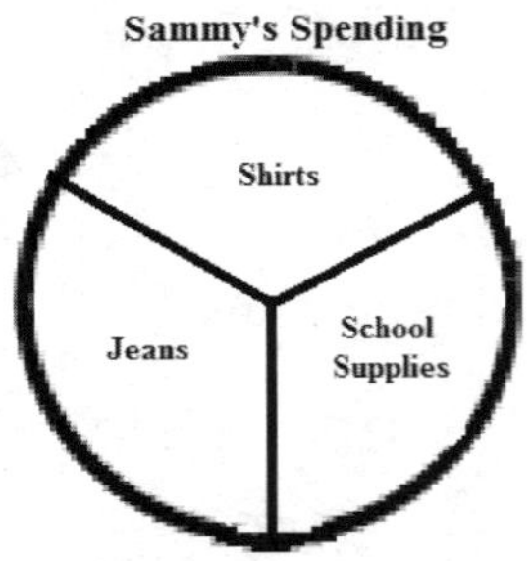

b.

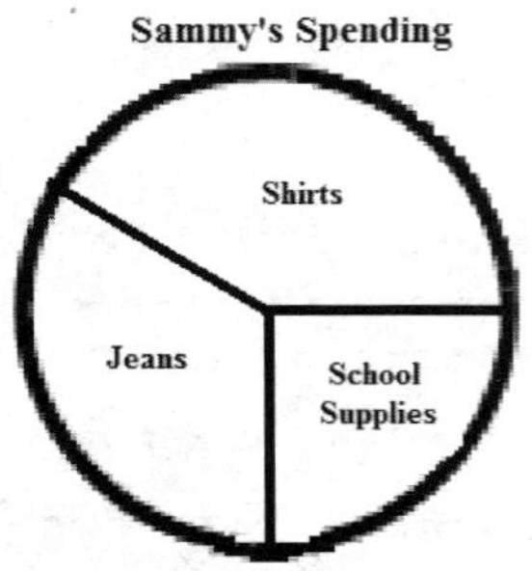

d.

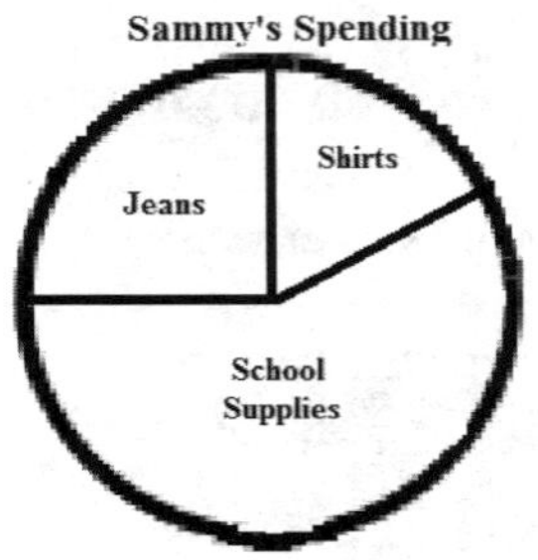

27. James and his driving partner, Larissa, recently drove a truck from Dallas, TX to Los Angeles, CA. The total distance they drove was 1,380 miles. James is paid $0.35 per mile he drives and Larissa is paid $0.30 per mile she drives. What additional information is needed to find the amount James should be paid for the trip?

a. The total number of hours each person drove
b. The total number of miles each person drove
c. The total amount of fuel the truck used
d. The total weight of the truck and cargo

28. Petra installed 10 light fixtures at a new warehouse that was being built. Each of the fixtures required 3 light bulbs. The bulbs come in packages of 5 and cost $8 per package. What was the total cost for the bulbs required for all of the fixtures Petra installed at the warehouse?

a. $16
b. $48
c. $120
d. $240

29. Anna and other members of her club sold caps to commemorate their city's 100th birthday. The caps sold for $14 and came in four colors. The club made $3,360 in total sales from selling the caps. The graph below shows the part of the total sales that each color represented.

Colors of Caps Sold

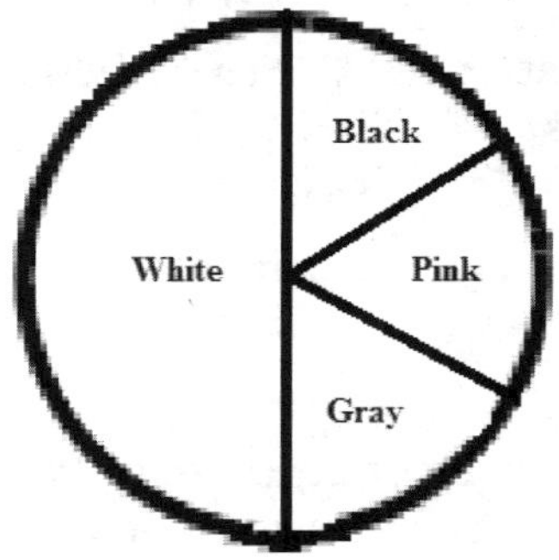

Which number is closest to the combined number of white and pink caps sold by Anna's club members?

a. 40
b. 80
c. 120
d. 160

30. Gabe has 6 pencils. The lengths of his pencils in inches are shown on the number line below. What is the mean length of the pencils?

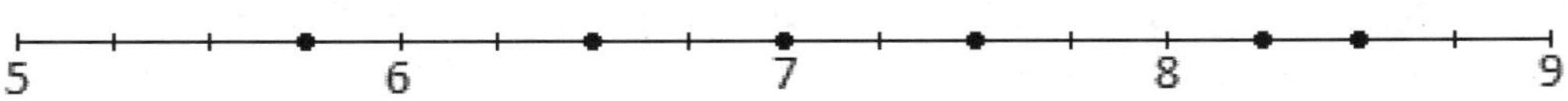

a. 7 in.
b. $7\frac{1}{4}$ in.
c. $7\frac{1}{2}$ in.
d. $6\frac{3}{4}$ in.

Refer to the following for question 31-32:

Jason wants to put dry fertilizer on the grass in his front yard. The yard is 20 feet wide and 45 feet long. Each pound of the fertilizer he plans to use is enough for 150 square feet.

31. Which expression could Jason use to determine the correct amount of fertilizer to use on the entire yard?

a. $(20 \times 45) \div 150$
b. $(20 \times 150) \div 45$
c. $150 \div (20 \times 45)$
d. $150 \times (20 \times 45)$

32. **How many pounds of fertilizer will Jason need?**

a. 0.17
b. 67
c. 135,000
d. 6

33. **The ratio of boys to girls in a math class is 3 to 4. If there are 12 boys in the class, how many total students are in the class?**

a. 7 students
b. 16 students
c. 24 students
d. 28students

34. **Mark is leaving a job site and moving equipment to Phoenix which is located 210 miles north. He drives the first ten miles in 12 minutes. If he continues at the same rate, what will his total travel time be?**

a. 3 hours 15 minutes
b. 3 hours 45 minutes
c. 4 hours 12 minutes
d. 4 hours 20 minutes

35. **Point *A* is graphed on the coordinate plane below. What ordered pair matched the location of point A?**

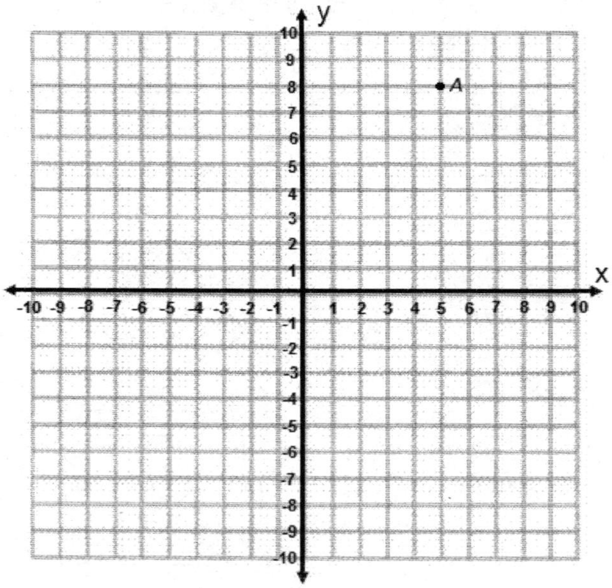

a. (8,5)
b. (5,8)
c. $(8,-5)$
d. $(5,-8)$

36. Candace's shoelace broke. She measured the unbroken shoelace and finds that she needs a replacement lace that is at least 16 inches long. The store has the following lengths available.

$$15\frac{7}{10}, 16.25, \frac{47}{3}, 15.5$$

Which one of the following lace lengths would be long enough to replace the broken shoelace?

a. $15\frac{7}{10}$
b. 16.25
c. $\frac{47}{3}$
d. 15.5

37. Nadia is working summer jobs. She earns $5 for every dog she walks, $2 for bringing back a trashcan, $1 for checking the mail, and $5 for watering the flowers. Nadia walks 3 dogs, brings back 5 trashcans, checks the mail for 10 neighbors, and waters the flowers at 6 houses. Which expression can be used to find out how much money Nadia earned?

a. $2(5) +$6(10) + $1
b. S10(6) + $1 + $5
c. S5(3+6) + $2(5) + $1(10)
d. $15 + $10 + $16

38. Only 8% of the dogs were solid white. Which decimal is equivalent to 8%?

a. 0.08
b. 80.0
c. 8.0
d. 0.8

39. Use this grid to answer the question.

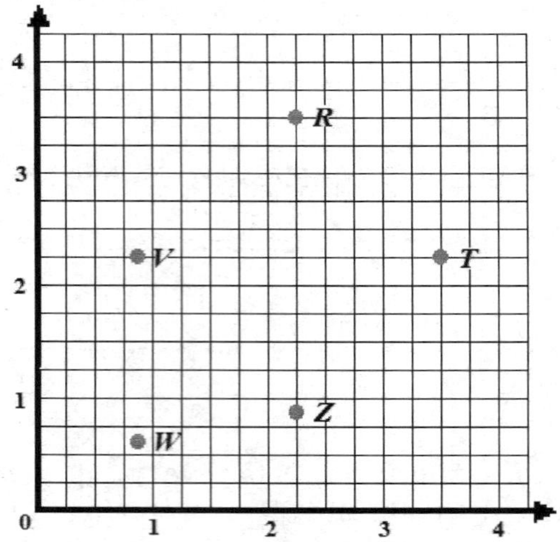

Which of the points on the grid best represents the point at $(2\frac{1}{4}, \frac{7}{8})$?

a. T
b. V
c. W
d. Z

40. The Charleston Recycling Company collects 50,000 tons of recyclable materials every month. The char shows the kinds of materials that are collected by the company's five trucks.

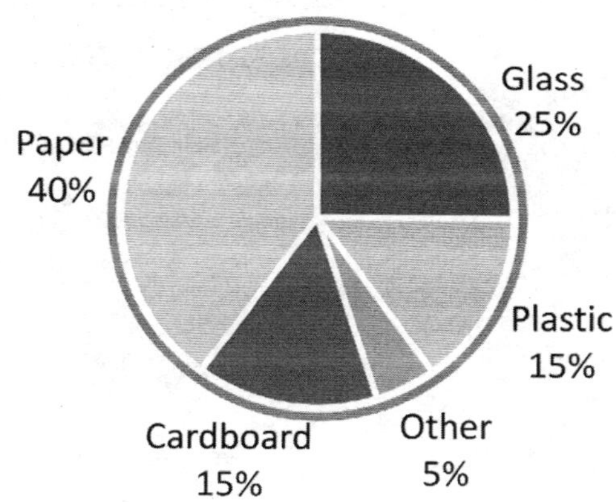

What is the second most common material that is recycled?

a. Cardboard
b. Glass
c. Paper
d. Plastic

41. What is the value of w in this equation: $3w = -6$

a. 2
b. -2
c. 18
d. -18

42. The 180 campers in Group A got to choose which kind of sandwich they wanted on the picnic. The results of the choice are given in the table below

Sandwich	# of Campers
PB & J	60
Turkey	45
Egg salad	15
Veggie	60

Which expression correctly provides the ratio of campers who chose veggie sandwiches to those who chose turkey?

a. 1:3
b. 1:4
c. 3:2
d. 4:3

43. If $x - 6 = 0$, then what is the value of x?

a. 0
b. 3
c. 6
d. 9

44. What is the value of r in the following equation?

$$29 + r = 420$$

a. $r = \frac{29}{420}$
b. $r = \frac{420}{29}$
c. $r = 391$
d. $r = 449$

45.What is a good estimate for the circumference of the circle shown below?

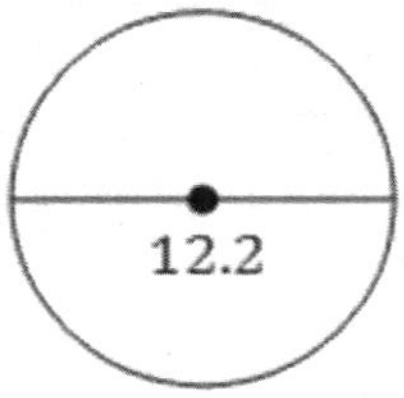

a. 6
b. 12
c. 24
d. 36

46. Hannah spends at least \$16 on 4 packages of coffee. Which of the following expresses this relationship in terms of the cost of a package of coffee, p?

a. $16 \geq 4p$
b. $16 < 4p$
c. $16 > 4p$
d. $16 \leq 4p$

47. What is the area of the triangle *RST*?

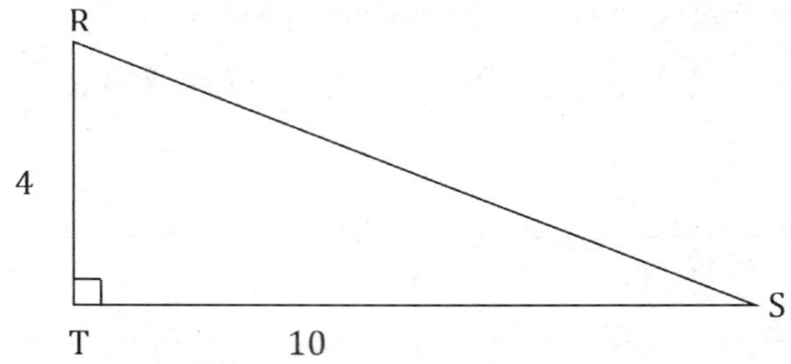

Record your answer in the griddable below.

–	0	0
+	1	1
	2	2
	3	3
	4	4
	5	5
	6	6
	7	7
	8	8
	9	9

48. Stefan's scores on his English essays were 75, 65, 80, 95, and 65. What is his average score?

a. 65
b. 66
c. 75
d. 76

49. Joshua has to earn more than 92 points on the state test in order to qualify for an academic scholarship. Each question is worth 4 points, and the test has a total of 30 questions. Let *x* represent the number of test questions Joshua answers correctly. Which of the following inequalities can be solved to determine the number of questions Joshua must answer correctly?

a. $4x < 30$
b. $4x < 92$
c. $4x > 30$
d. $4x > 92$

50. The radius of a circle is 6 inches. What is the area?

a. 18.84 in^2
b. 36.68 in^2
c. 87.98 in^2
d. 113.04 in^2

Answer Key and Explanations for the Mathematics Test

1. C: To answer this question correctly, convert all numbers to decimal form to make them easy to compare. Since two of the numbers are already in decimal form, we only need to convert $1\frac{7}{10}$ and $1\frac{3}{4}$ to decimal form.

$$7 \div 10 = 0.7, \text{so } 1\frac{7}{10} = 1.7$$
$$\text{and } 3 \div 4 = 0.75, \text{so } 1\frac{3}{4} = 1.75$$

Therefore, by comparing place values from left to right of 1.7, 1.72, 1.75 and 1.695, we see that 1.695 is least, 1.7 is next greatest, 1.72 is next, and 1.75 is greatest. So, Antonio should buy the border that is $1\frac{3}{4}$ inches wide.

2. B: To answer this question, one method that can be used is to convert all the fractions to decimal form so it is easier to compare them to each other. This can be done by simply dividing, since the fraction sign means division.

$$7 \div 8 = 0.875$$
$$3 \div 8 = 0.375$$
$$7 \div 5 = 1.4$$
$$4 \div 5 = 0.8$$

So, the only pair of numbers in which the fraction is equivalent to the decimal is in answer B.

3. B: She starts with 21 ounces. Create a proportion to figure out how many ounces she pours into each shaker. The first shaker is $\frac{1}{7} = \frac{x}{21}$. Since 7 times 3 is 21, the numerator can also be multiplied by 3. Therefore, the first shaker had 3 ounces. The second shaker is $\frac{1}{3} = \frac{x}{21}$. Since 3 times 7 is 21, the numerator can also be multiplied by 7. Therefore, the second shaker had 7 ounces. The third shaker is $\frac{3}{7} = \frac{x}{21}$. Since 7 times 3 is 21, the numerator can also be multiplied by 3. Therefore, the third shaker had 9 ounces. Add all of the ounces together and subtract from the original amount of ounces: $21 - (3 + 7 + 9) = 2$.

4. B: The total amount that Ms. Henderson spends on the clothing is equal to the sum of the individual pieces of clothing. The total equals $24.99 + $24.99 + $17.99 + $17.99 + $17.99 = $103.95.

5. C: To solve this formula, follow the order of operations. First, add what is in the parenthesis, 4.25 + 2.60, to get 6.85. Then, multiply the 6.85 by 35 to get 239.75. Last, we should add 20.00 + 239.75 + 47.00 to get 306.75. Be sure to line up the decimal points when adding.

6. D: Note that the ratio asked for is the number of people who ordered milk to the number who ordered juice. The number of people who ordered coffee does not matter here. This compares 10 to 25, and the order is important here. Since the ratio is with the number of people who ordered milk first, the 10 must come first. So, the ratio is 10 to 25, but the ratio can be written in simpler form by dividing both numbers in the ratio by 5, to get the ratio: 2 to 5.

7. A: One way to answer this question is to name the ratio: 200 to 240, then write the ratio in simplest terms by dividing both terms by the greatest common factor, 40, to get 5 to 6. It should be noted that the number of Grade 7 students is not important for this problem. Also, the order of the ratio matters. Since it asks for the ratio using the number of Grade 8 students first, the ratio is 200 to 240 and not the other way around.

8. D: To correctly write a percent as a decimal, the percent sign is dropped and the number is rewritten with the decimal point two places to the left. This is because a percent is always a value out of 100 and the second place after the decimal point is the hundredths place. So, 70% = 0.70 and the zero at the end after the decimal can be dropped.

9. D: There are 15 of the 20 assignments with check marks indicating a finished assignment. Since the fraction $\frac{1}{20}$ represents 5%, then 15 times 5% gives 75% of the assignments finished.

10. C: One way to find this answer is to set up a proportion: $\frac{6}{10} = \frac{G}{240}$, in which G represents the number of Grade 6 students living within two miles of the school. To solve the proportion, we should cross-multiply. So, 10 times G = 6 times 240. This gives the equation: $10G$ = 1,440. To solve the equation we divide both sides of the equation by 10, which gives G = 144.

11. C: Looking at the chart, a pattern can be seen in the relationship between the number of gills and the number of fluid ounces. Each number of gills in the first column, when multiplied by 4, gives the number of fluid ounces in the second column. So, f equals 4 times g, or $f = 4g$.

12. B: The formula for the area of trapezoids is not necessarily needed here to do this problem. Since the relationship between the area, A, and the height, h, can be seen in the chart, looking at the third and fourth columns to see if there is a pattern will show a relationship between the variables. Each value in the area column is equal to 6 times the value in the height column. So, we get $A = 6h$.

13. B: To answer this question, start with the perimeter formula, $P = 2(l + w)$ and substitute values that are known to remain the same. So, $P = 2(l + w)$ becomes $P = 2(40 + w)$. Then we distribute, multiplying both numbers inside the parenthesis by 2 and get $P = 80 + 2w$. Writing the variable first in the expression gives us: $P = 2w + 80$.

14. D: Congruent angles are angles that have the same measure. Therefore, angle A, angle B, and angle D are all congruent angles.

15. A: In order for two figures to be congruent, they must have the same size and shape. The two triangles in choice A have the same size and shape, even though the second triangle is rotated counterclockwise compared to the first triangle. The rectangles in choice B are the same shape, but they are not the same size. In choice C, the second circle has been vertically stretched, so the figures are not the same shape or size. In choice D, the second trapezoid has been horizontally stretched so it is not the same size as the first trapezoid.

16. D: The angles opposite each other in a parallelogram are congruent which means they are equal in measure. So, $\angle R$ has an equal measure to $\angle T$, or 35°.

17. B: Use inverse operations to solve for the variable in the inequality. Subtract 8 on both sides of the inequality to keep it balanced. $56 - 8 = 48$; therefore, $x \leq 48$.

18. D: To order these numbers, first order the negative numbers from least to greatest. Remember, the farther a negative number is from 0, the smaller it is.

19. C: A close estimate for the total time for all five runners is 125 seconds, which is found by adding 25.1 + 24.9 + 25.2 + 24.8 + 25.0. Then, to convert seconds to minutes, divide by 60 seconds (since there are 60 seconds in a minute) to get 2 with remainder of 5, or 2 minutes and 5 seconds.

20. C: The ruler is used to determine the length of one side of the triangle, which is about 4.5 centimeters. Since this is an equilateral triangle, all three sides are of equal length. To find the perimeter, we add up all of the sides. However, since they are all the same length, we can just multiply 4.5 centimeters by 3 to get 13.5 centimeters.

21. A: One of the easiest ways to solve this is to convert all fractions and percents to decimals, and then order from least to greatest. It is also possible to make all the decimals and percents into fractions and compare, or you can make all the fractions and decimals into percents to compare. When converting fractions to decimals, divide the numerator by the denominator. $\frac{1}{2} = 0.5, \frac{4}{5} = 0.8,$ $1\frac{3}{8} = 1.375, \frac{9}{12} = 0.75$. When converting a percentage to a decimal, divide by 100: $85\% = 0.85$. Therefore, the order from least to greatest is 0.5, 0.56, 0.75, 0.8, 0.85, 1.375, 1.6.

22. -68: First plug all of the numbers into the equation. Then follow the order of operations using integer operation rules.

$$(-2)^2 + (2(-5) - 8) \times 4$$
$$(-2)^2 + (-10 - 8) \times 4$$
$$(-2)^2 + (-18) \times 4$$
$$4 + (-18) \times 4$$
$$4 + (-72)$$
$$-68$$

23. C: The proportion can be written as $\frac{\text{data analysis problems}}{\text{algebra problems}} = \frac{4}{2} = \frac{x}{18}$. Cross multiplying gives $2x = 72$. This can be solved by dividing both sides by 2, which results in $x = 36$. Thus, there are 36 data analysis problems on the test.

24. D: The mean is just the average. To calculate this, find the total of all 10 numbers by adding. Then, divide that total by 10 because that is the number of data points. The total is 750, so the mean of this group of numbers is 75

25. B: The only chart that shows these values is B. Language has 25 out of 135. This is approximately 0.18 which equals 18%. Math has 20 out of 135. This is approximately 0.15 which equals 15%. Science has 30 out 135. This is approximately 0.22 which equals 22%. Social Studies has 20 out of 135. This is approximately 0.15 which equals 15%. Music has 15 out of 135. This is approximately 0.11 which equals 11%. Sports Activities have 25 out of 135. This is approximately 0.18 which equals 18%.

26. A: The appropriate fractions can be found by putting the amount of money spent on each category over the total amount of money spent. $\frac{50}{120}$ is a little less than half, since half of 120 is 60. $\frac{30}{120}$ simplifies to $\frac{1}{4}$ and $\frac{40}{120}$ simplifies to $\frac{1}{3}$. This means that Sammy spent almost $\frac{1}{2}$ his money on shirts,

$\frac{1}{4}$ of his money on jeans, and $\frac{1}{3}$ of his money on school supplies. The graph in A best represents those fractions.

27. B: Since each person is paid by the number of miles driven, one must know not the total miles for the trip, but the miles each person drove. The fuel, weight, or hours do not matter for this problem.

28. B: To answer this question, find the total number of bulbs required by multiplying 10 by 3. The number of packages of bulbs required can be found by dividing this total number of bulbs, 30, by 5, to find that 6 packages are needed. Then, multiplying 6 by the cost per package, 8, we find that the total cost for all the bulbs needed was $48.

29. D: To answer this question, the total number of caps sold must be found by dividing the total sales, 3,360, by the price of each cap, 14. 3,360 ÷ 14 = 240, so 240 caps were sold in total. So, looking at the graph, it appears that about half of the caps were white, around 120. The graph also shows that the other 3 colors were sold in about equal numbers, so dividing the other half, 120, by 3, gives around 40. Then, adding 120 white caps and 40 pink caps, gives an answer of 160. The club had close to 160 combined sales of white and pink caps.

30. B: First add all of the lengths together to get $43\frac{1}{2}$ inches. Then divide by 6 to get the mean. $43\frac{1}{2} \div 6 = 7\frac{1}{4}$

31. A: This procedure first finds the area to be fertilized, by multiplying the length and width of the rectangular yard: (20×45). Then, it divides that area by the area each pound of fertilizer will cover: $(20 \times 45) \div 150$.

32. D: Following order of operations, the multiplication inside the parenthesis should be done first. The product will be 900. Then division should be performed next. The quotient will be 6.

$$(20 \times 45) \div 150$$
$$900 \div 150$$
$$6$$

33. D: We know the ratio of boys to girls is 3 to 4, which means there are 3 boys for every 7 students (because $3 + 4 = 7$). We can write the ratio of boys to total students as $\frac{3}{7}$. We also know that there are 12 boys in the class, so we can create the following proportion.

$$\frac{3}{7} = \frac{12}{x}$$

To solve for x, use cross multiplication, and then solve as a regular equation

$$3x = 12 \times 7$$
$$3x = 84$$
$$x = 28$$

Since $x = 28$, this means there is a total of 28 students in the class.

34. C: Since the rate, in miles per minute, is constant, this can be solved by setting up a proportion

$$\frac{\text{miles}}{\text{min}} = \frac{10}{12} = \frac{210}{t}$$

Now, solve for t by using cross multiplication.

$$t = \frac{210 \times 12}{10} = 252$$

Mark will take 252 minutes to reach his destination. From here, convert the time to hours and minutes. Start by dividing 252 by 60.

$$252 \div 60 = 4.2$$

He will take 4 hours and 0.2 of another hour. To convert the partial hour, 0.2, to minutes, multiply it by 60.

$$0.2 \times 60 = 12$$

Therefore, it will take him 4 hours and 12 minutes to reach his destination.

35. B: Ordered pairs are written in the form of (x,y). The horizontal axis is the x-axis, and the vertical axis is the y-axis. Point A is in Quadrant I on the coordinate plane, so both values have to be positive.

36. B: It is easier to think as the required 16 inches as 16.00 and convert all answer choices to a decimal to compare. Anything greater than 16.00 would be sufficient. $15\frac{7}{10}$ is equal to 15.7, $\frac{47}{3}$ is equivalent to 15.67 and 15.5 remains 15.5. These three choices are all slightly less than the required 16.00 inches; therefore making 16.25 inches the only adequate choice.

37. C: Since she earns $5 for walking dogs and watering flowers, this term can be combined to simplify the equation. The other terms for bringing back trashcans and checking the mail are straight multiplication.

38. A: To correctly write a percent as a decimal, the percent sign is dropped and the number is rewritten with the decimal point two places to the left. If there is not two digits in the percent, a zero is used as a place holder. This is because a percent is always a value out of 100 and the second place after the decimal point is the hundredths place. So, 8% = 0.08.

39. D: Each of the units represents $\frac{1}{4}$. The point Z is 9 units right of the y-axis or $\frac{9}{4}$ units, which is equivalent to $2\frac{1}{4}$. The point R is also 9 units from the y-axis, or $\frac{9}{4}$, which is equivalent to $2\frac{1}{4}$. Be careful to notice that coordinate pairs always come in the order of the x-coordinate and then the y-coordinate, and is defined by the pair of numbers. The y- coordinate for Z is $\frac{7}{8}$, while Point R has a y-coordinate of $3\frac{1}{2}$.

40. B: This pie chart shows the percentage of the total recyclable material that each material represents. The larger percentages have larger slices of the circle. Also, the percentage for each material is shown next to each slice. In this chart, paper is the most recycled material because it has the largest slice. This is 40% of the total. The next most common is glass at 25% of the total. All of the other materials stand for smaller portions of the total.

41. B: When solving for variables in equations, use inverse operations. Perform these operations on both sides of the equation to keep it balanced. Follow integer rules when solving.

$$\frac{3w}{3} = \frac{-6}{3}$$

$$w = -2$$

42. D: The ratio indicates the number of people who chose veggie (60) to the number of people who chose turkey (45). Write the ratio 60 : 45 and then reduce it by dividing both parts by 15 so that it becomes 4 : 3.

43. C: To solve for x, simply add 6 to both sides.

$$x - 6 = 0$$
$$x - 6 + 6 = 0 + 6$$
$$x = 6$$

44. C: Subtract 29 from both sides of the equation to isolate r.

$$29 + r = 420$$
$$29 + r - 29 = 420 - 29$$
$$r = 391$$

The value of r is 391.

45. D: Use the formula for circumference:

$$\text{Circumference} = \pi \times \text{diameter}$$
$$\pi \text{ is approximately equal to } 3.14$$

To give the best estimate, round to the nearest whole number:

3.14 rounds to 3

12.2, the diameter, rounds to 12

$$3 \times 12 = 36$$

46. D: Since Hannah spends at least $16, the relation of the cost of a package of coffee to the minimum cost may be written as $4p \geq 16$. Alternatively, the inequality may be written as $16 \leq 4p$.

47. +20: Area of a triangle is one-half base times height.

$$\frac{1}{2}(10)(4) = 20 \text{ inches squared}$$

48. D: The average is the sum of all the scores divided by the number of scores:

$$\frac{75 + 65 + 80 + 95 + 65}{5} = 76$$

49. D: To determine the number of questions Joshua must answer correctly, consider the number of points he must earn. Joshua will receive 4 points for each question he answers correctly, and x represents the number of questions. Therefore, Joshua will receive a total of $4x$ points for all the questions he answers correctly. Joshua must earn more than 92 points. Therefore, to determine the number of questions he must answer correctly, solve the inequality $4x > 92$.

50. D: The formula for the area of a circle is $A = \pi r^2$.

$$A = \pi \times r \times r$$
$$A = 3.14 \times (6 \text{ in}) \times (6 \text{ in})$$
$$A = 3.14 \times (36 \text{ in}^2)$$
$$A = 113.04 \text{ in}^2$$

Reading Practice Test

Refer to the following for questions 1–12:

A World of White: The Iditarod Trail

(1) Imagine clinging desperately to your sled as brutal winds batter your body. The path ahead appears and disappears like a mirage, frequently obscured by blowing curtains of snow. You are freezing and sweating at the same time. Your throat burns with thirst, and your body aches with fatigue. You know your dogs must feel it too, so you encourage them to press on to the next checkpoint. All around you, the world is endless, empty, and white. Welcome to the Iditarod Trail.

(2) Alaska's Iditarod Trail is the world's most famous sled dog racing venue. But the trail is older than the sport of sled dog racing. In fact, the Iditarod Trail was first established in the early 1900s, during the Alaskan gold rush. In those days, dog teams were used for work, hauling thousands of pounds of gold from landlocked Iditarod to the port of Anchorage. But in faraway Nome, also known for gold, six-year-old George Allen had the idea to put together a race to see whose sled dogs were fastest, and the sport of sled dog racing was born.

(3) Though the Iditarod Trail race is the most famous race in the sport of sled dog racing, the first race along the trail was actually a race to save lives. In 1925, a diphtheria outbreak began in Nome. To prevent an epidemic that could kill thousands, doctors were desperate for the vaccine serum, but the closest serum was in Anchorage. The train ran from Anchorage to the village of Nenana, but that was still 674 miles from Nome. A cry for help was sent by the doctors, and in the midst of the blizzards and windstorms of January, the call was answered. Twenty brave mushers drove their dogs in a frantic relay, carrying 300,000 bottles of serum from Nenana to Nome. They followed the Iditarod Trail.

(4) Dog sledding, or "mushing," became quite popular after that heroic journey, but by the 1960s, it had lost popularity and the Iditarod Trail had been largely forgotten. There were a few lovers of mushing, however, who worked tirelessly to reestablish the Iditarod Trail and create a new sled dog race that used the trail as its course. The first official race was held in 1967 to celebrate the centennial of the purchase of Alaska from Russia. The race involved 58 drivers who mushed 56 miles in two days. This race was a success, but the popularity and future of the Iditarod Trail was still in question.

(5) In March of 1973, the first Anchorage to Nome Iditarod Trail race was organized and held. This race was much longer than previous races, covering more than 1,000 miles—the whole Iditarod Trail. Thirty-four mushers began the race, but only 22 were able to finish. After the 1973 race, the popularity of the Iditarod Trail finally grew and was firmly established. In 1978, the Iditarod Trail became a National Historic Trail.

(6) The modern Iditarod Trail race is open to mushers over 18 years old who have qualified in a recognized race of 200 miles or more. For younger mushers between 14 and 18 years old, the Junior Iditarod offers a 130-mile version of the race. Many Junior Iditarod participants go on to compete in the Iditarod Trail race, as the Junior

Iditarod is good practice for the grueling trek of the main race. All mushers must prepare for the race extensively, often for months before the race. Many mushers run their dogs more than 1,500 miles in preparation, giving them experience in all types of weather and terrain.

(7) To enter the Iditarod Trail race, participants must pay an entrance fee. Then they must travel to Anchorage with their dogs. In Anchorage, they attend a mushers' banquet where they are given their racing order numbers. Afterwards, all participating dogs are checked by a veterinarian and marked by race officials to prevent dog switching mid-race, which is not allowed. The dogs are even drug tested at the beginning and at checkpoints throughout the race to prevent cheating! Finally, the sleds and equipment are checked. Then participants are ready to start the race.

(8) On the morning of the Iditarod Trail race, mushers leave Anchorage in their assigned racing order. They are sent out one at a time, at two-minute intervals. For more than a week—sometimes up to three weeks—they travel throughout Alaska, stopping at designated checkpoints all along the Iditarod Trail as they make their way to Nome. When all participants have reached Nome, another mushers' banquet is held. Awards are given, and everyone is applauded for their achievement. Win or lose, the mushers know that only the toughest of the tough have what it takes to finish the race and conquer the great Iditarod Trail.

1. What does the simile in paragraph 1 describe?

a. The snow
b. The path
c. The musher's throat
d. The dogs

2. What does "landlocked" mean in paragraph 2?

a. Barricaded by hills
b. Built underground
c. Not on a waterway
d. In the mountains

3. What two cities are on the ends of the Iditarod Trail?

a. Anchorage and Nome
b. Nome and Nenana
c. Iditarod and Anchorage
d. Nenana and Iditarod

4. What is the author's main purpose in writing this article?

a. To encourage mushers to race on the Iditarod Trail
b. To inform the reader about the 1925 diphtheria outbreak
c. To describe the terrain of Alaska
d. To educate the reader about the Iditarod Trail

5. In paragraph 3, which words best convey the feelings of the doctors in Nome in 1925?

a. "Epidemic" and "diphtheria"
b. "Blizzards" and "windstorms"
c. "Brave" and "frantic relay"
d. "Desperate" and "cry for help"

6. Why did the author choose to write this article in third-person point of view?

a. Historical overviews are best written in third person
b. The author has never been to Alaska
c. Third person is the required point of view in nonfiction writing
d. This article is not written in third-person point of view

7. In what year did the Iditarod Trail become a National Historic Trail?

a. 1967
b. 1973
c. 1978
d. 1981

8. Which of the following is the best summary of the history of the Iditarod Trail race?

a. After the Iditarod Trail became a National Historic Trail, the race became more popular, and today many mushers participate each year
b. After a slow start in 1967, the Iditarod Trail race became firmly established in 1973, and it continues in popularity today
c. In the first race in 1973, 34 mushers began the race, but only 22 were able to finish, proving that the race was just too hard
d. Mushers between 14 and 18 years of age can race in the Junior Iditarod, while those over 18 can participate in the main race if they qualify

9. How is this article organized?

a. Chronologically
b. Geographically
c. Randomly
d. Spatially

10. Which of the following is a supporting detail in this article?

a. Alaska's Iditarod Trail is the world's most famous sled dog racing venue
b. After the heroic journey of 1925, mushing became more popular
c. Some mushers run their dogs over 1,500 miles to prepare for the race
d. There are specific requirements to enter the Iditarod Trail race

11. What do participants receive at the first mushers' banquet?

a. Awards
b. Racing order numbers
c. Supplies
d. Trail maps

12. What is the interval used to separate mushers as they begin the Iditarod Trail race?

a. Five minutes
b. One minute
c. Ten minutes
d. Two minutes

Refer to the following for questions 13–21:

THE RIGHT THING TO DO

Characters (in order of appearance):
JESSICA—a sixth-grade girl, Amy's friend
GROUP OF FRIENDS—a group of sixth-grade girls
AMY—a sixth-grade girl, Jessica's friend
SALES CLERK—a clerk in the store Amy and Jessica visit

Scene 1

(1) Jessica stands with a group of friends on the school steps. The group is chatting and laughing. Amy approaches from stage right.
(2) AMY: Jessica! Jessica!
(3) JESSICA: (turning away from her friends and taking a step toward Amy) Hi, Amy. What's up?
(4) AMY: I'm headed to the mall, and I thought you might want to come.
(5) JESSICA: Why me? I thought we weren't friends anymore.
(6) AMY: (waving her hand and shaking her head) That old fight? Ancient history. So ... do you want to come or not?
(7) JESSICA: (glancing back at her friends) Sure. I'll come. Just give me a minute.
(8) Jessica runs back and talks with her friends for a moment, then rejoins Amy. Amy and Jessica exit stage right.

Scene 2

(9) Amy and Jessica are looking at a shelf full of lipstick in a cosmetics store in the mall.
(10) AMY: Look at this one, Jess. Don't you just love this color? (She picks up a lipstick tube.)
(11) JESSICA: It's nice, but I like this one better. (She picks up a different tube of lipstick.)
(12) A sales clerk enters from stage left.
(13) SALES CLERK: (stopping by the girls) Can I help you ladies find something?
(14) AMY: Oh, no. We're just looking.
(15) JESSICA: Thank you, though.
(16) SALES CLERK: Okay. Well, let me know if you need anything. (He/she exits stage right.)
(17) AMY: So, which one are you going to get?
(18) JESSICA: (looking at the floor and shaking her head) I'm not getting one. They're a little spendy for me. Besides, I'm saving up for something special.
(19) AMY: (laughing) Who said anything about money? (She slips her favorite lipstick into her pocket.) I didn't ask you which one you were going to buy. I asked which one you were going to get. So, which one will it be?
(20) JESSICA: But—but—that's stealing!
(21) AMY: Look at all these tubes of lipstick. They'll never miss a couple.

(22) JESSICA: (looking around nervously) What if that sales clerk comes back and catches us?
(23) AMY: You worry too much. (She picks up two tubes of lipstick.) Now, was this the one you liked? Or was it this one? Never mind. We'll take them both. (She slips them both into her pocket.)
(24) JESSICA: Amy! This is wrong. We shouldn't be doing this.
(25) AMY: (glaring at Jessica) Do you even want to be my friend again? It sure doesn't sound like it.
(26) JESSICA: Of course I want to be your friend. It's just—
(27) AMY: Then come on. Let's go. (She starts to walk away, and then turns and looks back.) Are you coming?
(28) JESSICA: Fine. (She follows Amy.) But what if the alarm goes off?
(29) AMY: For a couple of tubes of lipstick? Not gonna happen. Now, follow me. And for heaven's sake, don't look so nervous.
(30) The girls exit stage right.

Scene 3

(31) Jessica reenters the cosmetics store from stage right. She stops at the shelf of lipsticks and looks around. The sales clerk enters from stage left.
(32) JESSICA: Excuse me ...
(33) SALES CLERK: (stopping) Did you need help with something?
(34) JESSICA: Yes. (She looks at the floor.) My friend who was just with me, um, she took—well, actually, she stole three tubes of lipstick. I'm not okay with that. So, um, I wanted to pay for them.
(35) SALES CLERK: That's impressive. I've never seen that happen before. And kids take stuff from this store all the time. What made you come back?
(36) JESSICA: (shrugging) I don't know. I guess it was just the right thing to do.

13. In paragraph 6, what does Amy mean when she calls her fight with Jessica "ancient history"?

a. It happened thousands of years ago
b. It happened in history class
c. Amy has totally forgotten about the fight
d. They were arguing about events in ancient history

14. What is the setting for Scene 1?

a. The school steps
b. The mall
c. A cosmetics store
d. Amy's house

15. What is the setting for Scene 2 and Scene 3?

a. The school steps
b. Jessica's house
c. A cosmetics store
d. Amy's house

16. Which scene contains the climax of this play?

a. Scene 1
b. Scene 2
c. Scene 3
d. All of the above

17. In paragraph 29, why is the word "gonna" considered acceptable?

a. It shows Amy's pattern of slang speech
b. It is always acceptable in written English
c. It is a different language spoken by Amy
d. It is not acceptable; it is a misspelling

18. In paragraph 6, what type of figurative language is used when Amy says "ancient history"?

a. Metaphor
b. Simile
c. Personification
d. Hyperbole

19. Which of the following best describes the overall tone of this play?

a. Formal
b. Conversational
c. Classical
d. Musical

20. What is the underlying theme of this play?

a. Amy and Jessica are best friends
b. Doing the right thing is always a good decision
c. It is okay to steal if you are not caught
d. Shopping for cosmetics increases peer pressure

21. Which of the following is the best summary of this play?

a. Jessica leaves her other friends to be friends with Amy again, and she and Amy go to the mall
b. Amy teaches Jessica how to steal lipstick without getting caught, being a bad influence on Jessica
c. Jessica agrees to go to the mall with Amy, but when Amy steals lipstick, Jessica goes back to pay for it
d. Jessica thinks stealing is wrong, and she thinks Amy is a bad influence because she is a thief

Refer to the following for questions 22–24:

The Talent Show

(1) The first notes floated from the piano. Megan smiled, warm and excited beneath the glaring stage lights. This was her moment. She had practiced. She had prepared. She was ready. As the introduction ended, Megan opened her mouth and began to sing.

(2) The song flowed along, and Megan relaxed, scanning the faces of the audience. But somewhere in the middle of the second verse, her mind suddenly went blank. The music went on, but the words were gone. Megan's smile faded. She stood silently with her mouth hanging open. When the music finally trickled to a stop, Megan ran from the stage.

(3) In a cramped dressing room backstage, Megan buried her face in her hands. She had wanted so much to win this talent show. Tears seeped between her fingers. Her confidence and pride and excitement had been replaced by utter disappointment. She felt a hand on her shoulder and lifted her damp face.

(4) "Ella and Kaylee are here," Megan's mom said, giving her shoulder a quick squeeze.

(5) Ella and Kaylee, Megan's two best friends, pulled folding chairs over to face Megan. She looked at them forlornly.

(6) "I'm a total failure," she moaned.

(7) Ella and Kaylee exchanged glances. Kaylee reached out and squeezed Megan's hand.

(8) "What are you talking about?" Kaylee said. "That first verse was some of your best singing ever."

(9) "Thanks," Megan said. "But the problem is that the first verse is all I sang. Then I totally bombed. I can't believe I forgot the words after all that practice."

(10) "You didn't totally bomb," Ella said. "You just forgot the words. That happens to everybody. Besides, don't the pros say you should leave your audience wanting more?"

(11) "I guess so," Megan admitted.

(12) "Well, trust me," Ella said. "I guarantee they wanted more—like the rest of the song! You probably did, too."

(13) Megan smiled a little. "So, you guys don't think I'm a total dork for forgetting the words?"

(14) "Of course not," Kaylee said. "Forgetting the words doesn't make you a dork. It just makes you human. And you're still the most talented person I know."

(15) Ella nodded in agreement. Megan pulled Ella and Kaylee into a quick hug. Then she wiped her eyes and managed a genuine smile.

(16) "I'm so lucky to have best friends like you two," Megan said. "It's nice to know that you'll be my friends forever, no matter what!"

Questions 22-24 pertain to "The Talent Show" short story:

22. Which of the following is the best definition of "forlornly" as it is used in paragraph 5?

a. With a happy spirit
b. With a sad spirit
c. With a lonely spirit
d. With an angry spirit

23. What is the main theme of this story?

a. Real friends support you, no matter what
b. It is easy to forget the words of a song
c. Performing in a talent show can be embarrassing
d. Megan feels like a failure

24. What point of view is used to tell this story?

a. First person
b. Second person
c. Third person
d. None of the above

Refer to the following for questions 25–29:

The Tournament

(1) Looking for a hole in the defense, Scott dribbled the ball, shifting it from hand to hand. A trickle of sweat ran down his back. No one was open. There were only seconds left on the clock, and Scott knew he had a difficult decision to make.

(2) The other team was leading by two points, and Scott was just outside the three-point line. If he could make the shot, the Eagles would be state champions again. But if he missed … Scott didn't want to think about that. He knew what he had to do.

(3) It was a classic jump shot. The ball left his hands and sailed toward the basket in a perfect arc. The crowd, the other players, the whole stadium seemed frozen in time. All eyes were on the ball as it struck the rim and bounced off. The buzzer blared. The game was over. Scott had missed, and the Eagles had lost.

(4) Scott stood like a statue on the court as people surged around him. Elated family members swarmed the winning team. Teammates hugged and slapped each other on the back. Even Scott's own teammates joined in the celebration.

(5) Suddenly, Scott felt himself being hoisted unsteadily onto the shoulders of his friends. Over the loudspeaker, the announcer proclaimed that Scott had been named the most valuable player of the championship game. Everyone cheered, and the Eagles took a victory lap with Scott on their shoulders. Finally, Scott's friends put him back on solid ground.

(6) Scott was bewildered. He was the one who missed the most important shot of the game. How could anyone call him the most valuable player? He didn't feel very valuable at the moment. Scott approached Coach Travis.

(7) "Coach," Scott said, "there must be some mistake. I can't be the most valuable player."

(8) "There's no mistake," Coach Travis said. "You had 26 points, 11 rebounds, and 8 assists. I'd say that makes you a very valuable player."

(9) "But I missed that last shot," Scott said. "We lost the game because of me."

(10) "I don't know about that," said Coach Travis. "Everybody misses a shot from time to time. Don't be so hard on yourself. It's all about perspective."

(11) "What do you mean?" Scott asked.

(12) "Well," Coach Travis answered, "you could say you are the reason we lost the game because you missed that last shot. On the other hand, you could say you are the reason we almost won because of your awesome performance throughout the game. How you look at it is up to you."

(13) Scott's teammates came running over and surrounded Coach Travis. They jostled one another playfully, talking and laughing.

(14) "Hey, Coach," one player called out, "how about treating your team to pizza?"

(15) "I don't know," said Coach Travis. "Do you think you deserve pizza?"

(16) Scott piped up. "Of course we do! After all, we almost won the game."

(17) Coach Travis smiled. "You're right, Scott. We did almost win. Okay. Pizza for everyone!"

25. In paragraph 4, what does "elated" mean?

a. Happy and excited
b. Frustrated and angry
c. Loud and rowdy
d. Pushy and proud

26. In the first sentence of paragraph 4, what type of figurative language is used?

a. Hyperbole
b. Metaphor
c. Personification
d. Simile

27. Which of the following best expresses the theme of this story?

a. The Eagles want to be the state champions
b. There are different ways to look at any situation
c. Winning isn't everything
d. Scott is a very good basketball player

28. Which of the following is the best summary of this story?

a. At the buzzer, Scott misses an important basket because he isn't a very good basketball player
b. Coach Travis feels Scott is the most valuable player in the game because he scored 26 points
c. When Scott misses an important shot, he is disappointed, but Coach Travis shows him there are different ways to look at the situation
d. The Eagles lose the state championship because of Scott, but Coach Travis sees things differently and makes Scott the most valuable player

29. Why is Scott so upset in this story?

a. He feels responsible for losing the game
b. He thinks he is a bad basketball player
c. He doesn't like Coach Travis
d. He doesn't want to play basketball anymore

Questions 30-31 pertain to both "The Talent Show" and "The Tournament" short stories:

30. In what ways are Scott and Megan most similar in these stories?

a. They are both performers.
b. They are both very active.
c. They are both disappointed in themselves.
d. They both have good friends.

31. What general theme is evident in both stories?

a. Winning is important, but it isn't everything
b. Good friends are the most valuable thing in life
c. Coaches can offer good perspective on tough situations
d. When you try your best, you shouldn't be disappointed in yourself

Questions 32-40 pertain to the following story:

Everybody's Problem

(1) I used to think homeless people were dirty and lazy and mean. I thought they were all old men with scraggly beards and mangy dogs. I thought they lived on the street because they wanted to. I thought they were all drug addicts and alcoholics who ate from garbage cans and slept in boxes. I used to think homelessness wasn't my problem. Then I met Chris, and he showed me I was wrong—about everything. Homelessness is everybody's problem.

(2) The sun was climbing into the bright blue sky as we loaded up the bus at the youth center. It was a crisp, cold Thanksgiving morning, and our youth group was headed down to a local shelter called The Lighthouse. We were going to serve Thanksgiving dinner to more than a hundred homeless people. It seemed like an appropriate way to spend Thanksgiving Day.

(3) When we arrived at the shelter, we were each given a job to do. My job was peeling potatoes. The shelter director gave me a peeler and a garbage can and sat me down in front of a giant pile of potatoes. I had never seen so many potatoes in one place before. They rose from the tray like Mt. Everest. By the time I had peeled them all, my hands and arms and shoulders ached.

(4) When the kitchen work was done, we were given our serving stations. The director explained that this was the only meal many of the homeless people would eat that day, and for some, it was the only hot meal they would have that week. Even so, there wasn't a lot of food for so many people. We were supposed to give each person one slice of turkey, one scoop of mashed potatoes, one scoop of stuffing, a small drizzle of gravy, a few green beans, and a sliver of pumpkin pie.

(5) I was plodding along, dishing up mashed potatoes with an ice cream scoop, when I happened to look up at the person I was serving. He wasn't a dirty, bearded old

man. He was a boy about my age, with brown hair and brown eyes and a patched green jacket.

(6) "Hi," the boy said. "I'm Chris."

(7) "I'm Ben," I said as I scooped some potatoes onto his plate. "Happy Thanksgiving."

(8) "Thanks," Chris said, and then he was gone.

(9) As Chris moved down the line, I began to look around, really seeing things for the first time. Very few of the homeless people fit my stereotype. There were men and women, old and young. Children played in a corner of the dining room. At one table, teenagers talked in a tight group. People chatted and smiled. A few were even laughing. This was not what I had pictured a homeless shelter would be like.

(10) When everyone had been served, I began to help clean up. I couldn't help watching Chris as I cleared the tables and wiped them down. He was playing peek-a-boo with a little girl in a high chair. I wondered if it was his little sister.

(11) I was so lost in thought that I jumped when the shelter director tapped my shoulder. She laughed.

(12) "I'll finish cleaning up here," she said. "Why don't you go talk to Chris? He's very nice."

(13) As I approached the table where Chris was sitting, I felt nervous. What would I say? Could we possibly have anything to talk about? Would he even want to talk to me? I sat cautiously beside him.

(14) "Hi, Ben," he said.

(15) "Hi, Chris. Is that your little sister?"

(16) Chris smiled. "Yep. This is Sophia. And over there is my little brother, Dane." Chris motioned toward the corner where the smaller children were playing. Then he pointed to a dark-haired woman at a nearby table. "That's my mom."

(17) "Are you all homeless?" I asked.

(18) "Yep," answered Chris. "We've been here at The Lighthouse for almost two months now. It's okay here, but I miss my old school and my friends. I hope we can move back to a real house soon."

(19) "I didn't know there was such a thing as homeless kids," I admitted.

(20) "Me neither," said Chris. "At least, not until I became one."

(21) "How did it happen?" I asked. Then I had second thoughts. "I mean, you don't have to tell me if you don't want to. I was just wondering."

(22) "It's okay," Chris said. "I don't mind talking about it. About a year ago, my dad got really sick. He was in the hospital for a few months. Then he died. We didn't have

any insurance or anything, and my mom couldn't get a job. Besides, she was really sad, and she was trying to take care of me and Dane and Sophia."

(23) "So, how did you end up homeless?" I wondered.

(24) "Mom says there were just too many bills and not enough money. First, we got our lights turned off. Then we couldn't pay our rent, so we had to move out of our house. We stayed with friends for a while, but eventually there was nobody left to stay with. So, we came here."

(25) "Will you stay here forever?" I asked.

(26) "No," Chris said. "My mom is in a program to give her training and help her get a job. When she finds a job, we can get a new place to live. Then things can be normal again."

(27) I heard my youth leader calling for us to load the bus. I wanted to talk to Chris more and ask him more questions, but I knew I had to leave. I stood up.

(28) "I have to go," I said. "I'm glad I got to meet you, Chris. I hope you get a new house soon."

(29) "Thanks, Ben," Chris said. "It was nice to meet you, too. Thanks for hanging out with me for a while. Happy Thanksgiving."

(30) "Happy Thanksgiving," I echoed as I headed toward the door. When I looked back, Chris waved. Then he started playing peek-a-boo with Sophia again.

(31) I will probably never see Chris again, but I have thought of him many times since that day. In just a few minutes together, he taught me so much about the problem of homelessness. It isn't just a problem that affects lazy, mean old men. It affects men and women of all ages. It affects children. It affects whole families. It affected Chris. And because I got the chance to see homelessness through his eyes, it affects me now, too. I think I'll go back again next Thanksgiving ... or maybe sooner. After all, now I know that homelessness is everybody's problem.

32. What is the setting for this story?

a. A youth center
b. A homeless shelter
c. A community center
d. A school

33. If you were describing this story, what classification would you use?

a. Memoir
b. Biography
c. Autobiography
d. Fiction

34. In paragraph 9, what does the word "stereotype" mean?

a. A textbook definition of a concept
b. Height, weight, and physical features
c. A generalized idea of what something is like
d. A description given by an authority figure

35. What point of view is used to tell this story?

a. First person
b. Second person
c. Third person
d. All of the above

36. What is the main theme of this story?

a. Kids can be homeless
b. Potatoes are difficult to peel
c. Serving at a homeless shelter is a good Thanksgiving project
d. Homelessness is everybody's problem

37. What does the author compare the potatoes to in paragraph 3?

a. A tower
b. A mountain range
c. Mt. Everest
d. A mound

38. Which of the following items was not included in the Thanksgiving dinner at the shelter?

a. Turkey
b. Cranberry sauce
c. Mashed potatoes and gravy
d. Pumpkin pie

39. What major event in the life of Chris's family led to their homelessness?

a. Their house burned down
b. Chris's mom lost her job
c. They had to live in their car
d. Chris's dad got sick and died

40. How does meeting Chris change Ben's mind about homelessness?

a. It doesn't change Ben's mind at all
b. It makes Ben afraid of being homeless
c. It helps Ben see that homelessness affects everyone
d. It keeps Ben from ever helping in a homeless shelter again

Questions 41-45 pertain to the following story:

A Call for Canines

(1) Dogs truly are man's best friend, and getting one comes with a lot of responsibility. However, the responsibility that comes with dog ownership is not a bad thing. It is actually an opportunity for kids to learn how to be responsible. In fact, having a dog can teach a child many valuable lessons. More parents should allow their child to have a dog so that they can learn these lessons in a fun, safe way.

(2) The biggest lesson a child can learn through having a dog is responsibility. Dogs need food, water, exercise, attention, and a place to relieve themselves. A child must remember to provide these things for the dog so that the dog stays happy and healthy. Dogs must learn that they cannot bite people, eat things that are not good for them, or destroy things. A child must pay attention to the dog, and possibly train it, to help it learn to behave well and get used to a new environment. Overall, dogs can help children learn to be selfless and responsible because they require them to choose to care for a pet instead of doing other activities they may prefer.

(3) Another reason that children should be allowed to have dogs is that it is a safe way for children to learn to be responsible. If the child fails to give the dog what it needs, the child can see the real consequences of their actions. This can be an opportunity for parents to tell their child what they did wrong and help them learn the consequences in a safe way. For example, once when I was young, my brother was watching television and forgot to take his dog for a walk. The dog made a mess in the house because he needed exercise and attention. Once my brother learned what had happened, he had to clean up the mess. However, he never forgot to take the dog for a walk again after that day. The consequences of his poor choice were easily fixed, and no one was hurt. He was able to learn a lesson without having to face serious consequences.

(4) Caring for a dog is also a fun and memorable way for children to learn how to be responsible. Dogs usually love to play and are often very affectionate, and most children enjoy petting and playing with dogs. Because children often enjoy and love their dogs, they are more likely to want to care for them. When a dog whines because it is hungry or wants attention, the child will want to make the dog happy by giving it what it needs. The child's love for the dog can also help them remember the lessons they learn as they care for it. Lessons about responsibility or uninteresting tasks that teach it are likely to be forgotten by a child. However, the child will remember both the good and bad memories they make with a beloved pet.

(5) Some may argue that getting a pet that is easier to care for, like a fish, will bring their child the same benefits with fewer risks. However, a fish will not love the child the way that a dog will. This means that the child will not bond with a fish the way he or she would with a dog. This can cause the child to be less invested in caring for the fish. The child will have a less memorable experience with the fish, so he or she may not remember the lessons that come with caring for it. Additionally, caring for a fish requires a lot less responsibility than caring for a dog. A fish will not teach a child the same lessons or make them as memorable as a dog will.

(6) Caring for a dog is one of the best ways to teach a child how to be responsible. Children must put forth effort to care for a dog, and they will see real consequences

when they choose not to. They will also learn to be selfless because they will truly care for and love the dog. This will also help the child remember the lessons he or she has learned. Allowing a child to get a dog clearly has great benefits for the child's growth. Parents, what are you waiting for?

41. Which sentence from the passage supports the idea that caring for a dog can be fun?

a. A child must pay attention to the dog, and possibly train it, to help it learn to behave well and get used to a new environment.
b. If the child fails to give the dog what it needs, the child can see the real consequences of their actions.
c. Dogs usually love to play and are often very affectionate, and most children enjoy petting and playing with dogs.
d. The child's love for the dog can also help them remember the lessons they learn as they care for it.

42. Which of the following best states the claim the author is making in "A Call for Canines"?

a. Dogs are the best pets because they are fun to play with and come with few risks.
b. Fish are only good pets for adults because children are easily bored by them.
c. Children should be allowed to have dogs so they can learn responsibility.
d. Responsibility must be learned using lessons and activities that are safe and fun.

43. Read the last sentence of the passage:

Parents, what are you waiting for?

Why did the author end the passage with this rhetorical question?

a. To invite parents to share their reasons for not getting their child a dog
b. To show parents that they have been convinced to get their child a dog
c. To help parents begin looking for a dog to get their child
d. To encourage parents to choose to get a dog for their child

44. In Latin, *bene* means *well*. Considering this, what is the meaning of the word *benefits* in paragraph 5?

a. Effects that are good for a person or thing
b. The possibility that something will go wrong
c. Actions that have no clear result
d. Pets that are healthy and well behaved

45. Which of the following sentences would be best to include in a summary of this essay?

a. Caring for a dog teaches children responsibility.
b. Dogs may need training to get used to a new space.
c. Most messes made by dogs can be cleaned up easily.
d. Fish do not need as much attention as dogs do.

Answer Key and Explanations for the Reading Test

1. B: A simile compares one thing to another by using "like" or "as"; the only simile in paragraph 1—"like a mirage"—refers to the path.

2. C: "Landlocked" means "not on a waterway."

3. A: This information is found in Paragraph 5: "In March of 1973, the first Anchorage to Nome Iditarod Trail race was organized and held. This race was much longer than previous races, covering more than 1,000 miles—the whole Iditarod Trail."

4. D: This is an informational article – the author's main purpose in writing this article is to educate the reader about the Iditarod Trail.

5. D: The descriptive word "desperate" and the descriptive phrase "cry for help" are used in reference to the doctors in Nome in 1925.

6. A: Historical overviews, like this one, are best written in the third-person point of view.

7. C: We learn in Paragraph 5 that the Iditarod Trail became a National Historic Trail in 1978.

8. B: This answer offers the most accurate summary of the history of the Iditarod Trail race.

9. A: This article is organized chronologically, from earliest to latest dates.

10. C: is a supporting detail that expands on a main idea from the article. A, B, and D are not the best choices because they are all main points in the article instead of supporting details.

11. B: is We learn in Paragraph 7 that the race participants receive their racing order numbers at the first mushers' banquet.

12. D: We learn in Paragraph 8 that, as they begin the Iditarod Trail race, mushers are separated by two-minute intervals.

13. C: The phrase "ancient history" is a figure of speech. Amy uses it to communicate that she has totally forgotten about the fight.

14. A: Scene 1 is set on the school steps.

15. C: Scene 2 and Scene 3 take place in a cosmetics store.

16. B: Scene 2 contains the climax of the play, when Jessica must decide whether to go along with Amy or not. In a story, the climax is the most exciting part of the story, when the action or tension builds to a zenith. This occurred when Jessica learned that Amy was planning on stealing the lipstick.

17. A: The word "gonna" is used to show Amy's slang speech pattern.

18. D: The use of "ancient history" in paragraph 6 is a hyperbole, a major exaggeration.

19. B: The tone of this play is conversational.

20. B: The underlying theme of the play is that you should always do the right thing, even when it's difficult. This could also be called the moral of the story.

21. C: Choice C is the most accurate and complete summary of the play.

22. B: "Forlornly" is best defined as "with a sad spirit."

23. A: Choice A most accurately represents the main theme of the story.

24. C: This story is written in the third person. That means the author is writing from the point of view of a narrator – someone who knows all the details of the story but isn't involved in it.

25. A: If someone is "elated", they are extremely happy and excited about something.

26. D: The first sentence of paragraph 4 uses a simile when it says Scott "stood like a statue." A simile uses "like" or "as" to compare one thing to another.

27. B: most clearly and completely expresses the theme of the story. Coach Travis tells Scott that "it's all about perspective", and then says that how Scott decides to look at it is up to him.

28. C: Choice C is the most complete and accurate summary of the story overall. A, B, and D are incorrect because they cover only part of the story or some of the main ideas and concepts.

29. A: Scott is upset in the story because he feels responsible for the team's loss.

30. C: Scott and Megan are most similar in their feelings of disappointment in themselves.

31. D: clearly reflects a general theme found in both stories.

32. B: This story is set at a homeless shelter.

33. A: This story is written in the style of a memoir, as evidenced by the first-person, reflective tone.

34. C: offers the best definition of "stereotype" as it is used in paragraph 9.

35. A: This story is written in first person. That means the author is involved in the events of the story and is telling it from his point of view.

36. D: The main theme of the story is that homelessness is everybody's problem. One clue that this is the main point of the story is that the author clearly states it in the last line of the story. It's not always true that the last line of a short piece contains the main point, but that is often the case.

37. C: In paragraph 3 the author uses a simile to compare the size of the pile of potatoes to Mt. Everest.

38. B: Cranberry sauce was not served as part of the Thanksgiving dinner at the shelter.

39. D: The death of Chris's dad was the major problem the family had to deal with that eventually led to their homelessness.

40. C: After meeting Chris, Ben had a completely different view of homelessness. Prior to the Thanksgiving meal, Ben thought homeless people were nothing but a bunch of old, filthy drunks and drug addicts. Meeting Ben and his family helped him understand that homelessness can happen to all kinds of people.

41. C: The sentence in choice C says that dogs like to play and that children enjoy playing with them. Most children would say that playing with a dog is fun, so choice C is correct. Choice A only describes a couple of responsibilities that come with owning a dog. These are not clearly fun activities, so choice A is incorrect. Choice B explains why owning a dog can teach children about consequences. This is not an example of having fun with a pet dog, so choice B is incorrect. Choice D explains why a child's love for the dog can impact how well they learn responsibility. This does not describe the activities that are part of caring for a dog, so choice D is incorrect.

42. C: The author uses the information in this essay to prove that owning a dog can help children learn how to be responsible. This is stated in choice C, so it is the correct answer. The author does say that dogs can help children learn responsibility better than other pets can. However, the author does not say that dogs are the best pets in general. The author's claim is also related to how dogs help children learn, not how fun or easy they are to care for, so choice A is incorrect. The essay only mentions fish in paragraph 5, and this paragraph presents a counterargument. This is not the author's claim, so choice B is incorrect. The claim is related to how owning a dog teaches responsibility, not responsibility in general, so choice D is incorrect.

43. D: This rhetorical question asks parents why they have not allowed their child to have a dog yet. This implies that parents know the reasons that they should allow their child to have a pet dog. The question is meant to encourage parents to decide that their child can have a pet dog, so choice D is correct. The author is not truly asking parents why they have not allowed their child to have a dog. Rhetorical questions are not meant to be answered, so choice A is incorrect. Some parents may read the essay and still not be convinced to allow their child to have a dog, so choice B is incorrect. The essay does not include information about how to search for a dog. The author also does not use the rhetorical question to offer to help parents find a dog for their child, so choice C is incorrect.

44. A: *Well* is a synonym of *good* or *right*. In paragraph 5, the author says that some parents think owning a fish can have the same benefits as owning a dog. It also says that owning a fish has fewer risks than owning dogs. This shows that benefits and risks are opposites. Benefits are something parents want to have, and risks are something they do not want to have. The Latin root in *benefit* and the way it is used in the passage show that a benefit is a good effect. Choice A is correct. Benefits are positive. Something going wrong is usually bad, or negative, and an action with no clear result is neither good nor bad, and neither positive nor negative. This means that choices B and C are incorrect. Benefits are something that can come from owning a pet, but they are not pets, so choice D is incorrect.

45.A: A summary of this passage should mention the author's claim and the main reasons the author gives to support this claim. Choice A restates the author's claim, so it would be an appropriate sentence to include in a summary of this essay. Choices B and C are details that are related to possible problems that may come with owning a dog. These details do not directly support the claim, and they are not among the main reasons the author uses to support the claim. Choices B and C are incorrect. Choice D is a detail from the author's counterargument. This should not be included in a summary of the essay because it does not help the reader understand what the essay is about. Choice D is incorrect.

Online Resources

Due to our efforts to try to keep this book to a manageable length, we've created a link that will give you access to all of your online resources:

mometrix.com/resources719/vsolg6

It's Your Moment, Let's Celebrate It!

Share your story @mometrixtestpreparation